Praise for *Freeways to Flip-Flops*

"Sonia Marsh and her family give new meaning to the term "flipping out!" Sombreros off to them for showing us the roads less traveled can often be the most rewarding — even when our trips don't go as planned."

—FRANZ WISNER, *NEW YORK TIMES* BESTSELLING AUTHOR OF
HONEYMOON WITH MY BROTHER AND *HOW THE WORLD MAKES LOVE*

If you're dreaming of escaping to a tropical island, or to any foreign land, don't miss Sonia Marsh's candid and vivid recounting of the ups and downs of life abroad. Part adventure tale, part romance, part family saga and part travel guide, *Freeways to Flip-Flops* is a memoir that reads like a novel.

—LAN SLUDER (*EASY BELIZE, FODOR'S BELIZE, LIVING ABROAD IN BELIZE*)

In her revealing memoir, Sonia Marsh invites us along as she and her family leave the Southern California rat race for what they hope will be a more satisfying existence in Belize. Sonia and her family bounce between disillusionment and joy as they learn that island life is more complicated than anticipated. In the end, Sonia realizes that paradise isn't a place — it's a state of mind. I loved the story and Sonia's courage in telling it."

—SUSAN POHLMAN, AUTHOR OF *HALFWAY TO EACH OTHER:
HOW A YEAR IN ITALY BROUGHT OUR FAMILY HOME*

Sonia Marsh's *Freeways to Flip-Flops* isn't just a page turner about an American family that takes off for a tropical island adventure. It's a fascinating exploration of how complicated relationships can be within a family, between friends, and across cultures. In her astonishingly honest memoir, Sonia recounts the family crisis that compelled her to take the risk, and the less than idyllic Caribbean life that followed. As Sonia draws you into her story, you'll root for the family at every high and low, finally cheering that even though the adventure didn't end as she had hoped, Sonia brought back the ultimate treasure: a healthy family that cherishes each other.

—REBECCA RAMSEY, AUTHOR OF *FRENCH BY HEART*

"A book that reads like a breath of fresh air — a tale of love, courage, and laughter and the strength of family bonds despite enormous pressures."
—LYNNETE BRASFIELD, AUTHOR OF *NATURE LESSONS*

"Have you ever dreamt of changing your life with one dramatic decision? How many of us have contemplated leaving it all behind and moving to paradise? Sonia Marsh is one of the few who have risked everything to make that dramatic change in order to save her family from falling apart. With great candor, she bares her heart and soul, and deep concern for her family's issues that compelled their move from Orange County, CA (center of the materialistic world) to a rustic beach house in the developing third-world country of Belize. The unexpected surprises, trials, and tribulations of such a dramatic change are told with drama and wit. *Freeways to Flip-Flops* engages the reader immediately and tells the adventure with short, easy to read vignettes which compel turning of the page to delight in the next story. Marsh's final conclusion that "Paradise is a state of mind," encourages others to seek adventure, but to know that happiness is only found within. Highly recommended for anyone considering, or simply dreaming about leaving it all behind."
—LARRY JACOBSON, AWARD-WINNING AUTHOR OF *THE BOY BEHIND THE GATE, A SIX-YEAR ODYSSEY OF SAILING AROUND THE WORLD*

Feels like I've been to Belize after reading this intriguing tale. *Freeways to Flip-Flops* is a desperate attempt to reconnect a torn family by seeking paradise in the third world, a gutsy move with school-age kids immersed in the flashy lifestyle of Orange County, California. I loved every scene and am grateful the author kept a detailed journal of her experience. Brilliant story, wonderful writing.
—JASON MATTHEWS, AUTHOR OF NOVELS AND HOW-TO GUIDES FOR SELF PUBLISHING, HTTP://WWW.THELITTLEUNIVERSE.COM/

SONIA MARSH

Freeways to Flip-Flops

A Family's Year of Gutsy Living on a Tropical Island

GUTSY
PUBLICATIONS

Freeways to Flip-Flops: A Family's Year of Gutsy Living on a Tropical Island

Copyright © 2012 by Sonia Marsh/Gutsy Publications. All Rights Reserved.

For information about this title or to order other books and/or electronic media, contact the publisher:
Gutsy Publications
23785 El Toro Road, # 131, Lake Forest, CA 92630
www.GutsyPublications.com
Info@GutsyPublications.com

ISBN: 978-0-9854039-1-1

Printed in the United States of America

Cover and Interior design: 1106 Design

Cover image: © iStockphoto.com/jlvphoto
Author photo on page 315 by Kira Robles kirarobles.com
Author photo on back cover by www.erikfischerphotography.com

Publisher's Cataloging-in-Publication
(Provided by Quality Books, Inc.)
Marsh, Sonia.
    Freeways to flip-flops : a family's year of gutsy
living on a tropical island / Sonia Marsh.
    p. cm.
    ISBN 978-0-9854039-1-1

    1. Marsh, Sonia—Travel—Belize. 2. Marsh, Sonia—
Family—Travel—Belize. 3. Americans—Belize—
Biography. 4. Voyages and travels. 5. Families—United
States. 6. Belize—Description and travel. I. Title.

CT214.M26A3 2012   972.8205'092
                        QBI12-600093

Dedication

For Duke and my three wonderful sons

Contents

Author's Note

THE FOLLOWING IS A TRUE STORY. Several names have been changed to protect the privacy of individuals, businesses and locations. Conversations are written as accurately as I can remember them and are not intended to be exact quotations.

CHAPTER ONE

The Storm

"Duke, we can't take the boat out. It's too dangerous," I said, my entire body quivering with fear. I tugged on the lines, squatting and leaning back, fighting the undertow so intent on snatching our boat from the dock. My wrists throbbed, and the skin on my palms felt raw. The lines slipped from my clenched fists and, sensing my loosening grip, Duke shouted, "Hang on, Sonia, just two more lines to go."

This was torture, and, in case I hadn't suffered enough, a massive black cloud smeared the entire sky and catapulted bullet-sized rain pellets onto my bare back. This was the first storm since we'd uprooted our family to live on an island in Belize, Central America. I punched my way through the wind, skidded along the slippery planks of our wooden pier and made it back to our house. Although only mid-afternoon, it felt dark and eerie, and I couldn't stop thinking about the safety of my three boys.

Why the hell did we leave Orange County, California, and move to this godforsaken island where our lives were now at risk? Did I really think this was going to save my family?

I had to get hold of Josh's school and let Jasmine, the secretary, know we were trapped by the storm. I wanted her to grab Josh before he scurried out of class to David's pier, where we normally docked our boat. I was freaking out at the thought of not being able to pick up our youngest son, age ten, after only a few days at the expatriate school in San Pedro. *What if some Creole drug dealer found Josh lost in San Pedro and kidnapped him? What if he locked him up in one of those shacks bordering the mangrove swamps next to the lagoon?*

I knew I shouldn't let my imagination run wild, but I couldn't help it. Our boat was the only way my husband, Duke, and I could get to town. All I could do now was pray that the storm wouldn't turn into a hurricane.

Once inside and protected from the painful rain, I dried myself off and hurled Duke a towel from the stack we kept by the front door. "Look what the rain did," I said, poking at one of many welts on my forearm.

I dashed to the phone across the living room and dialed the school. I heard one ring, then nothing. I pushed the button several times, pressed it firmly against my ear, even whacked it against the counter, but it was dead.

"Try the cell phone," Duke said. "It should be in my nightstand."

I hadn't used my cell phone since we left California, two months ago, and prayed it still worked. There was no reception in the house, so I covered my head with a towel and slid along the planks to the end of our dock.

This time Jasmine answered. "We're stuck in the storm," I said, out of breath. "I'm worried about Josh getting home."

"Don't worry," Jasmine said in her melodic Belizean voice. I almost expected her to say, "Be happy." Belizeans have a way of remaining calm. Island time had not infiltrated my cells yet, and I found it more natural to be myself: an anxiety-ridden mom from Orange County, California.

Embarrassed that Jasmine might think I sounded overly panicky, I told her we'd try again when the rain stopped.

"Call me back later," Jasmine said. "I'll be here till four."

By 3:35 P.M., the dark blanket had blown away, and Duke suggested we give it a shot. Barefoot, we slipped down the soggy, exterior staircase flanking our beach house, grasping the railing for support.

In the distance, I could hear the roar of the local *Island Ferry's* 250-horsepower double engines fighting their way through choppy water and scattered debris as the ferry approached our dock. Our older sons, Steve, sixteen, and Alec, fourteen, were positioning themselves on the bow, ready to jump off.

"Are you guys nuts?" Steve said, when he saw his dad and me untying the lines on our brand new boat. Steve and Alec had taken the *Island Ferry* home once before, but not Josh. I watched the *Island Ferry's* experienced captain, Roberto, struggle as he jerked the throttle into reverse, trying to maneuver his way out of our narrow channel before the waves slammed his expensive boat into our dock. Now Duke and I were attempting to drive our 95-horsepower lanchon, the *Island Rider,* to San Pedro — with no other boats on the water that day except for the *Island Ferry.* Surely we weren't so stupid we thought our boating skills comparable to Roberto's?

"Roberto almost hit the reef," Alec said, his pencil-thin body fighting the wind as he skidded on the wooden dock, heading for the safety of our house.

"You sure it's safe?" I asked Duke.

"Hurry! Jump in," Duke shouted, as the undertow suctioned our boat away from the dock.

Debris kept piling up on the beach, and I tried to ignore the ten-foot tree trunk floating a few feet from the bow. We had to get Josh home.

Duke turned the engine on. A massive dose of adrenaline flooded my veins as we rode the sea like a roller coaster toward the reef, salt spray splashing our faces. Our boat crashed through oncoming waves, and, a few feet after Duke turned south toward town, I heard two horrific noises. The first sounded like a machine grinding rocks. Next came a clamor like a loud train screeching to a halt. Our engine quit; then a creepy silence followed, despite the howling winds and thunderous waves. "What the hell's that?" I yelled, clinging to the boat's vinyl seat with a white-knuckled grip.

"The engine's slipping because of cavitation," Duke said, staying calm.

"What does that mean?"

"Air's getting in, and the blade's losing its bite."

"What now?"

"We head home before we lose power."

Each time Duke pushed the throttle forward, the horrific screeching resumed. Without power, the *Island Rider* flitted around like an indecisive hummingbird, and the sharp coral reef sucked us in. That's when I realized we might capsize. Salty waves stung my eyes as they slopped over the gunnels, slowly flooding the bottom. I closed my eyes to relieve the burn, and there, right in front of me, in fresh ink, I saw the headlines of tomorrow's *San Pedro Sun:* "Inexperienced boaters Duke and Sonia Marsh perish on reef. The *Island Rider* capsized while trying to reach San Pedro, where their youngest son attends the Island Academy." I was more afraid of abandoning Josh than I was of us capsizing.

A scraping sound right underneath me forced me to open my eyes. The bottom of our boat grated against the coral heads, and each wave wedged us more firmly into the sharp reef.

Duke placed his hand on the throttle and cranked it all the way forward, ignoring the sound of our engine grinding itself to shreds. He couldn't afford to lose a second by lifting the propeller to fix the problem at sea. But during those few seconds of power, Duke brought us close enough to our shallow channel to grab the long wooden pole we kept on board to propel our boat toward our dock.

My knees wobbled as I jumped onto the bow and started waving my arms like a windmill for Steve and Alec to see. I knew they would be watching from the large patio glass doors, which opened to a magnificent view of the normally peaceful Caribbean Sea. Both of them ran outside to help. Alec and I barely held onto the line as Duke attempted to turn the boat so the bow faced the incoming waves. Meanwhile, Steve jumped into the sea to push the boat around.

"Look at the propeller," Steve shouted. "You've got a fishing net caught in it."

Steve took his pocketknife and starting cutting the wire. For a split second, I couldn't believe this was the same Steve who'd caused me so much grief and angst in Orange County.

As soon as I'd fastened the lines onto the cleats, I ran back for the cell phone and called Jasmine just in time. "We're stuck," I said. "Can you drop Josh off at the *Island Ferry* dock?"

"I'll take him in my golf cart," she said. "No worries."

After hanging up, I realized Josh didn't know the name of our boat dock. Instead of addresses, houses on the islands had names like *Villa del Sol* or *Casa Tortuga,* and boat captains knew all of them. I would have to call the ferry office. Figuring it would take Jasmine fifteen minutes to drive Josh to the *Island Ferry* boat dock, however, I waited what seemed an interminable time before making that call.

"Can you see a small boy waiting for the ferry?" I asked the Belizean woman who answered.

"I don't see no small boy," she said.

"Please check. His name is Josh."

"Hold on, Ma'am." I sat, dangling my feet off the edge of our pier.

"No, Ma'am. No small boy here."

Racing back to tell Duke, I flew up the staircase. "Jasmine must have missed him. You know how he rushes out of the classroom as soon as the bell rings."

"He's probably waiting for us at David's dock," Duke said. Scary visions of Josh searching for our boat were heightened by my own childhood experience. I found myself reliving the fearsome episode when my babysitter abandoned me to run off with a guy and left me roaming the streets of Paris alone. I was only four.

Sandy, our Realtor, was the only other mother I knew who had a kid at Josh's school. Duke thumbed through the phone book — no thicker than a *Reader's Digest* — for her number.

"Sandy, you've got to find Josh," I pleaded.

My heart thumped so loudly, I figured she could probably hear it.

"Call me back in ten minutes," she said. "I'll look for him."

At nine minutes and fifty-nine seconds, I called her back.

"Josh hasn't left school yet," she said. "Jasmine's taking him right now. He'll be home in twenty minutes."

For thirty minutes, all I could see were white caps pounding the reef; there wasn't a single boat in sight.

"Oh, my God, perhaps the *Island Ferry* couldn't leave," I shrieked. Duke and Alec ran out to our dock with towels over their heads. I scanned the horizon from our upstairs patio and felt relieved when a speck in the distance seemed to be heading toward our house. This had to be the *Island Ferry*.

Turn now, come on, turn. The boat went straight past our dock.

"Bloody hell! Josh wasn't on the boat," I screamed. With cell phone clutched and ready, I dialed the *Island Ferry* and recognized the same Belizean woman's voice.

"Sorry, Ma'am. No small boy on the boat."

"You have to page Roberto. I see the boat. It stopped at Emerald dock."

"I can't," she replied, sounding fed up with my calls.

"Please," I begged.

Finally, I heard her page Roberto and understood enough Spanish to figure out that Roberto dropped Josh off at Emerald, the dock just north of ours. Apparently, our channel was too shallow and dangerous.

I ran along the beach toward Emerald Resort, barefoot. Scrunched up seaweed, empty plastic bottles, syringes and other debris now covered the entire path. Scared that I would step on broken glass, I stopped.

A small figure emerged in the distance, carrying a dark blue backpack. As he got closer, Josh's unmistakable, freckled smile calmed me down.

"Mom, that boat ride was awesome," he beamed. "Are you crying?"

CHAPTER TWO

Orange County Christmas

Two months after Steve turned thirteen, life in our household changed.

A large truck pulled onto our driveway. It was a typical winter day in Southern California, the kind where December gets confused with August and you end up wearing a tank top and shorts while there's a decorated Christmas tree in your living room.

I opened the garage door and saw the man. A short, dark-haired male with tattooed biceps stepped down from one of those cranked-up trucks with oversized tires.

"Are you Steve's mom?" the man asked, angling his neck upward to make eye contact. This did not feel like the start of a pleasant conversation, and I debated whether to say "no" just to get rid of him, or at least postpone our talk until Duke returned from Home Depot.

"Yes," I said. "Why?"

"Steve broke into my house at 2 A.M. on Christmas morning," he said. I leaned against the frame of the garage door for support, my heart racing. *So that's why Steve had slept in. Who was this man?*

"He jumped into my daughter's bedroom window," the stranger continued.

I half expected him to say, "I caught them having sex."

Steve's teenage hormones had kicked in earlier than his classmates', and at six foot one, he fooled adults who thought he was in high school, not seventh grade. Even Duke and I had fallen into the trap of treating him as older.

"What's your name?" I asked.

"Greg."

"Do you live in the neighborhood?"

"No. We live by the 5 freeway."

Steve didn't know anyone over there.

"I'll get him," I said, wishing Duke were here to take charge. I kept thinking the police would show up any minute. I didn't grow up in the U.S., so American cops terrified me. They made me feel like a criminal, even for a simple speeding ticket. I preferred the French cops I encountered during my years in Paris; they seemed more approachable, more human.

How could this be happening? Steve had never run away before, and he certainly hadn't been dating. Shaking, I barged into Steve's room. As he turned to face me, I asked, "Who's Greg?"

Steve froze.

"Did you break into his daughter's bedroom?"

He nodded.

"Come with me," I ordered.

Greg appeared tiny next to Steve.

"Hi, Steve," Greg said, grinning.

What the hell was going on?

"You're lucky Kari locked Killer in the kitchen, or he would have bit your ass."

For a second, I thought I was in a bar instead of my driveway. Greg's demeanor had changed. *Why was he acting confrontational toward me and friendly toward my son?*

"Kari told me she'd lock Killer up," Steve said with a smirk.

"Next time, ring the doorbell, will ya?" Greg advised, cackling.

I wish I'd had the guts to tell Greg, "I don't want Steve dating your daughter. His education comes first." Instead, I apologized for his behavior.

"Where you from? Australia?"

I'd heard this question a thousand times since I landed at Los Angeles International Airport in 1983.

"I was born in Denmark, lived in West Africa, then moved to Paris and college in England."

"I thought you sounded South African," Greg said.

Why wasn't Duke back? His large frame and previous prison guard experience might shut Greg up.

Finally, opening the truck door, Greg lifted his right leg onto the shiny silver platform. Once seated, he could finally look down at us from his perch. He turned the key in the ignition, revved the engine and cranked open his window. "Happy Holidays," he said, grinning. His muffler growled all the way down Bake Parkway.

I turned to face Steve, but he'd already disappeared.

What should I do now?

After closing the garage door, I stormed into his room.

"How could you do this?" I snarled.

"Do what?"

"Come on, Steve!"

"For the adrenaline rush," he said, smirking again.

I skirted his desk and sat on the edge of his bed. "Steve, you're only thirteen; you could've been arrested."

"I was totally safe, Mom."

"Turn around," I ordered. "I refuse to talk to your back."

Steve grunted, something he did more often than speak these days.

"I won't have you on the streets in the middle of the night, is that clear?"

"Whatever."

"Not 'whatever.' I mean it," I hollered.

I was dying to ask my son if he was having sex but couldn't get the words out.

Why else would he run to Kari's house in the middle of the night? Teen pregnancy terrified me, especially here in the U.S. Duke told me that if our son got a girl pregnant he — or, more realistically, Duke and I — would have to pay for the baby until the child turned eighteen. As a workers' compensation attorney, Duke was well aware of child support issues and garnishing of wages, and how the system made it virtually impossible for a young man to get out of debt.

Like many of my European friends, I often compared the U.S. to Europe and made sweeping statements such as, "Europeans would never force a teenage dad to pay. I'm sure the government would offer assistance to the pregnant girl."

I let it go for the moment and headed to the kitchen to make a pot of coffee. On my way, I could hear Josh's fingers tapping the controller of his new video game. How could his fingers move so fast? I wondered what skills these games were teaching him. Would his obsession lead to a profession down the road? Or was this just a passing phase he would outgrow? Heaven knows I was tired of ordering him to "go do homework" or "go read."

Josh kept whining for new game systems advertised on TV, and I hated the way I, and so many parents like me, caved in to kids' requests, especially during the holidays. I often wondered what this was doing to our society; we were raising a generation of children who felt entitled, who expected the latest in electronics and a nice car that Mom and Dad should pay for. I saw this all around me in Orange County, and I wanted to get my kids away from it.

Happily, I didn't have to worry about Alec. His closest friends, Jeff and Jake, lived across the street. Some parents asked me if they could "adopt" Alec, hoping his personality and study skills would rub off on their own kids. As I watched him fish from our boat dock, he reminded me of Duke in so many ways; both were quiet and intellectual.

The coffee machine gurgled as it finished brewing, and Cookie, our rat terrier, barked down the hallway to greet Duke.

"You'll never guess what happened," I blurted, as Duke strolled in and gave me his customary peck on the cheek.

"Not till you tell me."

"It's about Steve. Let's talk on the boat."

I poured us each a coffee and handed Duke his *Star Trek* mug.

"I'll replace the lights bulbs later," Duke said, emptying the Home Depot bags on the kitchen counter.

Our kitchen and living room opened up to a view of our neighborhood lake. As with most houses in Orange County, ours fit like a puzzle piece with the houses around us. If I opened my kitchen window, I could shake hands with my neighbor.

The only way we could escape people, and the busyness of life, was to jump into our small, electric boat. I called this "boat therapy" because we often discussed our dream of chucking it all one day and moving to a Caribbean island. Duke needed these coping dreams to get through his courtroom battles and hellish commutes on gridlocked freeways.

"Here's the key," I said. We climbed inside and, as soon as Duke turned the engine on, our favorite Bob Marley CD, *"Legend,"* started playing.

"So what happened?" Duke asked, turning our battery-powered Duffy down the first finger of the lake. I spewed out the tale of my encounter with Greg, while Duke listened in silence.

Turning toward him, I waited, then tapped his forearm to get a reaction. "Should we give him condoms or refuse to let him see her?"

"Let me talk to him first," Duke said.

Fifteen minutes after they spoke, Duke returned from our local pharmacy and handed me the bag of condoms.

Why did he give them to me? Did he think Steve would be embarrassed if I gave him the condoms?

"Here, Steve," I said, dumping condoms into his cupped palms. I remembered doing this with Starburst candy not that long ago.

"You know Dad and I don't approve of sex at your age," I said, crumpling the paper bag. I was hoping he'd say, *"Mom, don't worry, I'm not going to have sex,"* but he opened his nightstand drawer and tossed the condoms inside without saying a word.

That is when I realized that all my years of being a stay-at-home mom to raise my sons did not guarantee a close relationship and mutual respect between us. How wrong I had been to think it would.

A year later, when Steve started as a freshman in high school, he met Mandy. She was three years older, and, at seventeen, Mandy planned to move into Steve's bedroom.

CHAPTER THREE

Poisonwood Tree

IT DIDN'T TAKE ME LONG to get used to the half-inch ants carrying twigs and leaves across my wooden kitchen countertop, and the families of geckos scampering up and down the walls of our hut in Belize.

Every morning I'd find something in Duke's empty beer bottle from the night before. Tipping the bottle upside down, I thumped the bottom with the palm of my hand and watched the ugly roaches weave their way to an imaginary finish line. I then sprayed them. Long tentacles twitched while a cloud of white fumes rose from the sink.

"Mom, that's poison. Don't spray it in the sink," Alec said. I spun around and noticed a red, swollen patch underneath his left eye.

"What's that?" I asked, tapping lightly on the spot.

"I dunno."

"Does it hurt?"

"No. It just itches a little."

After sweeping critter droppings off our dark wood floors, I heard Alec yell, "Mom, my face is on fire." I raced down the hut's screened hallway to his bedroom and wasn't prepared for what I saw. In less than twenty minutes, his entire face had turned deep sangria red and bubble-wrap blisters had erupted on his neck and at the base of his hairline.

"It burns," he cried.

I inspected his skin and discovered a black oval on his knuckle. Though flat, unlike the neck blisters, it reminded me of an ink stain from a leaking fountain pen.

"Let me get the peroxide," I said. I dipped a cotton ball into the liquid and lightly patted the stain. Nothing happened, not even a bubble.

"Maybe you touched a poisonwood tree," Duke said after Googling the symptoms. For once, they popped up quickly on his computer screen, which meant our satellite dish was free of dense cloud cover.

"What's that?" Alec asked.

"Here, come take a look," Duke said. "It says the leaves are extremely toxic, causing blisters and rashes."

"I never saw one of those trees," Alec said.

"Some people are highly allergic and can break out just by standing next to the tree," Duke advised, continuing to read.

"It's probably the Belizean version of poison ivy," I said. "Remember, you used to get that on your camping trips with Jeff and Jake," friends who lived across the street from us in Orange County.

I had no idea what to do.

Were there special pills for Poisonwood? We didn't have a local doctor, so I called Evelyn, the property manager at Consejo Shores.

"I'll send my husband over right away," she said. "He can tell if it's poisonwood. Don't worry."

I started realizing that no one worries in Belize; however, that did not apply to me.

We waited fifteen minutes, but Carlos never showed up. We already knew that "urgent" had a different meaning in Belize.

"Go get Carlos," I told Duke. Alec could no longer open his left eye. It had puffed up like a crimson sea anemone.

Duke sprinted across the overgrown grass between our huts. He returned two minutes later with Carlos, who immediately poked Alec's blisters, then examined his hands.

"Ahaa," he said looking at the black spot. "You need sap from gumbo-limbo tree; it's cure for poisonwood."

I breathed a sigh of relief, until Carlos, shaking his head sideways, added, "I'm not sure it work now. You waited too long, but we try."

What did he mean too long? He took forever to come over.

Duke followed Carlos outside to look for a gumbo-limbo tree. It might come in handy in the future. Five minutes later, they were back with a small chunk of bark and handfuls of feather-like leaves. The red bark looked dry and peeled like sunburned skin. Carlos told us it was nicknamed "the tourist tree" because it reminded locals of tourists' skin after sunburns.

"So where's the gumbo-limbo tree?" I asked Duke, curious to know where to find it.

"It's next to Carlos' clothesline," he said. "A poisonwood tree used to grow right beside it, but Carlos cut it down. They always grow next to one another."

"Isn't nature marvelous?" I said, trying to cover up my fear. "God placed gumbo-limbo trees next to poisonwood trees." No one commented.

Carlos asked Duke for his Swiss army knife and proceeded to scrape the bark.

"You get sap from it," he said. To me it looked like Carlos grated half a teaspoon of sawdust from a sheet of sandpaper. There was no sap. Duke tried rubbing the powder onto Alec's burning face, but nothing changed. I guess we expected instant results: the American way. Fortunately, Carlos had a backup plan. "We boil the leaves," he said.

"You mean Alec's supposed to drink the tea?" I asked.

"No, you make mush with leaves and spread it on body," Carlos said.

I removed a saucepan from the cabinet, tossed a dead cockroach into the trash, and used bottled water instead of our stinky well water to boil the leaves. When the water bubbled, I threw all the leaves in and let them simmer until they turned velvety. Without a blender, I used a fork against the edge of the saucepan, crushing the leaves into a spinach-like mush.

"Alec, take all your clothes off except your boxers," Duke said.

"Why?" he asked.

"We're going to try the leaves instead of the bark," Duke replied.

I placed a towel on Alec's bed so as not to mess up his sheets. He lay flat on his back, and, with the back of a teaspoon, Duke smeared a thin layer of "spinach" over Alec's body.

"That looks gross." Josh wrinkled his nose.

We could have been filming an episode for the Discovery Channel called "Modern-Day Family Experiments with Ancient Tribal Remedies."

Alec felt worse afterward.

"I bet Alec touched the tree on purpose so you'd send him back to California," Josh said.

"Stop it," Duke snapped. "You're not helping."

Carlos leaned over Alec and said, "Tomorrow all your red patches turn black." Alec stared at his black knuckle, then turned his head away. Perhaps this was Belizean humor; we didn't find it funny. Carlos then dug a tube of hydrocortisone out of his pocket and handed it to Duke before leaving.

"Alec, don't worry, only the first spot stays black," Duke said. What we hadn't told Alec was that his skin condition could take a good five weeks to clear up.

The following morning, Alec's blisters had grown into half-inch raised mounds of yellow liquid.

"Mom, it hurts so bad. I can't move," he said with a groan.

I worried. He hadn't eaten in more than twenty-four hours.

"Duke, he's burning hot and needs a doctor." At six foot three and 135 pounds, Alec could not afford to lose another ounce. He'd had a huge growth spurt between his thirteenth and fourteenth birthdays. Being a picky eater, especially in Belize, didn't help. Duke agreed we had to get him to a doctor right away.

"I can't walk," Alec sobbed as I helped him get dressed.

How could I have put my son's health at risk by taking him to Belize? What if the doctors weren't qualified? What if hospitals didn't use sterilized equipment? What about AIDS?

"We'll carry you," I said.

"Don't be silly," Duke said. "He needs to walk to the car. You know what the roads are like here. He's going to be tossed around no matter how slowly I drive."

"Here, Alec, lie down in the front seat," I said, adjusting the angle of the passenger seat.

Where was Steve? Did he feel guilty about asking Alec to cut down a tree trunk for his crocodile-hunting spear? That must have been how Alec touched the poisonwood tree.

"Can I go?" Josh asked. "I want to see them poke needles in Alec."

"No. You stay with me," I replied. "You need a shower anyway."

"I hate our stinky water," Josh said.

"I know. I can't stand the smell, either," I said, feeling guilty about complaining to my nine-year-old son.

"Mom, it's better here than Iraq," Josh said, surprising me with his mature comment. He'd seen photos of the war on the Internet. Josh made me realize it's how you choose to look at things in life that matter.

It took a good three hours before I heard Duke's truck on our dirt path.

"Where's Alec?" I asked, running down the steps.

"In the hospital," Duke said.

"Oh-my-God! You left him?" I yelled.

Duke grabbed my hand and led me back inside the hut. He sat me down and explained how two doctors examined Alec. One doctor was Cuban, the other Pakistani, and they both agreed that he needed hospital care.

"Did they start an IV?" I asked.

"No, nothing. They just made him lie on a bed that didn't look too clean."

"How the hell could you leave your son alone in a dirty third-world hospital? What were you thinking?" I screamed.

"Sonia, he was in bad shape; we had to do something."

"Go get him," I ordered.

I had not yet plucked up the courage to drive the seven-mile, pot-holed dirt road to Corozal, the closest town.

Duke drove straight back to the hospital, and, during the hour and a half he was gone, I visualized doctors starting an IV and Alec getting infected with AIDS.

The phone rang. I jumped, startled by the sound. It was Evelyn asking me if Duke had come back yet.

"Not yet. I'm worried something's terribly wrong," I said, too embarrassed to tell her I didn't trust Belizean hospitals.

"Call the hospital," she said. Evelyn gave me the number, and I dialed. After only five seconds, they put me straight through to Duke. "Why are you still there? Is something wrong?"

"It's too long to go into now; I'll tell you later."

"Now," I yelled. "What the hell's going on?"

"Okay, they started an IV on Alec, gave him three shots, and the doctors aren't too thrilled about me yanking him out of the hospital after they just started treating him. I'll wait for the drip to finish, and then I'll bring him home."

"Are you sure the needle was clean?"

"Stop being silly," Duke said.

"Thank God he's OK. Why didn't you call me to let me know?"

"It's not easy to call. You know that."

An hour later I heard the sound of Duke's tires on gravel. I bolted out the door and flew down the steps. Hugging Alec lightly, so as not to squeeze his blisters, I noticed he could open his left eye again. An oversized cotton ball and Band-Aid marked where they'd placed the IV on the inside of his left elbow.

"I'm so happy you're home," I said. Although slouching, Alec was able to walk without flinching with each step.

Once back in the hut, he told me the hospital wasn't that bad. "The only problem was the Cuban doctor didn't speak English, so I couldn't understand him. The nurse told me I can't drink orange juice or Coke, and to ice the blisters instead of putting hydrocortisone cream on them."

"You look so much better," I said, wanting to shower him with kisses.

The following morning Alec called me to his room.

"Mom, I'm starving. Can you make pancakes, please?"

"Sure," I said, keeping my fingers crossed that the bugs had stayed out of my flour and sugar containers.

CHAPTER FOUR

The Leaking Toilet

"YOU SAW THE LEAK? Call the plumber; I've got a trial in L.A.,"
Duke said, rushing out the door.

At 8:30 A.M., Graham, a stout, red-faced plumber, showed up. As
soon as he opened his mouth, I felt like I was back in Glasgow, Scotland,
where I got my first job after college.

"How long have you lived in California?" I asked.

"Long enough," he said. "As soon as I can afford to retire, my wife
and I are moving to the Caribbean."

"Really! My husband and I have been longing to move to the
Caribbean, but everything seems so expensive. Have you found a place?"

"Belize," Graham said.

I shrugged, feeling geographically incompetent.

"It used to be British Honduras," he explained. I paused, uncertain
what to say. I had gone to school in the United Kingdom. *Why didn't I
know where British Honduras was?* Graham came to my rescue. "It's the
next country south of Mexico. They speak English there, and you can
buy beachfront property for $15,000." My heart leaped.

"You're kidding. That sounds dirt cheap," I said. "Is it like Mexico, where the government can take away your property?"

"Not in Belize," Graham said, looking sincere. "It's under British Common Law, so you get title of your property."

This sounded way too good to be true.

As soon as Graham left, I Googled Belize and checked his facts. He was right. There were parcels of oceanfront land for a mere $15,000, even islands for under $100,000. I drove straight to my local library and checked out a book on Belize. I felt like a child who'd learned to ride a two-wheel bike for the first time.

Cookie barked, my signal that Duke was home from work. I pounced on him in the hallway. "I found an island we could move to," I said, grinning from ear to ear. Duke loosened his tie.

"The plumber," I began.

"Is the toilet fixed?" he asked, interrupting me.

"Yes. Are you listening to me?"

Duke nodded.

"So the plumber told me about Belize, south of Mexico. He said beachfront land is dirt cheap, and English is their official language. Belize sounds like the perfect place."

"Let me get out of my suit."

I couldn't believe Duke's lack of reaction.

Why wasn't he more interested, considering I'd discovered a Caribbean location that seemed to have everything we'd been looking for? I shouldn't have been surprised. Like most men, Duke focused on one thing at a time. Once he was satisfied that the toilet was fixed and I hadn't paid the plumber a fortune, he'd be eager to hear about Belize.

"How much did he charge?" Duke asked, returning in his comfy, old jeans and the ragged T-shirt he wouldn't get rid of because it grew softer with age.

"Not much, but worth every penny considering I discovered Belize."

Now ready to consider Caribbean islands, Duke turned on his computer. "B-A-Y-L-E-E-Z, is that how you spell it?" Duke's spelling had always sucked. He counted on me to be his walking dictionary.

"B-E-L-I-Z-E," I said. "I spent the day researching properties and e-mailed you some links. I also found this great book at the library on Belize," I added, placing it on his desk so he'd thumb through it.

Over the next few days I devoured Lan Sluder's book, *Living Abroad in Belize,* while Duke spent his evenings looking at potential properties, and reading expat forums and other websites.

"Let's get a coffee and go to the beach," I suggested one Saturday morning. "Alec's at Jeff and Jake's house, and Josh's at Ryan's."

Duke dropped me off at our local Starbucks and waited in the car. It seemed like years since we'd enjoyed a coffee at the beach, and now that we'd spent time researching Belize, I wanted to discuss the pros and cons of moving our family there. I decided, on impulse, to ask the manager at Starbucks if the company had a store in Belize. "Where's Belize?" he asked.

Since Belize had become our obsession, I constantly searched for business opportunities. Through extensive reading, I discovered that Duke and I could work in Belize as long as we filed for the QRP (Qualified Retirement Program.) This didn't mean we were retiring. What it meant is that we could start our own business, as long as we hired local Belizeans. All we had to do was pay the BTB (Belize Tourist Board) $5,000 upfront, for our entire family, and the law guaranteed we'd have our QRP cards within six weeks. Though the cards were not cheap, we wanted job security and were thrilled to discover this program.

"There aren't any Starbucks in Belize," I told Duke as I stepped into our van.

"There's probably not enough of a demand for it."

"You'd think with tourism, there might be a need for one," I said, placing my coffee in the cup holder.

"We should get a better idea if we decide to check it out," Duke said as he drove along Laguna Canyon highway to the beach.

"You mean, when we check it out?" I said with a twinkle in my eye. He nodded.

Duke parked in front of the multimillion-dollar mansions that hugged the cliffs of Shaws Cove in Laguna Beach. We grabbed our coffees and strolled down the steps to the beach below. It was high tide, and the salt spray misted our faces as we looked for a spot to prop up our umbrella and unfold our beach chairs. I glanced at the cool Pacific Ocean, pretending it was the warm, turquoise Caribbean and remembering the first time I had visited Eleuthera Island with my parents when I was eighteen. I was smitten; I knew that one day, I would live on a Caribbean island.

After a few minutes of quiet, I said, "I wish I knew how we could make money in Belize."

"Actually, I've been thinking about a legal transcription business," Duke replied. "You know Belize has a very high literacy rate, something like 97 percent, so we can hire local secretaries to do the proof-reading, and I'd oversee their work."

"Why didn't you tell me?" I said, admiring Duke for his creativity. "I just did."

I took a sip of coffee and pointed to some scuba divers in the distance, their heads bobbing out of the water.

"I need to learn how to scuba dive if we decide to move," I said.

"We should both get certified," Duke said, digging his bare feet into the sand.

"I thought you already were."

"That was years ago. I need a refresher course."

As I watched the scuba divers, I wondered how difficult it would be to get the hang of breathing through a tube. *Would I feel claustrophobic?*

I loved water, but something scared me about breathing through a tube. Still, I had to learn. I couldn't let Duke — or myself — down.

"It'd be good for our boys to experience adventures they'd never get in the U.S.," Duke said. "Did you check out the schools?"

"Looks like schools are better in Corozal," I told him. "They even have a junior college for Steve after high school."

"I found an expat community in Consejo Shores," Duke said. "It's close to Corozal, and there are some nice waterfront properties for under $50,000."

"That sounds too good to be true," I said.

It seemed ironic to be sitting on a beach in Southern California surrounded by stunning, multimillion-dollar homes — the envy of people around the world — and to be longing for a simple, non-materialistic life in the Caribbean.

We folded our beach chairs, kicked the sand off our flip-flops and tossed our empty Starbucks cups in the nearest trash can. Duke turned to look at me. "So are we really serious about Belize?" he asked.

"I think so, don't you?"

"Yes." We both smiled.

CHAPTER FIVE

Crossing the Line

"MANDY'S NAKED IN STEVE'S BED," Josh said, bolting into the kitchen. His light blue eyes beamed with delight at squealing on his older brother.

"I saw her boobs," he said, snickering.

Coffee gushed out my nostrils and mouth, splattering on the tiled floor as I gasped for air.

"That's gross, Mom," Josh said, leaping back to avoid the spray. Duke ripped some paper towels off the roll and handed them to me as I crouched on the floor mopping coffee splatters.

"Duke, you handle Steve. I'll go talk to Mandy."

Alec and Josh pretended to watch television, but I could tell they were listening. The line had been crossed, and I didn't want my sons to think we condoned this behavior.

I heard the back door slam and dialed Mandy's cell phone. "Mandy, we need to talk now. Meet me at Starbucks in The Grove shopping center."

"Sure," she replied, charming as usual.

Mandy's angelic face and blue eyes looked so innocent, but after our meeting, I finally saw the manipulator behind her sweet smile.

My head felt fuzzy as I drove home.

I hit the remote and listened to the garage door squeak and struggle as it rose.

"Where the hell you've been?" Steve demanded, puffing up his chest. "You talked to Mandy, didn't you?"

I squeezed past him as he tried to block the entry. "Yes I did," I snarled, spinning around to face him. "I won't have her sleeping here. Is that clear?"

"Fuck you. I don't care what you think."

I never thought I could fear my own son. How could I love and hate him at the same time?

I ran upstairs, tears streaming down my cheeks, needing Duke to comfort me.

"We have to talk," I said as I dropped to the cold, tiled floor next to the bathtub, sobbing.

"What happened?" Duke said, stroking my shoulder.

"You won't believe what Steve just said." My voice trembled as I repeated Steve's ugly words. Duke grabbed a tissue and wiped my tears.

"Did you talk to him while I was gone?" I whimpered.

"He was taking a shower. I didn't get a chance."

"Come on, Duke. He wasn't in the shower the whole time."

I got off the tile and rinsed my face.

"Mandy told me she's manic-depressive and tried to kill herself," I said, hoping this would get Duke to react.

He headed downstairs, but Steve was gone.

During our fifteen-year marriage, Duke rarely spoke about his childhood. But one day he'd confessed that he'd felt angry and unloved as a child, and rebelled as a teenager. He told me his job as a prison guard helped him overcome some of his issues. Duke had broken up numerous fights among inmates, which made me wonder whether he'd picked the job in order to get rid of his own aggression. *Was this why he hated confrontations at home?* I remembered a conversation when Duke told me, "You never want to see me angry." And I believed him.

Josh burst through the front door, his nose and cheeks smeared with dirt and grass stains.

"Dad, come play football with Alec and me," he said, panting.

"Not now, Josh. I'm too tired."

"You're always tired," Josh said.

I felt a pang of guilt and sadness as Josh shuffled out the front door, his chin dipped toward his chest.

"Duke, I'm worried about Alec and Josh. You're not spending time with them anymore."

"I know," he said grabbing a couple of oatmeal-raisin cookies from the large Costco container on our kitchen counter and heading toward the couch.

Stress and exhaustion had become permanent fixtures in Duke's life, which led to him snacking on anything he could find in the pantry. He ate mindlessly, and now all that was left from his years of being in great shape as a high school varsity swimmer were his wide shoulders.

I worried constantly about a heart attack or a stroke, and it frustrated me that Duke didn't seem to care. Steve's issues made everything worse for all of us.

When Duke returned from work, I showed him Steve's room.

"What's all that?" he asked.

"It gets worse," I said. "Come listen to the answering machine." I played back a message from the high school attendance line. Steve had been absent all day.

"Where is he now?" Duke asked.

"I don't know. He hasn't come home."

"What's for dinner?" Alec asked, packing his books away after finishing homework.

I'd forgotten about dinner.

Alec, now twelve, made it easy to forget he existed. He never asked for much, and his room remained tidy and organized. I shall never forget the essay he wrote in fourth grade entitled, "My Future." I read it and, already at age nine, he had high expectations. "I never want a grade below an A, and after I graduate college, I shall get married and have two kids: a boy and a girl."

Duke confronted Steve when he marched into the kitchen later that evening.

"You ditched school today."

"Only one class," Steve said, wearing what seemed to be his ever-present smirk.

"Your school called and said you were absent all day."

"They screwed up."

Steve opened the refrigerator door and searched for food.

"Don't lie," I said. "I already spoke to attendance."

Steve shrugged, then crammed a slice of pizza in his mouth.

"Why's Mandy's stuff in your room?" I asked.

"She wanted to decorate it," he grinned, and jumped onto a barstool.

"This is our house, not hers," Duke said.

"It's my room. I can do what the hell I please."

"You've got till tomorrow to get rid of it, or I will," Duke said, his face turning bright red. Steve surged forward and kicked the barstool. It crashed to the tile floor, almost hitting Cookie.

"Poor Cookie," Josh said, pouncing on top of her like a protective shield.

"What the hell do you think you're doing?" Duke yelled. "I'm getting sick and tired of your crap."

Steve balled his fist and ran out the back door.

"Knock it off," Duke yelled.

I ran down the hallway and out the garage door just in time to hear tires screeching and see Mandy's BMW veering round the corner. She'd been waiting for him.

Sinking between Alec and Josh on the couch, I squeezed them both against my chest. Had it not been for the familiar warm bodies of my two sons, I could have been sitting in a complete stranger's house. I longed to give Alec and Josh the love and attention they deserved and knew Steve was sapping our family's energy, like a bad virus.

Several hours later, Steve tiptoed back into the kitchen, staring at his hands to avoid looking at me. I noticed dark circles under his eyes. I just wanted to hug him and say, "I love you." I longed for my old Steve, the one who smiled and played basketball with his brothers, the one who threw tennis balls for Cookie to catch, the smart kid who made people laugh. I got off the couch, and he turned his back to me. I caught a glimpse of a black star inside a circle on his right shoulder blade. It looked like fresh black ink bleeding through his white T-shirt. *This couldn't be a tattoo—surely not?*

He sat down on the couch with his brothers and watched the last few minutes of a Discovery Channel show.

I had to tell Duke. He was already asleep.

"I think Steve got a tattoo," I whispered.

Duke sprung up instantly. "Where?"

"His right shoulder blade."

Duke was seething. He stomped downstairs and caught a glimpse of Steve's back.

"Is that a tattoo on your back?" Duke demanded.

Steve didn't respond. "Show me your back." Still silence.

"Now!" The tension was so thick I covered Josh's ears with my hands. Alec ran upstairs to his room. He hated yelling.

"Duke, go to Steve's room," I pleaded.

I finally witnessed the side of Duke's personality he wasn't proud of. He'd been pushed past his limit.

"Fuck you, fuck you, fuck you!" Steve yelled. I heard a loud thud against the wall and Duke's voice, "Don't you dare!" Finally, a door slammed so hard that I felt the vibration down the length of the hallway.

"Why is Steve being so bad?" Josh asked, threading his fingers inside mine.

"I wish I knew. I hope you never get that way when you're a teenager."

"I won't, Mom; I promise," he said.

After tucking Josh into bed, I knocked on Alec's door.

"Go away," he whimpered.

"Alec, I'm so sorry," I said, and headed back to my bedroom, trembling.

"What happened?" I asked Duke as soon as he stepped inside.

"He ran away."

"Where? Where did he go?" It was pitch dark, and I panicked.

"He took off full-speed."

"Was she outside?"

"I didn't see her."

"Should we call the police?"

"No. He'll come back once his temper cools off. You realize Steve got a Satanic tattoo," Duke said, his body tense and face red with anger. "I'll make sure he gets it lasered off."

Steve didn't come home that night.

I couldn't sleep, so I sat on the couch hugging the pillow against my chest.

My cell phone rang at midnight, "Mom, it's me. Don't call the police, I'm OK," Steve said, as though reading my mind.

"Where are you?

"I'm OK," he repeated. "Just bring my backpack to school tomorrow. I'll meet you in front of the school parking lot." Then he hung up.

I crawled upstairs and collapsed into bed. Duke stirred and slid his hand toward mine. Our fingers locked, and I told him Steve had called.

Hearing Steve's voice gave me hope that he still cared about his family, that he didn't want me to worry. It was possible, of course, that he was only concerned about himself and what might happen to him if we called the police. I didn't want to accept that. As a mother, I had to believe my son loved me. I brushed aside his hurtful comments, always hopeful that the teeniest act of kindness would prove that my son always had, and always will, love me.

The following morning Duke brought me a cup of coffee in bed.

"Don't you think it's time to check out Belize?" Duke whispered.

"Yes," I replied.

In a way, it felt selfish even to consider uprooting our kids from their familiar life to adapt to a foreign one in a third-world country. But Duke and I had to resolve the problems we faced with Steve. Taking him away, rather than shipping him off seemed like the right thing to do. Alec and Josh were suffering from lack of attention; if we left Orange County, Duke would have more time to spend with our boys.

All I wanted now was to save my family. I was confident that getting out of our comfort zone and starting a new life in Belize would help us reconnect as a family.

When I looked back at my own childhood in Africa and Europe, I realized that my parents had offered me a wonderful *gift*. Traveling and living in different parts of the world made me grow up emotionally, become independent and take charge of my life. What harm could there be in letting my kids experience life in another part of the world? Belize was not a rich country, so perhaps our kids would learn gratitude, humility and other noble values. This might be the best remedy for all of us, and I felt fortunate that Duke agreed.

I think Duke craved adventure more than I realized, and I longed to discover my paradise.

We knew we had to go; but we still had to work out the answer to our question, *"Can we move our family to Belize?"*

CHAPTER SIX

Scouting Trip

"We're not moving to Belize, are we?" Alec asked when he saw me pack. He'd heard us talk about the possibility of moving but must have thought it was simply a threat to get Steve back on track. Strangely, Steve had not said a word about our potential move. But Alec always knew how to pull on my heartstrings.

"Dad and I want to check it out first," I said, trying to reassure him.

"I hope you hate it," Alec said, pacing back and forth.

"Why do you say that?"

"It's all because of Steve that you and Dad want to move," he said and stormed out before I had time to respond.

I looked for him, but knew he'd run off to Jeff and Jake's house.

Out of my three sons, Alec worried me the most when it came to moving; he hated change.

I had crammed ten days' worth of clothing into a single carry-on, thanks to Duke's years of nagging about my packing. "I hope we won't need anything too dressy," I said, not yet realizing that "dressy" in Belize meant an unstained tank top.

On June 7, 2003, our taxi arrived at 4:30 A.M., and I felt like a kid running away from home. Duke saw me heading toward Alec's room and grabbed my hand before I grasped the doorknob. "Don't wake him," he whispered, "It'll make things worse."

Thankfully, Paul, my cousin's thirty-two-year-old son, had agreed to supervise our boys during our ten-day scouting trip. At six foot five and a hefty three hundred pounds, he could both intimidate Steve and act like a giant teddy bear with Alec and Josh. He was like a big kid himself, who enjoyed pizza, ice cream and video games.

Duke and I held hands in the taxi, like lovebirds on our second honeymoon.

"Think Paul can handle Steve?" I asked on the way to the airport.

"Don't worry; everything will be fine," Duke said, giving my hand a reassuring squeeze.

I couldn't wait to explore Belize and secretly hoped we'd both love it. My resentment toward Orange County had grown stronger with each passing day, and I deliberately started focusing on what I hated about our life in Orange County to justify a potential move. Things like road rage, stressed-out people who had everything but still looked miserable and over-scheduled kids who grew up too fast.

Belize is a tiny country the size of Massachusetts, south of Mexico and east of Guatemala. Unlike Southern California, it's sparsely populated, with only 280,000 people in the entire country. What attracted me to Belize was its eco-friendliness, with more than five hundred species of birds and seven hundred species of butterflies. It not only had jaguars roaming the jungles, but also the second-largest coral reef in the world, after the Australian Great Barrier Reef. Duke and I knew it would be hot and humid, with tropical storms and hurricanes during the time we'd picked to visit.

We planned to check out three main parts of Belize. The first was the popular tourist island of Ambergris Caye, with a population of eleven thousand, including about one thousand American, Canadian and European expats. The second place was another expat development, called Consejo Shores, which was far cheaper, had better schools nearby and was situated in northern Belize, next to the Mexican border. The last place, Placencia, is located in southern Belize, where the rainfall is much heavier, meaning more mosquitoes and bugs.

Thunderstorms in Houston delayed our connecting flight by two hours, but this was typical in the summer, and we were told not to worry; the puddle jumper would be waiting to take us to the island of Ambergris Caye.

As our flight approached Philip S.W. Goldson International Airport in Belize, I looked out the plane's oval window at the heavy tree canopies below. They gradually thinned out, and a brackish river meandered through swampland. Most houses looked as though they were only half-constructed, with rebar poking out the sides and dilapidated shacks thrown haphazardly in between swamp and grassland. I tried not to let my heart sink, but this landscape was nothing like the photos I'd drooled over of white sandy beaches and surrounding turquoise waters.

Had all those photos been Photoshopped? As the runway emerged beside steaming, tea-colored pools of water, I thought of mosquitoes breeding and remembered that we were in a third-world country.

Passengers complained about the ten-minute wait to get off the plane. I remained in my seat studying everything going on outside. Several dark-skinned Belizean men dressed in long pants and short-sleeved dress shirts seemed to be joking around at the entrance to the small airport building. After several minutes, they decided to push the staircase-on-wheels to the front and rear exits of our plane. I noticed the animated and happy-looking faces of families with children staring at our plane from a large outdoor terrace attached to the airport building. This brought back memories of when I was a child in Paris and my father and I enjoyed watching planes take off and land at Le Bourget airport. Dad knew every airline, every aircraft and their flight routes. I was so proud of him.

Once the doors of the aircraft finally opened, the plane turned into a giant sauna. My naturally frizzy hair immediately lost the "hip" Orange County look. I felt free, in a non-conformist, rebellious sort of way.

The Belizean woman who greeted us at the gate had a very round, dark face; the bottom half was concealed by a mask like the one my dentist wore when she cleaned my teeth. A small sign stated, "Severe Acute Respiratory Syndrome (SARS) outbreak in Asia," and I assumed she wore this to protect herself from tourist germs. A strange mixture of sweat; hot, humid air; and simmering chicken stew greeted us as we stood in line waiting for immigration to stamp our thirty-day tourist visas. Apparently, we had missed an immigration form and had to step aside to fill it out. Once we were back in line, the immigration officers didn't look happy to see us. "Where are all the welcoming Belizeans?" I whispered to Duke. All the books we'd read claimed that Belizeans were super-friendly.

We proceeded through customs and checked in for the *Tropic Air* flight to San Pedro, the only town on this 26-mile-long island of Ambergris Caye. All islands in Belize are called cayes, pronounced "key." *Ambergris* isn't a very pleasing sound to the ear and, according to the dictionary, means: "A wax-like substance that originates as a secretion in the intestines of the sperm whale, found floating in tropical seas and used in perfume manufacture." Not exactly romantic.

As we sat waiting on rock-hard plastic chairs at gate number four, my butt grew numb. I thought I heard a parrot screeching but soon realized it was a dwarf, the airport bartender, trying to drum up some business. "Rum, rum, anyone for rum?" he squealed. No one seemed interested in drinking rum.

Only two minutes before departure, a young woman spoke into a crackly sounding microphone. All we understood was "San Pedro," so Duke and I followed a single file of passengers walking toward a propeller plane on the tarmac. Everything seemed so casual, as though we were heading to our minivan in a Walmart parking lot. Our suitcases were loaded via wheelbarrow, and we could grab any seat we wanted, including the one next to the pilot.

The flight only climbed to 1,500 feet, allowing us to focus on some dark blobs below. We soon determined they were manatees and dolphins swimming in the transparent turquoise waters. I squeezed Duke's hand tightly, feeling a tingling in my chest.

Barely fifteen minutes later, our Cessna landed on a dirt strip in San Pedro, and two guys pushed rusty wheelbarrows loaded with suitcases over to us and our fellow passengers. Some grabbed their own bags; others waited for the baggage handlers to assist. Disorganized by our standards, their system worked as long as you accepted it. What Lan Sluder had written in his book, *Living Abroad in Belize,* now made sense. If you wanted everything organized and done to perfection, Belize would drive you bonkers. He mentioned spontaneous people did well in Belize. Duke and I belonged in that category.

Bicycles, golf carts and a few rust-colored Toyota taxi vans swarmed outside the open airport gate, leading to an unpaved road. From all appearances, traffic rules were based on instinct, not written code. With each step, clouds of chalky dust turned our feet light gray. We had no clue how to get to our hotel, but a teenage driver found us, and we followed him to a line of parked golf carts. I sat facing backward, my carry-on tucked under my feet, and used both hands to hold onto the flimsy, battery-powered vehicle. Our adventure had definitely begun.

I picked Coconuts Hotel because I liked the name, and our room pretty much fit the description in our guidebook, as well as our budget. A queen-size bed, tiled floor and no ocean view. A fur coat would have been nice for the icy temperature inside. Condensation from the air conditioner formed huge water droplets, making the drapes wet and moldy. But that didn't bother us; we were here to explore the outside world. After changing into shorts, I opened our door and the humidity slapped me in the face like a steamy washcloth after a facial. We followed the staircase down to an empty bar and searched for refreshments.

"Maybe the bartender's on the beach," I said. A few steps away, the wooden floor became sand and then the sand became sea.

Duke reminded me that June was the slow tourist season. Between Thanksgiving and Easter, the temperature and humidity became more tolerable.

I dipped my feet in the sea, walked a few steps further along the sea bed, and the level remained ankle deep. "It's really shallow."

"It's nice and warm," Duke said, swishing his foot back and forth. "We won't need wet-suits here."

"Look at all those coral heads," Duke said, pointing to some protruding mounds. "I'm sure there are tons of colorful fish swimming around."

We walked to the end of a long, uneven wooden pier where a ladder led to an open area for swimmers. The air smelled salty clean, and warm breezes caressed my face. I could feel my skin softening as it relaxed. I kicked off my flip-flops and let the silky sand massage my feet.

Back at the hotel bar, Duke asked our barefoot Creole bartender for our complimentary "welcome" drinks. He poured a heavy dose of rum, added a drop of punch and attached a chunk of fresh pineapple to the rim of the tall, skinny glass. We sipped our rum punches outside on lounge chairs, gazing at the beauty of the clear, unpolluted sky. I had forgotten how nature could entertain us with its twinkling stars. I rarely noticed the stars in the Orange County sky. Slowly, I started floating into *my paradise*, and when the bartender played the same Bob Marley CD we listened to on our boat at home, I said, "Duke, we're meant to be here." He smiled.

"I'm starving; let's go eat," he said.

We strolled toward town on the only street. Electric golf carts, bicycles and the occasional car skirted past us on this dusty lane. Since there weren't any sidewalks, we followed the gutter. The first restaurant, Jack's Place, looked lovely with its romantic, lantern-lit tables. No one greeted us, so we picked our own table. When a tall, blond man approached, I thought he was a tourist, not the waiter.

"What would you like to drink?" he asked. For a brief second, I was back in Europe, Germany to be precise. Our waiter was from Stuttgart and had lived fifteen years on the island.

"Do you miss Europe?" I asked.

"I wouldn't dream of moving back. Why would I want to go back to traffic and stress when I can live in paradise?" He said exactly what I wanted to hear.

"I'll get your rum punches."

What I really wanted was some bread and butter, to soak up my previous rum punch.

Fifteen minutes later, Günter still hadn't brought us a menu or drinks. "Maybe he went home," I joked. I got up looking for him, right when he emerged from the kitchen. Embarrassed, I zipped back to my seat. "We're very hungry, Günter," Duke said. "We want to order dinner now."

Günter frowned, baffled by our haste. Duke ordered the local grilled snapper.

"All I have is chicken, rice and beans." By now, even stale bread sounded delicious.

"How can they be out of fish?" I whispered after he left. "This is an island, for God's sake."

Clearly, we would have to adapt if we moved. This would be a good learning experience for our boys, since we planned on eating like the locals. We read that chicken, rice and beans, *fry jacks* (fried bread served at breakfast), *johnnycakes* (flat biscuits also served at breakfast) and *garnache* (crisp tortillas topped with cabbage, cheese and salsa) were part of the local fare. I wasn't too sure about eating *gibnut* (a brown, rat-like rodent the size of a large rabbit) or *cowfoot soup* and *stewed iguana*.

Duke and I agreed that if we moved, we'd no longer live the American way. We would switch from air conditioners to fans and local breezes, as the cost of electricity was too high. We would refuse to pay for imported filet mignons, cheeses, wines and ice creams, though perhaps we'd make an exception on birthdays and other special occasions. As Lan Sluder mentioned in his book, living the American lifestyle in

Belize will cost you more than back home. I wondered what my boys would say to thirty-second showers instead of thirty-minute ones.

When dinner arrived forty minutes later, our portions were tiny. This was not the night for a scrawny chicken leg. Duke joked that it was Uncle Jose's hormone-free chicken. We soon learned that in Belize you eat less and drink more. Duke called it, "The two-drink minimum country," as it took at least two cocktails before dinner was served. Perhaps Duke would lose weight without too much effort. I didn't object to smaller portions at all. I always thought American portions were huge, especially after returning from a visit to Paris.

The following morning we woke up to a cup of weak Maxwell House coffee, the local favorite served everywhere. Now I longed for a Starbucks.

We rented a golf cart for the day, and our adventure began. I was eager to explore the northern part of the island, supposedly more serene, for those who wanted *to get away from it all.* Though nothing like Los Angeles, downtown San Pedro still had its fair share of commotion. Traffic rules and one-way streets seemed to apply to tourists only, not the locals. Dust blasted from underneath the golf cart's tires, sticking to the sweat on our faces and bare skin. We laughed every time we hit a pothole and bounced off the seat. I imagined our boys enjoying the crazy ride through town.

A river bisected the island, and the only way to cross was on a wooden platform towed by three teenage boys. The crossing cost us twenty-five cents. They wore gardening gloves to protect their hands as they grasped a thick metal rope and pulled three golf carts and numerous bicycles on this floating piece of wood. Although primitive, the experience of drifting on a plank in a golf cart, with kids pulling us, was part of the island's charm. As we reached the other side of the river, a kid about Steve's age placed a worn sheet of plywood to block the gap where the barge met the road. I knew it would be good for my boys to see how these teenagers worked so hard and seemed happy with so little.

A pothole-ridden dirt path led to an area called *Tres Cocos*, where a small community of expats lived. With only one road you couldn't get lost, but this rickety ride probably kept golf cart repair shops in business. We hesitated at a fork and decided to follow an inviting, hand-painted sign pointing to the Palapa Bar. Once there, we discovered a two-story, palm-thatched structure and a bar, smack on top of the water. The three-hundred-sixty-degree view high above the turquoise sea was stunning. It made California's Pacific coast look dull by comparison. "Look how close the reef is. We can almost walk out and touch it," Duke said.

We ordered a couple of fresh-squeezed lime juices and stood there silently, hypnotized by the island and its beauty.

Duke pointed to a school of barracuda swimming right below us.

"I'm beginning to think I could really live here. Don't you think the boys would love it?" I asked.

Duke nodded. "It'd be great to have our own boat." His eyes glistened with excitement as he studied the skiffs speeding past us. I had no idea Duke was so keen on owning a motorboat. I guess after our electric boat, this seemed more like the real thing.

We continued along the trail until we reached a condo development called Belizean Shores. Two-story condos surrounded a pool with a swim-up bar. "This is so well-designed," Duke said. "Look how they've staggered the planters to protect from hurricane storm surges." We saw a sign, "Condos for Sale."

"Why not take a look?" I suggested. The sales guy was from San Diego, California.

"How do you like living here?" I asked.

"Love it," he said. "I don't plan on moving back to California." I was becoming more positive about the prospect of Belize by the minute. Though the condos were not huge — only one- or two-bedroom units — I tried convincing Duke that he and I could sleep in the master bedroom, Alec and Josh could share the second room and Steve could sleep on the couch in the living room. I was trying to fit five of us in 900 square feet — an adjustment after living in a 3,100-square-foot house with five bedrooms — but the view of the Caribbean and all the water activities were well worth giving up square footage. At least, that's what I felt at that moment.

"We could simplify our lives with less stuff, and I'd have less to clean," I said. "Look, there are even kids playing in the pool." I found out later they were on vacation; none of them lived here.

"You know, this is like the Orange County of Belize," Duke reminded me when we jumped back into our golf cart. I knew what he meant. There were several wealthy expats with second homes living on the island. "Perhaps if it was just the two of us, but we have to think of our kids," Duke said. "Besides, schools are better in Corozal than here."

Duke was right, but I knew the kids would enjoy the water activities and fishing here. "Perhaps we can stay an extra day and contact a Realtor," I said.

"Sonia, properties cost three times more on Ambergris Caye. They cater to tourists, so everything is more expensive."

A little disappointed, I decided I could always look on the Internet when we returned to California. "We should head back to our hotel before it gets dark," Duke said.

CHAPTER SEVEN

Northern Belize

THE FOLLOWING MORNING, we left Coconuts and caught the first puddle jumper back to Philip S.W. Goldson International Airport. Without a single reservation for the next seven days, we felt like true daredevils.

"What now?" I said, as we headed out the door of the last car rental agency — without a car.

"Wait," the car rental lady hollered, right before the door clanged shut. "I have one car left. It's the oldest one. Not so comfortable, no air-conditioning, no automatic windows, but much cheaper."

"We'll take it," we shrieked.

"It's old model Suzuki Samurai," she said.

"Is that the one that tips over?" I whispered to Duke. I recalled news reports alleging that the Suzuki Samurai had a tendency to flip over when turning corners.

"Yep," he said, with a shoulder shrug.

But as soon as we saw the white and rust-stained Suzuki Samurai, it was love at first sight. The vehicle had adventure written all over it. I would have felt like a materialistic tourist driving a luxury SUV in the heart of a third-world country. Besides, weren't we fleeing the world of SUVs? So with our free, photocopied map — which looked like a fourth grader's drawing of Belize and its skeletal road system — we buckled our sweaty bodies into our seats and let the adventure begin.

At the first intersection, Duke asked, "Right or left?"

"Left," I said. I couldn't wait to check out the properties up north.

Evelyn, a Realtor in the Consejo Shores expat development, was expecting us. She promised that her husband would show us some waterfront properties for sale whenever we showed up. I had high hopes, as Consejo Shores was not only affordable but also close to Mexico in case of a medical emergency. It was also a super-safe community, according to the guidebooks. We figured our kids could go to school in Corozal, only seven miles from Consejo Shores. Now that I'd fallen in love with the beauty and charm of Ambergris Caye, I hoped Consejo Shores would be equally nice but less of a strain on our budget.

We soon discovered that roads in Belize could be classified according to what we called "the three P's": paved, potholed or perilous. Driving north to Consejo Shores, we experienced all three P's. The Northern Highway, a one-lane road, was paved for eighty-five miles — a blessing — except that we got stuck behind a series of overflowing sugar cane trucks. We coughed our way through a noxious mixture of diesel fumes and smoke from burning fields of sugar cane. Beat-up trucks chugged and sputtered as they made their way to the only sugar mill factory in the north. Our eyes felt like they were on fire. We were practically driving blind, in a country where drivers hug beer bottles between their thighs and drive without headlights at dusk. Everything was different here, compared with accustomed safety standards in the U.S. But, as visitors in a foreign country, we knew we'd have to adapt.

Along the way, we passed several villages with piles of burning trash. That seemed to be the way families got rid of household waste. Old men sat smoking on worn-out porches, watching the cars go by. Chickens pecked the red clay soil looking for morsels of food, while women gathered around streams and rivers, pounding clothes on large rocks. They dried them on ropes tied between tree trunks.

Uniforms were mandatory in all public schools. Even in the more remote and destitute villages, children headed off to school, shoulders back, chest out, chin lifted, wearing bright white pants or skirts, white socks and crisp white shirts. These kids were experts at not getting one drop of terra cotta mud onto their clothes when it rained. Even while pedaling their old bikes through rust-colored, slushy mud, they somehow managed to prevent the tires from flinging dirt onto their starched white clothes. I wondered if the secret to white clothes was not bleach — as we believed in the U.S. — but the pounding action of clothes on a large rock.

My boys had never worn uniforms to school. I wondered what they would say when they had to dress in white like the local kids?

We drove through Corozal without stopping and found the seven-mile, potholed road leading to Consejo Shores. I was afraid the axle of our old, rusty car might break, but Duke drove cautiously around each pothole, taking forever to cover the seven miles. Only two cars passed us, zig-zagging around each pothole at about 50 miles per hour.

We found a pebbled path and followed it to a small cement building with an "office" sign above the door. We could see a noisy air-conditioner sticking out of the back window. I opened the door and felt as though I'd stepped into a freezer storage area. One metal desk sat in the center of the room, a woman sitting at it.

"Are you Evelyn?" I asked. She suddenly looked happy, and I got the impression it had been a while since she'd interacted with anyone.

"You must be Duke and Sonia," she said. We shook hands.

"My husband isn't here today. He can show you the properties tomorrow," she said.

Nothing seemed urgent in Belize.

"Is there a hotel close by?" I asked.

"Casablanca Hotel is in Consejo village. It's very nice," Evelyn said. "Just follow the road out. You'll find it; there's only one road. Carlos will meet you at ten tomorrow morning."

We drove along a dirt road to Casablanca Hotel. Our tires skidded as gravel popped underneath us. Another crack in the windshield would have made it even more difficult to see the road, so Duke slowed down to a crawl on the driveway leading to Casablanca's front gates. The hotel parking lot was empty, which was not reassuring. Duke pushed open a heavy wooden door that led straight into the bar and restaurant. No one showed up, so we each grabbed a stool and mopped the sweat off our foreheads with paper napkins from the bar. The place was quiet, except for the buzz of the refrigerator and a few geckoes scampering along the walls. After several minutes, a frail Belizean teenager appeared, holding a tray of clean glasses. She froze when she saw us.

"Do you have a room with a king bed for two nights?" Duke asked. Without a word, she placed the tray on the counter and reached for an old-fashioned silver key on a hook behind her. We followed her outside and up a cement staircase. There we had a view of Chetumal, a large city across the bay on the Mexican side of the border. Our hotel, which had a wrap-around balcony on both floors, looked to us like an unfinished apartment complex. Vertical rebar poked through the flat rooftop, giving it the *still under construction* look that seemed to be a trend in Belize.

Despite the unfinished exterior, Belizeans never skimped on their wood. Imagine a Motel 6 in the U.S. with custom-carved, solid mahogany doors. Our front door had a carving of a Mayan pyramid with steps leading to the summit. I could smell fresh varnish, which brought out the golden tones and rich shades of brown on the door.

Once inside the room, we were disappointed with the small bed — definitely not a king — and the musty smell that indicated it hadn't been occupied in months. We decided not to complain; In the Caribbean, you go with the flow.

"Let's get something to eat and a drink," Duke suggested.

After the translucent waters of Ambergris Caye, the cloudy, jade-colored bay of Chetumal was disappointing. I forced myself to think of the positives: better schools and medical facilities, and roads to escape a hurricane — the latter an important consideration when you live in Belize.

We joined the Canadian owner of the hotel, Betty, and her sister for a drink. "Is it always this quiet?" I asked.

"No, sometimes we have groups of fifteen or more staying," she replied.

"What's it like living here?"

"It beats the cold winters in Canada," Betty said, combing gray strands of hair off her face. The warm breeze picked up, offering a pleasant massage. "I like the slow pace of life here," she added.

I sensed her growing weariness with expat wannabes who always asked the same questions; but as one of those wannabes, I needed to hear the opinions of those who'd already taken the plunge and moved to Belize. Asking questions was my way of coming to a decision. Duke preferred to decide for himself; he didn't care as much about what others had to say.

"We lock the gates at ten o'clock, until eight the following morning. It's for your own safety," Betty said, raising her fleshy body off the bamboo bench. She then excused herself for dinner.

"I thought Consejo Shores was safe," I whispered, pulling on the straw in my glass.

"We're safe," Duke said, reminding me that Casablanca Hotel was in Consejo Village where the locals lived, not in Consejo Shores where the expats lived. "That's probably why they lock the gates." Duke always had answers to soothe my anxiety.

As the night sky took over, artificial lights flooded Chetumal. Now I felt the city vibes of Orange County instead of the serene beauty of paradise I desperately longed for.

Our waitress reappeared, notepad in hand. "You want to eat?"

We both said yes.

"The cook goes home soon. She can make fried fish and coleslaw for you."

"That's fine," Duke said. She wrote down our order slowly, as though her English teacher stood behind her and the handwriting had to be perfect.

After dinner, everything was dark and quiet. We were now prisoners of the hotel, so we went to bed.

Duke and I are both early risers. We never sleep in, not even on vacation. I longed for a cup of coffee when I awoke the next day, but the hotel was empty. The gates would remain locked until nine or so. We changed into our swimming trunks and took a quick dip in the bay, where I noticed the water tasted less salty than on Ambergris Caye. "Watch out for crocodiles," Duke yelled right after I got in.

"Where?" I screamed, reaching wildly for the ladder.

"This is brackish water where the crocs like to hang out," Duke said.

"Thanks a lot," I said, getting out. I knew Duke meant this as a tease, but I no longer felt like swimming.

Our boys loved Steve Irwin's TV show, *The Crocodile Hunter*, and would probably pretend to hunt crocodiles if we moved here.

"Maybe we can get coffee now," I said, picking up my towel and rushing back to the restaurant. The hotel was still empty. Now I really felt as though I were behind bars.

I got my first cup of coffee at 10 A.M. Our teenage waitress brought two tiny espresso cups with coffee the color of chamomile tea. It didn't even smell like coffee, and I swallowed it in one gulp before she'd even placed Duke's cup on the saucer. I asked if we could get an entire pot of coffee, but she looked at me as though I'd requested imported French truffles. Duke offered to share his coffee. He knew I needed my caffeine.

As we waited for Carlos to show up, a six-foot "Viking" appeared at the hotel gate, clad in dark blue overalls, a long-sleeved white shirt and a large straw hat. I couldn't figure out whether he was a lost tourist or an abducted farmer from Scandinavia.

"Is Betty here? I have come to fix the engine," he said to our waitress, enunciating each syllable with painful slowness. No one in Orange County would have the patience to listen to him.

"I think he might be a Mennonite," Duke said.

We were surprised to read about the large community of Mennonites living in northern Belize. They were the main producers of dairy, fruits, vegetables and furniture in the country. They had their own communities and schools, a bit like the Amish in Pennsylvania. It seemed strange that these blue-eyed blondes — with skin that never tanned — had picked a hot, humid third-world country to live in. I'd read that they represented 9 percent of Belize's population and had emigrated from Canada and Mexico in the 1950s.

Carlos showed up fifteen minutes late, in a rusty old Ford Astrovan. His English wasn't as good as that of his wife, Evelyn, but he still managed to throw in a lecture about his Mestizo heritage: "The Mexican race of Belizeans," he said. "We make up half the population." He was beaming with Mestizo pride. "Spanish is our first language and English, our second."

"Would you like a coffee?" I asked Carlos, gesturing for our waitress to come over.

"Yes, please," he said, happy as a child who'd been offered an ice cream cone. Fed up with waiting for her to come back, I chased our waitress inside the restaurant.

For some reason, Carlos quit talking after he'd delivered his Mestizo speech. I quizzed him about the properties he planned to show us, and he finally disclosed that he had three bay-front properties for sale.

We drove behind him to the first lot. "Look at the sinkholes," Duke muttered. "We don't want to put a foundation on this piece of land."

"Carlos, can you show us the other two?" Duke asked, raising his voice over the sound of the growing wind.

We drove to the northern tip of Consejo Shores. As soon as we parked, I knew this piece of land had a stunning view. Stumbling through overgrown grass and weeds, I swatted flies off my damp skin as I pushed my way to the water's edge. The wind pulled my curls out of the clips and started whipping my face. "Is it always this windy?" I had to shout so Carlos could hear me.

"Yes, lots of wind here."

I was somewhat disappointed by the murky water; I couldn't help but compare it to the turquoise waters of Ambergris Caye. The view was lovely, though; a tiny island covered with dense foliage lay a few hundred feet in front of the property. It made me think of Robinson Crusoe's island.

The third and last property looked promising. Carlos called it lot number eight. With its panoramic view of the bay and eighty feet of water frontage, it had great potential. The owner had built a five-foot seawall to protect the lot from storm surges. A small, jungle-like peninsula protruded, giving it a protected feel.

"So how much is this one?" Duke asked.

"Owner ask $55,000 US, but you can get for $48,000 US."

"It was listed for $45,000 US on your website," Duke said.

"Price go up since then."

I knew Duke wasn't happy with the price. He had planned on offering $38,000 US, but perhaps we could negotiate with the owner.

"What about that house?" I said pointing to what appeared to be an abandoned house, in good shape. "Does anyone live in it?"

"It belongs to liar in town." Carlos said. Duke and I glanced at one another.

"The *liar?*" I repeated.

"You know, like your husband."

"Oh, you mean lawyer," I said with a chuckle.

"Duke, I married a *liar*," I said, and we both laughed.

"The *liar*, she so busy she never come. She work in Belize City."

"Is she selling?" Duke asked. We both realized how much easier it would be to move our family into a finished house rather than build one.

"No. She not sell. It's empty fifteen years," he said.

As we peered through the windows, we noticed it was fully furnished. The kitchen cabinets were made of solid Belizean hardwood; I could easily see our family living in this house should we decide to move here. That would give us time to find the right property, I thought.

"Can you ask her if we can rent it?" I asked.

Carlos promised he'd call her.

We followed Carlos back to his wife's real estate office. "So which property did you like?" Evelyn asked.

I told her lot number eight, but that we also liked the lawyer's house.

"We rent houses, too," Evelyn said. "Carlos, show them John's house. That one you can rent when you move here."

We strolled along the dirt path to the rental. It was more like a hut on stilts than a house: rustic and somewhat charming, though a tad primitive for our family. The walls were made from skinny, pimento tree trunks. They had gaps, which I assumed would allow bugs to squeeze through. The roof was a thatched palapa — dried palm fronds woven together. We followed Carlos up four broken cement steps and waited for John to open the front door.

An old, caveman-like American expat greeted us. When he invited us in, I reluctantly placed my bottom on the worn fabric of his couch. The walls were bare, and the floors were charcoal-colored planks. "You plan on living here?" John asked.

"We're still looking," I said.

We strolled back to Evelyn's office. "You want to rent the palapa hut?" she asked.

"We prefer the lawyer's house," I replied, quickly.

"It's the right size for our family and already furnished," Duke added. "Please call and see if she's interested in renting it before we leave Consejo Shores."

"She's very difficult to get ahold of," Evelyn said.

"Do you have other houses for rent, in case she says no?" I asked.

"Not often," she said. "We mostly rent the huts, like the one you saw."

Duke told Evelyn we'd stop by after we checked out of our hotel to see if she'd contacted the lawyer.

The following morning, I called home. Josh answered the phone.

"How's everything?" I asked.

"Paul keeps playing my video games," Josh complained.

"Let me talk to Paul."

I really wanted to make sure Steve wasn't getting into trouble with Mandy.

"Everything's fine," Paul said. "Mandy hasn't been over once. I think they broke up."

"Really? I can't believe that," I said. "That's fantastic news."

With that, I joined Duke at a small table outside. We ordered breakfast and discussed Steve, reminding one another not to get our hopes up too soon.

"Something's a little weird about Consejo Shores, don't you think?" I said, buttering my Belizean johnnycake. "It's sort of dead compared to Ambergris Caye."

"It's a retirement community," Duke said.

"Think the boys will like it?"

"You heard Evelyn say there's a couple of Canadian kids in Consejo."

"Yeah, but I haven't seen them."

"They'll make friends at school," Duke said. I hoped he was right, as this community seemed sparsely populated.

We drove back to Evelyn's office and heard some promising news. "I got ahold of the lawyer. She said she might consider renting. You're lucky," Evelyn said. "She's never rented it before."

"That's wonderful," I said. "Can we take a look inside?"

"Sorry, but I don't have a key."

"Let's take another peek through the windows," I suggested.

Duke and I drove over and stared through the windows to get a feel for the inside of the house.

I had a feeling this might work out for our family, though I still preferred Ambergris Caye. But I had to be practical, and think of what was best for our family and our finances.

"Imagine if we rent her house while we build our own next door on lot eight," I said.

"My thought exactly," Duke said. "Now we need to negotiate the price of lot eight."

"We should wait before buying it," I said. "We might find something else we like even more."

"We saw all the properties," Duke said, wiping sweat off his forehead with the back of his hand.

"What if we like her house, and she says we can buy it?" I said.

We left Consejo Shores feeling confident about our decision to move here. We decided to check out Placencia, even though we hadn't found any properties we liked online. We wanted to be certain of the right decision.

CHAPTER EIGHT

Southern Belize

THE PAVED NORTHERN HIGHWAY ended way too soon. To continue south to Placencia, we had only one choice, the Western Highway, a 50-mile inland detour that took us past Hattieville Prison. In 2003, this jail was rated the worst in Central America. I read about the lack of a sewage system and how inmates were put twelve to a cell meant for two. I shuddered as we drove by and visualized inmates being served meals shoveled from a wheelbarrow.

We continued along the famous Hummingbird Highway, the most scenic route in Belize, and drove through the lush rainforests of the Maya Mountains. Barefoot kids walked alongside the road sucking on juicy mangos with orange flesh dripping like ice cream cones in the heat. Some kids stopped to stare at our white faces; others started running, as if trying to beat our car to the finish line. Solitary shacks appeared, with nothing but a hammock inside them. A few chickens roamed the premises, and sometimes a lone skinny cow or a horse remained close to a shack. I wondered whether the cow or horse represented a local status symbol — the Belizean version of a

Mercedes on the driveway. What a different environment from ours back home.

What would my boys think?

We reached Dangriga by late afternoon after crossing numerous speed bumps. These consisted of three sets of chunky ropes, each about eight inches thick and twenty feet apart. Villages placed them at their entrances and exits, forcing traffic to slow down. The ropes blended in with the dust, and Duke forgot to slow for them. This, together with our nonexistent suspension, resulted in major jolts to our spines.

Belize had such a diverse population, as if the tiny nation had swallowed many countries. Dangriga reminded me of Nigeria, West Africa, where I lived until the age of six. Garifunas were originally slaves from West Africa who intermarried with American Indians; they made up the population of Dangriga.

As Duke and I drove through town, ten barefoot young boys started chasing us. At a stop sign, the kids glued themselves to our Suzuki Samurai. They stuck their hands inside our windows and tried to grab our belongings. Duke and I cranked the windows closed, trying not to hurt them. I never thought I could fear children, but in this case, I did.

How would my boys react to seeing these kids, who were around their age?

It was getting dark, and although we'd planned on spending one night in Dangriga, we quickly changed our minds.

"Keep going south," I said.

Our paved road gradually turned into large potholes. Nothing was lighted, so we relied on our headlights to read any signs we could find.

"Look, there's a sign to Hamanasi Resort," I said. "Let's follow it. Maybe it's a nice place."

We drove in darkness on a dirt path that appeared to lead nowhere. After five miles of crappy road, we found Hamanasi Resort — and what a gem it was.

This was a scuba divers' resort catering to a well-to-do crowd, and the bar was obviously the place to be. I kept my fingers crossed that the resort would have a room available. Behind an impressive solid wooden counter, a friendly woman greeted us. She had the American customer service touch. I noticed a blackboard with "Lobster dinner tonight. Please pre-order" written in chalk. Starving and happy to find this place, we lucked out. It had one room and two lobster dinners left.

Our room was luxurious, contemporary with a tropical twist. Apart from the local Belizean mahogany beams across the ceiling and the gorgeous, heavily veined hardwood floors, we could have been in a five-star California resort. Even the bed — a true California king — had a sleek, modern look to it, with silky, scented sheets. I felt like we were back in Newport Beach, Orange County, among the rich and famous crowd — at least temporarily. Then I felt guilty. This was not why we'd come to Belize. However, Dangriga had scared me. I did not feel safe among those kids who tried to steal our stuff.

We slept beautifully, and after a quick swim in the pool and an expensive charge on our credit card, we were off in our Suzuki Samurai to Placencia, the last of the places we wanted to check out.

There was only one road south; we just weren't sure whether that road was supposed to be red and dusty. We kept going and found ourselves in the middle of a banana plantation.

"I don't think we're supposed to be here," Duke said. "Look at the sign; we're on private property."

"What are those black nets for?" I asked, pointing to the banana clusters.

"Probably to stop animals from eating them."

We drove on the dirt channels between rows of banana trees until we reached several wooden planks. Both of us got out to see what they covered. We peered down a ten-foot-deep crevice. The wood looked cracked and worn, with large gaps between each piece. After stomping on them, Duke asked, "Shall we risk it?"

"Why not?" I said. "I don't want to go all the way back."

Like a small kid, I stuck my index fingers in my ears and hummed so I wouldn't hear the creaking sounds our tires made as we drove slowly across the planks. We made it across, and several miles later a primitive sign pointed toward Placencia, a small town at the end of a twenty-mile peninsula. What appealed to us most about this peninsula was the statement we found in one of our guidebooks: "You'll love Placencia if you're looking for a little bit of the South Pacific in Central America." I'd never been to the South Pacific, but movies like *Blue Lagoon* and *Castaway* were filmed on some Fijian islands, and they sure looked appealing to me. We hadn't made reservations, so we went with our guts. More accurately, I went with my Orange County gut, which somehow picked the more expensive hotels.

"This one looks brand new," I said. "Let's see if they have room."

We parked in front of the Turtle Inn. A gorgeous hotel with a thatched palapa roof, it sat right on the Caribbean. We soon learned that film director Francis Ford Coppola owned the inn. The individual thatched *bures* — small dwellings — and the bar and restaurant were inspired by the style in Bali. Our credit card was safe, as there were no vacancies.

Not far away, we checked into the Inn at Robert's Grove, also a nice resort. We stopped at the bar on our way to the room. A talkative, dark-skinned Garifuna bartender asked us, "Where'yu from?"

"California."

"Which part?"

"Southern."

"I used to live in Anaheim and worked as a delivery guy for Crate and Barrel," he said.

"That's so weird to bump into you here," I said. "Are you going back or staying here?"

"Oh man! You guys are crazy over there. I'm staying here. Too much traffic, too many people in L.A.," he said.

When we told him we were planning to move to Belize for the same reasons, he replied, "It's too quiet here for you, especially after L.A." I almost said, "Oh, we're from Orange County, not L.A.," like that made a huge difference.

After dinner, we kicked off our flip-flops and strolled along the toasty sand before going to bed. A big mistake. Our ankles were bitten by microscopic no-see-ums. They thrive in areas like Placencia, where it rains a lot. Their bites itch like hell, causing some people to break out in welts. Fortunately, we weren't allergic to them, but our ankles itched for days.

The following morning, before breakfast, I decided to check out the ocean temperature. I jumped from the end of the pier and landed directly on something that stung me in the crotch. Screaming all the way up the ladder, I inspected my crotch to see if anything was attached to it. An embarrassing red patch spread down my inner thigh. *Was I going to die?* I ran the length of the pier to ask the lady at the hotel lobby. Pointing to my crotch, she said, "You were stung by jellyfish." She then turned to the shelf behind her and handed me a small soup bowl of white vinegar and some cotton balls. I started nursing my groin area in the hotel lobby, but after some funny stares, I realized I should go to my room to continue the treatment. The stinging continued for quite a while, and now I was scared to swim in the sea.

It didn't take long for us to realize that Placencia wasn't the right place for our family. There were no schools in the vicinity and only two convenience stores in town, both the size of a kitchen pantry. Rows of rusty canned vegetables and a few boxes of dust-covered cornflakes sat on a shelf. The remaining shelves had bottles of local rum. This wouldn't feed our three growing sons.

We gave up on house hunting and played tourist instead, taking a boat tour to Monkey River, where we hiked and heard screeching howler monkeys in the tree canopy.

"Perhaps Alec can have a pet monkey when we move," I said, looking for any way to make the transition easier for him.

We had finally made up our minds. Now we had to tell our boys.

CHAPTER NINE

Family Meeting

O N THE FLIGHT HOME, Duke and I discussed how to break the news to our boys. It was now the middle of June 2003, and the kids would soon be on summer break. We knew we couldn't move right away; there was too much to prepare.

"We need to sell our house," Duke said.

"How about renting in case things don't work out?" I suggested.

"If we keep the house," Duke said, "the kids won't try to adapt. They'll whine to come back."

He did have a point, and we needed the money to buy property and build in Belize. The *finality* of it scared me. *What if things didn't work out? We'd never be able to come back to this house.*

With the real estate market booming, we decided to wait until spring 2004 to put our house on the market. Duke wanted to relocate in April, three months before the kids' summer vacation. He thought he could persuade his boss to pay him to telecommute from Consejo Shores.

"What makes you think Phil will let you work from Belize?" I asked.

"One attorney in our office commutes from Montana," Duke said.

"Montana is in the U.S. Belize is another country."

"Phil knows I'm good at winning trials. I'll propose working three weeks in Belize, then one week back here to do my appearances."

"You won't have a secretary, though."

"I'll have the Internet, and my secretary can scan documents and e-mail them. Linda in Montana does it that way."

His plan did make some kind of sense, but would Phil agree to it?

After we moved and the kids started school in Corozal, Duke intended to quit working for Phil and open a legal transcription business. At least, that was his plan.

Duke wanted everything organized before we joined him. He had already arranged to trade in his car for a truck, then drive to Belize, a four-day trip through Mexico.

"Ask Carlos if he'll drive with you," I said.

"Why?"

"He speaks Spanish; plus, it's dangerous driving through Mexico alone."

"Not if you stay on the toll roads."

"I'm scared of you driving through Mexico," I said. "I'll e-mail Evelyn and see what she suggests. We'll have to pay for Carlos' flight. He can stay with us for a couple of days, and it might be good for the boys. They can ask him about Consejo Shores and the local high school."

As our flight started its descent toward Orange County, I thought about what Paul had told us.

"I hope Mandy and Steve split up."

"Well, don't get too excited," Duke said. "He might already have another girlfriend."

During our taxi ride home, I felt anxious about how the boys would react to our news. I was worried they would either get angry or sad. Especially Alec; I couldn't bear the thought of breaking his heart.

Cookie barked at the front door and peed with excitement as we entered. She bounced up and down like a yo-yo, and her yelps alerted the boys that we had arrived. I scanned our living room and kitchen, and my heart sank. The house was a disaster. Trash and dirt had accumulated during our ten-day trip.

Josh and Alec sprinted downstairs to greet us. I wrapped my arms around their shoulders, then couldn't stop hugging them. Paul marched downstairs with his suitcase.

"How did you like Belize?" he asked.

"Loved it," I said, right away.

Alec turned his back to me.

"Any trouble with Steve?" Duke asked as he pulled an envelope out of his back pocket.

"Nope. Everything went smoothly."

"So did they break up?" I asked, bending down to lift Cookie into my arms.

"Think so."

"You're kidding. How did that happen?" I said, trying to stop Cookie from licking my face.

"I told Steve I'd call the cops if he disobeyed me."

"That easy?" I said.

"I guess Mandy got fed up with Steve's strict curfew."

"We should have hired you two years ago," Duke said, handing Paul the envelope.

"Bye, Steve, I'm leaving," Paul shouted down the hallway. I heard Steve's door open and footsteps along the tiled hallway. What a change in less than two weeks. All three boys merged to say goodbye to Paul.

As soon as the door slammed, our boys asked, "So, are we moving to Belize?"

"We'll discuss it during dinner," Duke said.

There was nothing left in the fridge, so Duke picked up some Chinese food from our favorite take-out restaurant. As soon as he returned, he placed the Styrofoam boxes on the dining room table and shouted, "Dinner." It took a couple of minutes before all three boys arrived.

"We're not moving, are we?" Alec said, pulling his chair out.

Duke was silent. We waited for everyone to be seated. As I handed out plates and chopsticks, he said, "As you know, Mom and I have been talking about Belize for quite a while, and we think it's time to experience new adventures. So, yes, we are moving there."

"It'll be fun to have a boat, go fishing and scuba diving," I added.

"We can do that here," Alec protested.

"Yes, but it'll be different in Belize," I said. "Dad won't be stressed and can spend time with us."

"Aren't you going to work, Dad?" Alec asked with concern.

"Yes, but I'll no longer have to fight traffic."

"What about my driving lessons?" Steve said.

"You won't need to drive in Belize," I said.

"But I want to get my license."

"That can wait," Duke said.

"Dad and I saw howler monkeys, jaguars, crocodiles and toucans at a great zoo outside Belize City. You guys will love it."

"We hate zoos," Josh said.

"Perhaps you can get your own pet monkey," I added. Alec had always wanted a pet monkey, which is illegal in California.

"Yeah, Alec. Remember the monkey in Cancun?" Josh said.

"Why aren't you eating? I thought beef broccoli was your favorite," I said, eyeing Alec's untouched food.

"I'm not hungry," he said, chewing the end of the wooden chopstick.

Alec suddenly smiled. "Can I stay here with Jeff and Jake? I told Melanie that you and Dad might move to Belize, and she said I can live with them."

"We're all going to Belize," Duke repeated.

"Alec, you're coming. Jeff and Jake can visit us in Belize. I'm sure they'd love the adventure," I said.

"I'll only go if Cookie goes," Josh said. "And no more school."

"You'll be in fifth grade in Corozal," Duke said.

"I'm sure they're way behind over there," Steve added.

"Not according to what we've read and what the expats say. Corozal has good schools and a junior college," I continued.

After dinner, I encouraged Alec and Steve to look at the high school website. They followed me to my computer and peered over my shoulder.

"I'm not going to that school. Look at the uniforms. They look like a bunch of retards," Alec said after seeing photos of students dressed in white pants, white shirts and white socks. Steve laughed and said, "There's no way I'm wearing that."

"I think uniforms are great," I said. "I had to wear a gray skirt, white shirt and blue blazer when I went to the English School of Paris."

"Yeah, but that was ages ago," Alec said.

Despite the protests, I was relieved that our family meeting hadn't ended in a major argument, and that Steve did not throw a fit and run away. *Was Steve looking forward to moving?*

CHAPTER TEN

Preparations

I'D BECOME OBSESSED with Belize.

I'd tell anyone who cared to listen — including complete strangers in supermarket lines or at the gym — about how we were uprooting our family to live in Belize. Sometimes I imagined a glimpse of envy on a stranger's face. That's when I shifted into salesperson mode, trying to push them into doing the same. Duke warned me, "Don't tell everyone about Belize; we don't want people flocking there."

Some people thought we were crazy. Others were skeptical. "Yeah, sure," they said. "Let's see if you really go ahead with it." The second group always asked, "So what do your kids think?" to which I snapped back, "Who makes the decisions in your family, you or your kids?" Many looked shocked, but my European accent helped. It allowed people to classify me as an alien, despite my U.S. citizenship.

Months flew by as we handled all the necessary preparations. We applied for Qualified Retirement Cards (QRPs) from the Belize Tourist Board.

This involved the entire family getting blood work done and medical forms filled out. Josh had never had blood drawn before, and I asked Duke to take him and the boys to the clinic. I couldn't bear the thought of holding onto his arm while he screamed. Duke told me later that Josh didn't scream, he howled as the technician drew his blood. Cookie also required special paperwork and a signature from a Belizean veterinarian, which Duke planned on getting when he moved to Consejo Shores in April.

Evelyn became our liaison with the tourist board and called frequently to check on the status of our QRP cards. Duke needed his card, not only to enter Belize, but also to bring his truck and computers in, duty-free. Evelyn also helped with the rental property so Duke could set his office up in April, as planned. Everything took longer than anticipated, and we kept reminding ourselves that this was Belize, and things weren't done the American way.

Thanks to a search on the Internet, I found a Canadian expat mom living in Corozal. She became my link to daily life in Belize, and I quizzed her on many topics. Lydia warned me about what *not to* expect in the local stores. Our kids would have to adapt to powdered Mexican milk instead of fresh, "as you couldn't count on it being fresh," Lydia said. We could buy Mennonite ice cream and cheese, but I worried about the lack of fresh milk. Our boys consumed gallons each week. Fortunately, Mexican peanut butter and jelly were readily available at local mom and pop stores. As far as bread, Lydia said, "Bake your own." That advice prompted me to buy a bread maker, but Lydia forgot to tell me to bring whole grain flour from the U.S.

Duke spent weeks preparing his truck for the trip to Belize. He kept a detailed list of what he needed to take, and he double-checked with the Mexican authorities about driving through Mexico with four computers.

One morning I found Duke's feet dangling out the back of his silver Nissan truck. I ran to get the camera. "You try fitting everything in my truck," Duke said, as I poked fun at him for re-arranging our scuba-diving gear, the bread maker and his computers for the umpteenth time.

Fortunately, housing prices were on the rise, a huge advantage for us. Only two weeks before Duke left, he hammered a "For Sale by Owner" sign on our front lawn. Within an hour, we'd received an offer we could not resist. When Duke left, my job was to sell my old Saturn, our electric boat and all of our furniture before the boys and I relocated to Belize in July. I wasn't looking forward to all the garage sales and advertising in order to sell seventeen years' worth of accumulated *stuff*.

Carlos' flight landed late at night. I drank coffee to stay awake while Duke picked him up at the airport. He was shorter than I remembered. But excited to be in the U.S., he was in full party mode. Carlos guzzled three beers while Duke and I watched. Duke then offered a deafening yawn.

"Goodnight, Carlos," he said, picking up the empty beer bottles. "Sonia will show you to your room now."

Carlos followed me upstairs with his small suitcase. "Why you leaving?" he said. "You have beautiful house. Evelyn love to swap house with you." After his comment, I tossed in bed for hours. His words haunted me.

I cooked a special farewell dinner for Duke and Carlos the night before they left. I prepared all of Duke's favorites: Filet mignon with a red wine reduction sauce, fresh green beans with mushrooms in garlic butter and garlic mashed potatoes. For dessert, I baked my boys' favorite: a New York cheesecake with fresh strawberries, raspberries and blueberries.

Carlos piled food on his plate as though he were getting ready for a long hibernation. When Steve handed him the dish with green beans and mushrooms, Carlos held it under his nose and sniffed it.

"What are those?" he asked.

"Mushrooms," Steve replied.

"Can you get mushrooms in Belize?" I asked.

"Only in a tin," Carlos said.

I grinned, remembering the last time I'd used the word "tin" myself. When I moved to the U.S., I had to Americanize my vocabulary. I hated canned mushrooms.

"We don't get mushrooms, no green beans, no salad — and what are those?" Carlos asked, pointing to the cheesecake.

"Strawberries, raspberries and blueberries."

"You can't get in Corozal."

"So what do you and Evelyn eat?"

"We eat rice, beans and chicken."

Duke and the boys remained silent, savoring their meal.

"What kind of vegetables?"

"Onions, peppers, potatoes, avocados, cabbage and carrots. Sometimes you find broccoli."

"Well, I guess we'll adapt," I said. "I know you have delicious mangoes."

"Yes," he said.

I could always make coleslaw and baked potatoes with some Mennonite melted cheese on top. The boys would like that.

"Are there many bugs?" Alec asked Carlos. I cringed, aware of Alec's aversion to mosquitoes.

"You need bug zappers. Many, many mosquitoes in Consejo Shores," Carlos said. I glanced at Alec, who was pushing food around his plate while shifting in his seat.

"Don't worry, Alec," Duke said. "We've got mosquito nets to put over the beds."

I was grateful that Duke managed to appease Alec.

I tossed all night and woke up feeling exhausted. In a few hours, Duke would be off to start his new life in Belize. Cinnamon rolls were baking in the oven, filling the house with a mouth-watering aroma, but Carlos didn't want any. He preferred fruit for breakfast. "Can I have Carlos' cinnamon rolls?" Josh asked.

"Dad took 'em," I said.

The sky was a depressing pale gray, and the weather matched my mood.

"Carlos, can you take a photo of all of us in front of Duke's truck?" I asked.

"So, you're really doing this," a neighbor shouted from across the street. *Did our neighbors think these past months had been a charade?* "Tim, hurry over! Duke's leaving for Belize."

Duke squeezed me like a tube of toothpaste. Neither one of us wanted to let go. He kissed me hard, as though scooping out extra love to last him for a while. I sensed a smidgen of fear, though he tried to conceal it. After our kiss, I burst into tears. Josh carried Cookie over to me and placed her in my arms like a present. "Mom, why are you crying?"

"I'm sorry, Josh. I'm sad Dad's leaving."

I noticed a shiny teardrop forming in the corner of Duke's eye, but there was no turning back. We knew this was the right thing for our family.

Steve dribbled his basketball next to Duke's truck, as though this were another ordinary Saturday. My throat tightened as I watched Duke approach Steve and wrap his arms around his son. Duke had come a long way for a man who never received more than a handshake from his dad. Steve stood still, arms locked to his side while Duke muttered a few words. He then surprised Josh with a playful toss in the air, while Alec received an affectionate squeeze.

Reaching inside his pocket, Duke pulled out his car keys, buckled his seat belt and drove off with Carlos. I looked at my watch. It was 9:11. *I hope that's not a bad omen.* As soon as they turned left at the end of our street, a sudden downpour forced me to run back home. This was the first rain we'd had in months.

I felt empty, just like my house. This part of my life was over, with its memories of kids growing up and all the birthdays and Christmases we'd celebrated. This was the first time Duke and I had been apart during our seventeen-year marriage. *How would I fall asleep without the comfort of Duke's fingers interlocked with mine?*

I focused on remaining positive. I had to believe that Steve was not a ticking bomb, or I'd drive myself insane. Perhaps seeing Duke leave made Steve realize we meant business. I longed to ask him if he felt at all responsible for our move, but I wanted to keep the peace.

Duke called me several times that day. By nightfall, they had reached El Paso, Texas. He and Carlos hoped to cross the border into Mexico the following morning. As I stood naked, ready to step into the shower, the phone rang again.

"We're stuck at the Mexican border." Duke's voice sounded distant and exasperated.

"What happened?" I asked,

"Customs changed the rules. I can't bring any of my stuff through Mexico. It all has to be shipped."

"Even the computers?"

"Yes, everything."

Obviously irritated, he asked me for the shipping guy's phone number, which he'd left on his desk.

I rushed downstairs naked, hoping no one would see me. Duke's cell phone died. I waited a few seconds, dialed and gave him the number. After that, I didn't hear from him again. I had nightmares of Duke sitting on a cold cement floor in a Mexican jail.

Almost two days later, the phone rang in the afternoon. "Where are you?" I squealed, happy to hear his voice.

"I'm in the hut." The line sounded so clear.

"What hut?"

"Our hut," Duke said. "The lawyer changed her mind at the last minute."

"Are you serious?" I said. "Is it the same hut we saw with that expat caveman?"

"Yes, that's the one."

"Nothing else was available?"

"I tried to get another house, but Evelyn said this was all she has to rent."

"What are we going to do? The kids will be so pissed."

"And I had to sign a one-year lease on the hut."

"Shit, Duke. Can't you look for something else?"

"Sonia, I've got other problems to deal with right now, like how to get my work done without a computer."

"I'm sorry," I said. "I'm just upset."

I paused, waiting for Duke to respond.

"Evelyn never got our QRP cards. She called BTB many times, but they weren't ready, so I was forced to enter Belize as a tourist."

"What's taking them so long?"

"No idea."

It had been four months since we filed the application. Now he'd have to deal with customs.

"Do you have food?"

"I bought some cocktail sausages on the way."

"Does the hut have a view of the water?"

"The kitchen and our bedroom do."

"Think everything will be OK?"

"It's an adventure," Duke said. "I'm going for a swim in the bay to cool off."

"Wish I could be there with you," I said.

"You will soon."

CHAPTER ELEVEN

The Hut

"I THINK WE MADE A MISTAKE," Duke said, calling me after his first night in the hut.

"What do you mean?" My heart started racing.

"Don't panic." Duke knew me well. "It's just the hut. It's infested with bugs. You should see my legs. I look like I have chicken pox."

"Alec's going to freak out," I said.

"A scorpion landed on my pillow during the night."

"You're kidding, right?"

This didn't sound like my husband — the man who took me camping and got upset when I asked him, "Where's the tent?"

"Are they dangerous?" I asked, concerned for our kids.

"Evelyn says they sting, but don't kill you." Noticing my lack of response, Duke added, "The good news is mosquitoes only come out after rain. Normally, they stay in the jungle, behind our hut."

When Duke described our water supply, I thought he was exaggerating. "We only have cold water, and it stinks of sulfur from the well. The shower barely trickles. The pressure's too low. I hope I can fix that."

"Try to find another house that's less primitive!"

"Carlos said there's nothing in Consejo Shores but the huts."

"What about downtown Corozal?" I asked.

"Well, Consejo Shores is safer."

"I wish you hadn't signed the one-year lease."

"They gave me no choice."

Now I regretted not purchasing one of those 900-square-foot condos on Ambergris Caye. At least the kids would have enjoyed the beach. But as Duke kept reminding me, we wanted to live frugally. The hut, however, sounded a little too frugal.

Could we handle such a drastic change in lifestyle?

"Evelyn offered me her spare computer. I need to fix it first," Duke said. "Hopefully by tomorrow I can e-mail you."

I leaned back against the cushion, stroking Cookie as she lay curled up in a tight ball on my lap. I imagined Duke sitting on the dark wooden planks of the hut, wiping sweat off his brow with the bottom of his T-shirt, computer parts scattered all around him.

Phil expected Duke to bill 220 hours per month — the same number of hours billed from his comfy, leather Orange County swivel chair. If Phil caught a glimpse of Duke's new office, I knew he'd have a heart attack. Duke described a thriving community of iguanas and geckos scurrying up and down the walls and hiding in the palm-frond ceiling. Apparently the iguanas were the good guys, because they ate the mosquitoes.

The following day I received a sweet e-mail from Duke. "To my dear wife and best friend, I love you and miss you with all my heart." Now we had an Internet connection.

Not long after Duke left for Belize, Steve brought home his new girl-friend, Tina. My heart sank. When Tina's parents invited him over for dinner, I asked to meet them first. Keith and Laura seemed pleasant, though they treated Steve a little too much like a potential fiancé. Tina, a sweet, sixteen-year-old from Steve's high school, appeared smitten.

Whenever Steve paid attention to her, Tina combed her fingers through her shiny, brown hair and locked her spaniel eyes onto his. Steve did not seem as interested in her, perhaps due to our upcoming move to Belize.

One evening, before going to bed, I noticed two bottles of wine missing from the wine rack. I stopped to ask Steve whether he took them.

"I'm fed up with you checking on me," he said, raising his voice.

"I'm your mom. That's my job."

He lurched forward and yelled, "I'm sick of you." I took several steps back into the hallway as he balled his hands into fists. He swung his right fist toward my nose. At the last moment, he veered away from me, so the wall took the blow.

"Stop it," I screamed, feeling sick to my stomach. "Cut it out. You almost punched me," I sobbed. "Why? Why would you do that to me? Answer me," my voice quivered.

Steve's face was flushed. He looked vicious, and I felt nauseated by the encounter. He spun around and slammed the door. *Why the anger? Why the violence? Was it the alcohol? There had never been physical abuse in our family, so why?* I was desperate for Duke's help, but there was nothing he could do from Belize. So I picked up the phone and called Tina's dad for help.

"I'll come over right away," Keith said. Fifteen minutes later, the doorbell rang. Cookie's non-stop yapping woke Alec up. Keith flinched when he saw the punctured drywall. He knocked on Steve's door, entered and made sure it closed behind him. Steve towered over Keith, and I worried he might pick a fight with him.

A few minutes later, Steve came out of his room with his wallet.

"I'm taking him to Home Depot," Keith said, and gestured to Steve to head out the front door.

"He's going to repair the wall."

"Mom, what's going on?" Alec asked, rubbing his eyes at the top of the staircase. At thirteen, Alec had shot to six feet, yet he still longed for hugs and reassurance. I followed him to his room. After he curled up in bed, I wrapped my arms around him and said, in Danish, "Jeg knuser dig." My mom used to say that to me as a child, and it made me feel safe. It means "I'm giving you a big squeeze." Alec's mouth formed a faint smile, and I hoped he would soon fall asleep.

I collapsed on the couch and tried to focus on a magazine. Normally asleep by 9:30 P.M., I was exhausted. I had no idea Home Depot stayed open this late. The sound of Steve's flip-flops slapping the tile, followed by Keith's voice doling out instructions on how to patch the hole, calmed me down. Not wanting to interfere, I remained in the kitchen, grateful for Keith's help. "I won't allow you to see Tina until the wall is patched, painted and, more importantly, you apologize to your mom." Keith said in a firm tone. I knew he was concerned about his daughter. How could I blame him?

When Keith said he was leaving, Steve followed him to the front door and turned toward me. "Sorry, Mom," he said, and sprinted back to his room, closing the door.

I e-mailed Duke about the incident, and he reminded me that Steve was one of the reasons we were moving to Belize. He was right. We *had* to get Steve away.

Days went by, and I waited for Duke to say, "It's so beautiful here. You and the kids will love swimming in front of our house, and in the evening we'll sip a rum punch and watch the gorgeous sunsets." Not once had Duke mentioned anything that made me think this would be the paradise I was searching for.

"How come you haven't said anything positive about Consejo Shores? Are you having second thoughts about living there?" I asked.

"No, but you seem to be," Duke wrote back.

I sensed friction, so I chose my words carefully.

"You know Consejo Shores never really fit my vision of *paradise*," I wrote. "I always liked Ambergris Caye better, but I understand why we picked it."

"Don't think of it in terms of beauty but in terms of adventure," Duke replied. "The bay is beautiful even though the water's murky. The jungle has its own beauty, too. I think every day here is an adventure. Not all adventures are wonderful; they are always interesting, though."

Duke always amazed me with his logic. "As far as sipping rum punches outside, forget it," he continued. "We'd need a truckload of Deet." I forced myself to realize that *adventure,* and adapting, were more important than white sand and turquoise water.

Duke told me he'd met an expat couple with two kids, ages six and eight, from San Diego, California.

"Did you ask them about the schools?"

"Yes. They send them to elementary school in Corozal. They say the school is great on basic subjects, but not on music and art."

"That's the same as California," I said, happy to find an American couple who trusted the school system, even though their kids were much younger than ours.

Duke's priorities soon shifted from work to finding another house. He told Evelyn and Carlos he didn't think the hut would work for us, especially not for a whole year. What were our options? he asked them. Carlos mentioned a house that had just come up for sale in Consejo Shores and some properties closer to Corozal that he would show Duke. Evelyn did not seem too concerned about us breaking the one-year lease. She already had two people waiting to rent the hut.

Meanwhile, Duke contacted Sandy, a Realtor on Ambergris Caye, after realizing that the house Carlos showed him needed major repairs. The other properties were part of a project still in the planning stages. It could take years before the Canadian developer started building.

Duke decided to fly over to Ambergris Caye and meet Sandy. She convinced him she had "the perfect house for our family at a great price." He took the twenty-minute puddle jumper from the tiny Corozal airport to San Pedro, where he met Sandy at her beachfront office. She had arranged for a boat and driver to take him to *Villas Tropicales,* five miles north of town. Duke sent me photos of this three-bedroom Caribbean front house, and I loved it right away.

When Duke admitted he could not work as many hours as Phil expected, I worried he might get fired. "I can't wait for you to come over. I need help with the daily chores so I have more time to catch up with my work," Duke said. "I waste four hours a day just running errands. You remember what the road to Corozal is like?"

"Yeah, but I'm not sure I have the guts to drive in Belize," I said.

"You'll get the hang of it soon."

Little by little, I noticed Duke starting to slow down. It had only taken him ten days to swerve from life in the fast lane to life in the Belize lane. *How could he unwind that quickly from the rat race?* He wrote to me about the birds. "One sounds like a tea kettle with a whistle that goes on for a minute. The other bird mimics the telephone in our hut." He no longer talked about politics or world events. He was in a different world now.

Three weeks had passed since we last kissed. I stood in an almost empty Orange County airport waiting for Duke's flight to land from Houston. I dreamed that Duke would come running from the gate toward me, arms wide open, throwing me up and twirling me round like an ice skater. But that was not Duke. Instead, he strolled toward me wearing a new T-shirt with the words, "You Better Belize It." I smiled and noticed his relaxed face, but no tan, which struck me as odd since Belize is close to the Equator. My eyes meandered down towards his belly. *Had Belize made him healthier?*

It hadn't. How was that possible since he'd complained about constant sweating, running out of food and, once, jogging fourteen miles to town and back. He no longer spent hours sitting in freeway traffic, and there weren't any McDonald's or Taco Bells in Belize. So what the hell happened? I kept my mouth shut.

Back home I'd prepared his favorite steak dinner. Duke remained silent while eating. It was getting late, and the boys were anxious to hear what Dad had to say.

"Are there many bugs?" Alec asked.

"Outside, yes, but we'll bring a mosquito net to put on top of your beds," Duke said.

"Steve, there's a medical research lab being built in Consejo Shores. I spoke to Irina, a young Russian woman in charge of managing the place. Perhaps you can get a summer job there."

Steve shrugged.

"Are the expats friendly?" I asked.

"So far the ones I've met have been nice."

"Are there any kids?" Josh asked.

"Evelyn said there are three Canadian kids, perhaps nineteen and twenty-one, and then a girl around eleven."

"Does she go to the local school?" I asked.

"I'm not sure," Duke said.

Duke ate his dinner slowly. He was now on Belize time.

CHAPTER TWELVE

The Move From Hell

I T TOOK SEVERAL GLASSES OF WINE to numb me from the torture
of packing my life into two suitcases. This wasn't cram a bikini, flip-
flops, sunblock and a toothbrush into one carry-on. That I could handle.

"My trophies won't fit," Alec hollered from down the hallway.
"Grandma put too much newspaper around them."

"Try squeezing them in the corners," I offered, instead of speaking
my mind: *Do you really need to bring five identical swim trophies to Belize?*

The phone wouldn't shut up. "Mom, Kelley's on the phone. Catch,"
Josh said, hurling the phone, like a Frisbee, from the landing. *Shit,
why does she wait till the last minute to call me for an update? We haven't
spoken in two months.*

"Hi, Kelley, how are you?" I said, mad at myself for not instructing
Josh to tell her I'd e-mail her from Belize.

"I just wanted to wish you and Duke the best of luck in Belize. We
can't believe you're actually moving."

Neither can we, I almost blurted. "Yes, we're packing right now,
and everything has to fit in ten suitcases." I hoped my words sounded

normal, not slurred. *What would Kelley think if I sounded drunk?* But I felt overwhelmed and scared, and the wine relaxed me.

Duke zipped up our last suitcase at half past midnight, then checked on Steve's progress. "I'm not going to bed," Steve said. "It's not worth it for three hours."

Our wooden floor creaked as Duke approached his side of the bed. My body needed rest, but my mind kept scrolling down all my to-do lists. I finally had that wonderful sinking feeling just before sleep. Five minutes later, or so it seemed, the alarm hollered. My temples pounded with each beep.

"Here's coffee," Duke said, handing me my wake-up mug.

"You're already dressed?" I asked.

"Couldn't sleep. You were snoring."

I stubbed my toe, spilling coffee as I headed straight to the medicine cabinet for some Tylenol. *"Merde,"* I mumbled. Swearing in French or Danish didn't sound as bad.

"Duke," I yelled, expecting him to drop everything and come to my rescue. "I forgot to pack our medicine." *What else have I forgotten?*

Our airport shuttle driver showed up fifteen minutes early. I raced from room to room barking orders, an exercise that made me feel useful, although it accomplished zilch. There was no way our luggage could fit in the twelve-person van I'd reserved. I hid in the kitchen, unwilling to hear any complaints, and refused to step out until they called me.

Opening the fridge, I found milk, cheese and crème fraiche on the top shelf. The bottom drawers had lettuce, tomatoes, cucumber and carrots, enough to make a salad. *What was I thinking? That I would be back later on to clean up this mess?* I had booked a cleaning crew for the following week, when the new owners were supposed to move in. I started emptying the perishables, but I couldn't squeeze a single yogurt carton into the overflowing trash cans.

"Sonia, time to go," Duke shouted from the garage.

I gasped when I reached the van. The driver tried to slam the door shut several times. There was no way he could see out the rear or side windows.

"I'm squished; I can't breathe," Josh complained.

"Only fifteen minutes left," I fibbed. All of us kept quiet, except for Cookie. She whimpered and scratched the inside of her plastic crate.

Our van pulled up curbside in front of Continental Airlines, where two eager skycaps showed up, panting. Our luggage filled the sidewalk. Fortunately, we were first in line. Duke charged straight to Jeanie — our check-in lady — with a charming smile. Jeanie greeted us warmly, and Duke handed her our tickets and passports.

I searched my purse for the plastic vial of tranquilizers the vet had prescribed for Cookie. "Is that a sleeping pill?" Josh asked, studying the lentil-sized pill in my palm.

"No. It's to calm her down," I said, squatting to unlock the metal handle on her crate. Cookie tore out of her cage, tail wagging for a treat, not a pill.

"Can I give it to her?" Steve asked.

He held Cookie's mouth open and stuck the pill in her throat.

"Is that your dog?" Jeanie asked.

"Yes," Duke replied. "And here's her confirmation number," he said handing her the receipt. She studied it carefully.

"That crate's too big to bring on board, sir," remarked a uniformed employee, glasses perched on the end of her nose as she leaned over Jeanie's shoulder, inspecting our paperwork.

"It's the size Continental's website stated we could bring on board," Duke replied.

Jeanie squirmed in her seat. Her face had lost its welcoming glow.

"Sorry, sir, but you'll have to check your dog into cargo," Jeanie's colleague said and left Jeanie to take over.

Jeanie glanced over her shoulder, then leaned in closer. "If you come back with a soft Sherpa bag from Petco, your dog would be allowed under your seat."

"I'll catch a cab and buy one right now," I said.

"It's only 5:30. They're not open," Duke said.

I glanced around. Alec and Josh were snoozing on top of our suitcases in the midst of the growing check-in lines. We still hadn't checked in a single suitcase.

I refused to put Cookie in cargo after hearing the horror stories my vet told me about pets dying or getting lost in transit. I decided to stay with Cookie and catch a later flight once I'd purchased a Sherpa bag. Duke pulled my suitcases aside and gave me a hasty kiss goodbye. At that point, my brain quit functioning. I stood rooted to the cold marble tile, tears dribbling down my nose, and waved goodbye to my family.

What was Duke doing? I rubbed my eyes to bring the blurry world back into focus. This could not be happening. My adrenaline kicked in, and I raced toward the counter where Duke was handing our carry-on luggage to Jeanie. Our birth certificates, marriage license, investment papers and my mother's pearl and gold necklaces were in one of the carry-on's, but which one?

I flung myself on top of the three remaining carry-on's, even as two of them disappeared down the conveyor belt. While I unzipped them and rummaged through their contents on the airport floor, Duke looked down at me.

"What are you doing?" he asked, shaking his head. I whispered an explanation, trying to let Duke know what I needed without informing the entire airport, but Duke appeared deaf. I never found the bag and assumed Jeanie had checked it through. All I longed for at that moment was a bed to collapse into.

I clipped Cookie's leash back on and took the elevator down two levels to Enterprise Rent-A-Car. Within twenty minutes, I was back on the 405 freeway, now heavy with early-morning commuters, returning to "our" house. Already, I'd made a complete mental break from this house we'd owned for the past eight years. Now I felt uncomfortable returning and refused to park in "our" driveway.

During the past three hours, I'd visualized my new life in Belize, and now I was back, sliding open the patio door I'd forgotten to lock. *What a disaster! Was this my punishment for leaving a house that looked and smelled like a pigsty?* Overfilled trash cans infused the house with putrid odors, but I ignored that. Cookie's tranquilizer had finally kicked in, and I felt as if I'd taken several myself. Her legs buckled as she tried following me up the staircase. I lifted her and placed her on our bed. My eyes shut as soon as I hit the pillow.

Twenty minutes later, a nightmare woke me up. Our carry-on with all the important papers had been stolen. I woke up whimpering, with a growing migraine and stomach pain.

Perhaps I needed food. I tiptoed downstairs, scared to make noise. I felt like an intruder in my own home. A plain bagel remained in my bread bin, and I toasted it. I grabbed the cream cheese and jelly from the refrigerator and, after a couple of bites, felt worse. I wanted to sit on the couch but felt awkward, like a shoplifter caught on tape. Guilt made me start picking up the house; then I remembered why I was back. I had to purchase a Sherpa travel bag.

I scooped Cookie, still groggy, off the warm bed covers and laid her on the passenger seat of my rental SUV. She grew alert and, once we reached Petco, stood on all fours without falling. I discovered that Sherpa bags came in two sizes: nine inches and eleven inches. I had no idea which one fit airline regulations, and neither did the teenage store clerk. I figured the smaller the better, but Cookie refused to climb in. I forced her head down and quickly zipped up the bag, but even the eleven-inch bag scrunched her up.

To be safe, I drove straight to the airport and spotted Jeanie, still on duty.

"I got a Sherpa bag," I shouted, running toward her counter like a kid showing off a picture she'd drawn. Before Jeanie had time to respond, her supervisor walked over. "Please put your dog in the bag," she ordered. I obeyed. Cookie gave me the *hell no* look and, with a faint growl, allowed me to squish her body into this fabric bag with handles.

With my palm on top of her head, I managed to zip the bag. I felt like a magician making an animal disappear. I was rather pleased with my accomplishment, but the supervisor obviously felt differently. "The dog needs to do a complete turn inside the bag," she said.

Wasn't one magic trick enough?

"Only a Yorkie or a Chihuahua could possibly do a 360 in a bag this size," I said, trying to smile but grimacing instead. "You should tell people you only allow four-pound Yorkies and Chihuahuas on the plane."

Jeanie apologized and persuaded me to put Cookie in cargo. I had no options left. She booked me on a 9:15 P.M. flight to Newark that same evening with a connection to Belize the following morning. "That way you can join your family sooner," she said. I was too tired and frustrated to argue.

With several hours to kill before my flight, I drove to my vet's office, hoping she could comfort me. She assured me Cookie would be fine if I bought a crate large enough to hold water and food. A soft blanket and her favorite toy would help, too.

"Petco is close by, and they have some," she said. I cringed. Not another trip to Petco. But, of course, I followed her instructions.

Then I revisited the airport for the third time in one day. A fresh set of employees focused on my jumbo-sized crate and, by comparison, my miniscule rat terrier. "Where you flying to?" a loud voice in uniform called out.

"Belize, via Newark," I replied.

"Is that your dog?"

"Yes."

"Follow me," she said. Finally, I thought, someone was treating me with respect.

"Can I see the international cargo papers for your dog?"

"What do you mean?"

"You're taking your dog to Belize, so you need international cargo paperwork."

"I've had it," I shouted, pounding my fist on the counter. I felt my face flush, and heads turned. Within seconds, a supervisor raced over. After hearing me out, she had the nerve to ask me to catch a bus to international cargo.

"I'm going nowhere without one of your employees." The supervisor asked Brenda to take me there, but when I saw her, I knew there was no way I would make the flight to Newark. Brenda gasped for air, heaving her 350 pounds along as I dodged passengers, holding onto Cookie's crate. I had tranquilized her for the second time in one day.

With only ninety minutes until departure, Brenda informed me that international cargo could not fill out my paperwork. "Their type-writer broke."

"Who uses a typewriter these days?" I asked.

Brenda sensed I was ready to strangle her. "I have an idea," she exclaimed, beads of sweat dripping from her brow. "You can get your cargo papers filled out in Newark. You have a four-hour layover. That's enough time."

By 9 P.M., I was collapsed in seat 21A, with Cookie in cargo. With my ears on high alert, I thought I heard a yelp from under my seat — or was that the baby two rows back? The flight attendants appeared shortly after take-off, bumping their beverage cart into passenger elbows. I pur-chased a small bottle of wine to knock me out. This was the first time in my life I managed to sleep through an entire flight.

As soon as we landed, I darted to international cargo, skidding on the just-mopped floors. All along, I prayed Cookie was alive. When I found the office, it reminded me of my vet's waiting room, with dog and cat owners cuddling their pets and cooing over them. I pounced onto Cookie's green plastic crate and stuck my head in front of the metal grill that separated us.

"Can I let her out?" I asked the employee.

"Sure you can," he said.

Her tongue licked my fingers through the prison bars as she whined, almost howled, for me to open the latch. She refused to sit still on my lap while the international cargo papers were being processed. Fifteen minutes later, I took her for a quick walk outside Newark airport. Cookie rushed through the terminal as though late for her flight. We flew through the automatic doors into the hellish, concrete environment of roads, overpasses, tunnels and nearby runways. Not a single blade of grass. *What the hell am I doing here?* Cookie seemed to say. She sniffed the sidewalk, then glanced back at me. "Come on, Cookie, go potty," I pleaded. But she refused. I tried jogging with Cookie inside the terminal to give her a workout, but security informed me this was not allowed. After Cookie was back in her crate, I placed fresh ice cubes in her water bowl, hoping to combat dehydration and soaring temperatures while traveling to Belize.

Six hours later, we started our descent toward Belize City. Once again I noticed the dilapidated shacks with rebar poking out of the flat, cement rooftops, as well as yellow-colored pools of water in the marshlands. A sense of anticipation mixed with fear made me shudder as I thought about my boys and their initial reaction to Belize.

When the front and rear doors of the aircraft opened, I felt as though I'd stepped into a sauna, fully clothed. Poor Cookie would be stuck in the belly of the aircraft until the luggage handlers got their act together. Goodness knew how long that would take. Here pets were not regarded as family members; they were part of the animal kingdom.

I had no trouble spotting Duke, dressed in camouflage shorts, long-sleeved, mosquito-repellant shirt and a wide-brimmed straw hat.

He smiled and waved when he spotted me.

"How did it go? I was so worried about you," Duke said, giving me a kiss.

"I had to check Cookie into cargo after all that," I said. "Why didn't the boys come?"

"The drive takes too long, and there's no room in the truck."

"Where do we pick up Cookie?" I asked, pacing the luggage area, hoping to see Cookie's green crate.

"She should come out here by the suitcases." Within five minutes, suitcases spewed out onto the conveyor belt, and Cookie's crate arrived, twirling with the bags. Duke grabbed her crate before she got too dizzy. I opened the latch while Cookie struggled to stand up, sniffing the unfamiliar smells of Belize. Her small pink tongue flopped outside her mouth with heavy panting. I grabbed her empty plastic water bowl and filled it in the ladies' room. She refused to drink. Instead, she tugged on her leash, dragging me outside where the air smelled third world. Locals stopped and pointed at Cookie, and I soon realized why. They had never before seen a dog on a leash.

"So how did the boys react to the hut?" I asked Duke on our two-hour drive to Consejo Shores.

"The way I expected them to," Duke replied.

"Which is?"

"Alec said, 'It sucks,' and Josh whined about sharing a room with Alec."

"What did Steve say?"

"Not much. All they wanted was to hook up their computers and IM their friends."

"They didn't explore?"

"Give 'em time," Duke said.

"We're going to have to plan something on Sunday. It's the Fourth of July, and they'll be homesick," I said.

Cookie sat on my lap, her tongue still hanging out of her mouth. I opened the window so she could stick her head out. She took a sniff, looked at me, then sniffed again. The air smelled of smoke and burning trash, accented by the earthy aroma of red soils and the scent of pungent stews cooking in roadside huts. Orange County's smoggy air seemed sterile by comparison.

Here you could tell who was rich and who was poor by the materials used to build the houses. Painted cement houses with tin roofs sat next to primitive huts with a family hammock inside. Occasionally, you'd find a mansion on several acres of land, surrounded by a wrought-iron fence. We were told that government officials owned them.

I stared at all the stray dogs roaming the streets like scavengers on a hunt. *Had my boys seen them? Of course they had.* As we drove along, I kept wondering, *what did our boys think? How did they react?* I now viewed everything through their eyes rather than my own, recalling my perhaps overly rosy reaction during our scouting trip. I began to prepare myself mentally for the worst.

CHAPTER THIRTEEN

Complaining

"Mom, I hate this place," Alec said, as I walked in the front door. "The water stinks, there are bugs everywhere, and I found peanut husks on my bed."

"Yeah, Mom," Josh added. "Dad said a mouse made the mess on our beds. Why did you and Dad bring us here?" Steve remained surprisingly quiet.

"Cookie," Josh squealed, scooping her into his arms. "How's my Cookie?" he cooed.

"Well, we came for adventure," I said, refusing to let their moods affect mine. I gave my boys hugs, and even Steve allowed me to approach him.

"Look at Cookie; she's already searching for mice and rats," Duke said, pointing at her long muzzle sniffing the gaps in the walls.

"She'll keep busy in this hut," Steve said.

Josh continued hugging Cookie. "I'm so happy she's here."

"Let's eat," I said. "Dad and I stopped in Corozal to get some chicken, rice and beans. Did you taste fried plantains yet?"

"That's all we eat here," Alec said.

"You just got here yesterday," I remarked. "Think of it as Belizean fast food, only healthier."

"Mom, I can't sleep without air-conditioning," Alec said. "It's too hot."

"Well, at least we get a breeze from the bay," Duke said.

I noticed for the first time that we had no glass in the windows. Everything was screened in, including the walkways between our bedroom and the kids' rooms. The screens had gaps and tears in them, though.

"What shall we do tomorrow? It's July Fourth," I said, trying to remain upbeat.

"Can we get fireworks?" Steve asked, picking the chicken out of the Styrofoam box with his fingers.

"I doubt it," Duke said.

"But we're close to Mexico. You can get them there," Steve countered.

Knowing Duke had no desire to cross the border, I suggested the Belize zoo. Duke and I stumbled upon it during our scouting trip and thought it the best zoo we'd ever seen.

"Not the zoo," Alec and Josh moaned.

"Steve Irwin visited the zoo. There are photos of him in the gift shop," I said.

"Who cares?" Josh shouted.

"You've never seen a zoo like this one," Duke said. "It's like you're in the jungle with jaguars, toucans and howler monkeys only a couple of feet away from you."

"I want to be with Jeff and Jake," Alec whined.

"Well, it's time to explore Belize," Duke said.

The following morning, after a breakfast of scrambled eggs and toast, we told the kids to get ready for the trip to the zoo.

"Stop arguing and get in the car," Duke ordered, his finger pointing to the door.

"I'm staying," Steve said, refusing to get off his chair.

"We're all going," Duke said, opening the front door.

"What about Cookie?" Josh asked.

"I just took her out to pee; she'll be fine," I said, not quite reassured myself. Our hut didn't have a doggie door, which was probably a good thing since we were surrounded by wildlife. Still, I worried that a crocodile or coatimundi (a relative of the raccoon) would tear through our screens and kill Cookie. Coatimundi were known to rip screens out in search of food.

The boys stomped down the cement steps and paced around Duke's Nissan truck, swatting large dock flies off their legs. Our parking spot, only ten feet from our hut, consisted of an area of flattened weeds. Duke pressed the lever of the driver's seat, which catapulted forward with a grinding noise. The truck had two seats in front and one narrow slot behind, big enough for Josh if he squished in sideways. Still, he had the luxury of cool air from the truck's air-conditioner — unlike his brothers, who sat in the rear cab.

Duke unfolded a couple of beach chairs for Alec and Steve. "When are you getting real seats, Dad?" Steve asked, shoving the lightweight chair to one side.

"A guy in town said he'd get some salvaged ones, but so far he hasn't."

Alec and Steve tried fitting their long, teenage limbs into the cramped camper shell. Soon the shell would turn into a convection oven. I felt guilty about the lack of cool air, but this was all we had for now.

Everyone kept silent during the first seven miles of potholes to Corozal. The zoo was another eighty-five miles away, and now that we were living here, everything seemed so primitive. Stray anorexic dogs roamed the streets of Corozal, searching for food; grubby, shoeless kids played on mud-caked roads; and grandmas and grandpas with prune-like skin sat on crumbled steps in front of dilapidated shacks. A gringo once described the buildings in Belize as follows: "You never know if the building is going up or is being torn down." *Why hadn't I noticed all this poverty eleven months ago? Had the adventure blinded me?*

The drive to the zoo was ridiculously long. I had forgotten it was further than the airport and felt sorry that Duke had to drive this far three days in a row. But I thought it was important to do something with our kids rather than listen to them complain in the hut.

Only a third of the way there, and I wasn't sure whether I should scream or cry. The boys were uncomfortable, and they protested. Duke stopped the truck. I thought he was going to let the kids out for a breather. Instead, he bought two bags of homegrown cashews from what appeared to be four generations of the same family, huddled underneath a canopy. I enjoyed a few moments of silence while they ate.

Orange Walk Town was the only major town we passed. Steve spotted a large sign advertising motorcycles for sale. "Let's get a dirt bike," he said. By now, I yearned to give my boys anything to see them smile again. Adjusting to our frugal life would not be painless, and I believed we should ease our boys into it. Duke disagreed. He believed in instant immersion and drove straight past the motorcycle shop. My heart sank.

After three long hours on good and bad roads, Duke pulled over to a roadside restaurant. The tires made a popping sound on the gravel, reminding me of popcorn in the microwave. Most tables were empty, and the kids were so thirsty they opened the glass refrigerator door in the bar and helped themselves to Cokes. Duke grabbed a Belikin beer, and so did I. An old chalkboard had the *dish du jour*: chicken, rice and beans. What else? From the smeared writing, it probably never changed.

"Are we almost there?" Josh asked, tearing his paper napkin into narrow strips.

"No more than five minutes," Duke said.

"Is that the only thing we get to eat in Belize?" Alec grumbled.

"Yes, this is your local Taco Bell," I said. "You love Taco Bell."

With our bellies full, we piled back into the truck. No one spoke for several minutes. Thankfully, an arrow pointed toward the zoo, and we headed down a long dirt road lined with trees. At the end, we found another gravel parking lot with outhouses on top of stilts, and a small playground attached.

That's it?" Alec said, without even getting out of the truck.

"We drove *this* far to see *this* crappy place?" Josh added.

I knew better than to respond, so Duke and I strolled ahead, hoping the kids would follow. They did. We stepped inside a cold, musty-smelling cement building and paid our entrance fee to a woman sitting on a high stool, looking bored.

As soon as we headed outside the building into nature, I remembered why I had fallen in love with this zoo. Unlike the cages and cement surrounding me in American and European zoos, here I felt *free*, as did the sixty indigenous animals in their surroundings. Three jaguars roamed a few feet away from us. Although they were fenced in, the lush vegetation made me focus on the animals instead of their depressing "jails."

"Can we go home now?" Josh said. "This zoo sucks."

I pointed out Rambo the toucan and several howler monkeys high up in the treetops, but Josh continued bellyaching. Alec focused on the howler monkeys screeching above our heads. *Did I detect a slight smile? Perhaps he hoped he could finally get his own pet monkey.*

"Where's the gift shop?" Josh pestered, dragging me toward the exit.

"Come on, Josh, open your eyes. Look how close we are to all the animals." He quit for a few minutes, and I dreaded our long drive home. If only we could medicate the kids, like we'd done with Cookie.

The sun was setting by the time we reached our hut. Steve and Alec emerged from the rear cab, complaining that they felt like dough that had been kneaded for six hours.

"Why don't you get a shower?" I said. "It'll help you relax." They reeked of teenage hormones. "When did you last take a shower?" I asked.

"I haven't had one since California," Alec replied with pride.

"Me, neither," Josh said, as if he deserved a trophy.

"No wonder."

"The water stinks," Steve said, "but I've already had a couple."

"It stinks so bad I want to puke," Alec added.

"Pinch your nose, or breathe through your mouth. That's what I do," I advised.

Steve headed to his shower without further complaint. Strangely, taking him out of his element made him more compliant than his brothers.

Alec finally pulled off his T-shirt and shorts, and headed to the bathroom in his boxers.

Meanwhile, Duke and I relaxed with a well-deserved rum and Coke. We collapsed on the rental couch, too tired to comment on the stains and broken springs poking out of the fabric. My knees felt like they were above my head.

Alec bolted through the hallway and landed in front of us, shaking and speechless.

"What happened?" I asked, staring at my ashen-faced son, who looked like he'd lost two quarts of blood.

"There's a scorpion in the drain," he whimpered. "I'm never taking a shower here."

"I'll remove it," Duke said, as I gave him a shove to hoist him off the couch.

"Alec, use our shower." He tiptoed behind me, using my body as a shield against critters.

I realized we'd never smell clean again. Not even my Chanel perfume could mask the stench of perspiration.

How long would it take us to adapt? This was only our third day in the hut, and already I was tempted to fly over to Ambergris Caye to meet Sandy, the Realtor, and check out the beachfront villa Duke had sent photos of. I didn't want to give in so quickly, though. I felt the boys and I should put up with our new, frugal lifestyle and adapt, rather than jump into the comforts of a nicer home on Ambergris Caye. The thought was tempting, though.

CHAPTER FOURTEEN

Belize Expat Style

I FELT CLAUSTROPHOBIC in our hut and longed to get out.

"Why don't we have dinner with the expats?" Duke suggested. "They meet at Smuggler's Den on Friday nights."

"Let's go," I said. "Our fridge is empty anyway."

"I'll eat Top Ramen," Steve said.

"Come with us," I urged.

"Irina's usually there," Duke added.

"Not interested," Steve said, filling a saucepan with water and tearing open the bag of Top Ramen.

We could still bribe Alec and Josh with hamburgers and fries, but not Steve.

Duke introduced me to Irina and her friends, Inga from Germany and Rochelle from the U.S. They seemed a close-knit group, and as a newcomer I felt a bit like a high school student trying to break into the popular clique.

Fortunately, everyone seemed easygoing and friendly. I told Irina, a six-foot-tall young Russian woman, about Steve. She had recently been hired to supervise the construction of a stem-cell research lab in Consejo Shores. The lab was being built in our neighborhood, and we hoped Steve could get a summer job there.

I got my conversation fix that evening and regretted that Steve hadn't come with us. He seemed to be turning into a recluse, the opposite of who he was in Orange County.

Now my goal was to meet as many expats as possible. I missed talking to others, so on the second Tuesday of the month, Duke and I joined the expat group at TJ's restaurant for a potluck lunch. Most were retirees without kids, except for Joan and Matt from San Diego. I couldn't wait to ask Joan about the schools in Corozal, but I felt uncomfortable the minute I walked in. My new sundress was too sexy, too tight and too fuchsia.

Before leaving California, I had purchased three cotton/spandex sundresses from the Victoria's Secret catalog. I accessorized my dress with matching, beaded flip-flops. A group of women walked away as I approached them. Others started whispering to one another.

What had I done wrong? Duke was right to warn me about the gossipy expat crowd. He told me, "Be careful what you say to people; they'll instantly judge you."

I put my foot in it when I mentioned that an expat had recently been attacked at gunpoint in Consejo Village — a rumor heard over dinner at the Smuggler's Den — and one I should have kept to myself. One woman rolled her eyes. "For your information," she said coldly, "that person got robbed in Consejo Shores, not in the village."

"I've only been here a short while. What would I know?" I said, and quickly excused myself to look for Joan.

I spotted a younger woman sitting next to the pool with her eye on two young kids splashing one another.

"Are you Joan?"

"You must be Sonia," she replied. "Duke told me you brought your three sons with you to Consejo Shores."

"Yes. I'm dying to find out more about the schools here," I said pushing a lounge chair next to hers.

"Both my kids go to St. Francis Xavier. It's a really good school," she said, taking a sip of iced water.

"Our sixteen-year-old son thinks the schools here are way behind California schools."

"Tell him that when he applies to U.S. colleges. He'll stand out from the crowd from having studied in Belize." She picked an ice cube from her tall glass and dabbed it on the back of her neck.

"That's exactly what Duke and I said."

"He should volunteer in a Belizean school. American universities look for what you have to offer that's different. If he can show he helped kids in Belize, they would automatically be interested in him."

"I'll tell him," I said. "My boys are eager to see the school textbooks."

"You can buy them at the Ministry of Education in Corozal."

"Are they open tomorrow?"

"They should open around ten. Don't forget, everything closes for at least two hours during lunch."

"Where is it?"

"It's right next to the massage parlor on Seventh Street," she said.

Store locations kept surprising me; like Chuck the butcher located next to the vet, or Fred, the other butcher, sandwiched between two residential homes. It made no sense at all, but this was Belize, not the U.S.

I couldn't wait to share the news with Steve and Alec. Her validation made me relax and feel like we'd made the right decision to send our kids to school in Corozal. *But what if we moved to Ambergris Caye? We didn't want to stay in our hut much longer, and we hadn't found another house we liked in Consejo Shores. We knew nothing about the high school on Ambergris Caye.*

We started a new family ritual during dinner. Since we didn't have cable TV, Duke gave us a choice of five DVDs to vote on. Each of us was allowed to vote for two, and the one with the most votes won. That evening we voted for the movie *Contact*, starring Jodie Foster.

Duke started the DVD and, three minutes into the movie, the electricity shut off. Used to this from before we arrived, Duke grabbed his emergency flashlight from the shelf above the couch and lit a candle. The boys and I sat in darkness. "This usually happens on Saturdays and Sundays," Duke said, "not Tuesdays."

"Why did we move here? It's so backward," Alec said.

"It's different," I said. "How long does it last?"

"As long as they want it to," Duke said. "It depends if Juan is taking a break on the Mexican side."

"You're kidding!" I said. "So we get our electricity from Mexico?"

"Yeah, but it also depends on whether the Belizean government paid its bill."

"Who told you that?" I asked.

"A Belizean."

It got cozy with all of us huddled together with no TV, no music, no entertainment except our voices and a flickering candle. This would never have happened in Orange County. The kids would have found some excuse to leave; but now, we only had one another.

During the ten-minute blackout, I brought up what Joan had said about the schools, and about how our boys would stand out from other students in the U.S. when filling out their college applications.

"I'd like to see the schoolbooks," Alec said.

There was never a moment when Alec didn't think about his education. Even in preschool, Alec acted alarmed when his teacher recommended he wait a year before entering kindergarten. She believed he was academically but not emotionally ready, so she suggested a year of pre-kindergarten.

"We can get the books tomorrow," I said.

After a while, the kids enjoyed the blackout. There was something special about a candle's flickering flame; it felt soothing, and I noticed the first steps toward my family reconnecting. It was just the five of us talking, listening to the rain outside and accepting the way things were without complaining.

The following day, we drove to the Ministry of Education. An arrow guided us to a small office, where a clerk asked the boys which grades they would be entering. She then turned her swivel chair around and grasped one of the few remaining ninth-grade textbooks for Alec. "Here," she said, "Sorry, that's all I have. Come back later."

"When should we come back?" I asked

"Maybe in two weeks," she replied. We paid for the book, and Alec flipped through it on the way home. All of a sudden, Duke and I heard Alec's cry from the rear cab.

"What's going on?" I asked through the small window separating us.

"There's no way I'm going to school in Belize. There's a chapter on how to tell time."

Duke pulled the truck over to the side of the road. He thumbed through to the next chapter and said, "And here's a chapter on how to add 'ing' to the end of a word."

"Maybe that's Josh's fifth-grade book," I suggested.

"No, it's the ninth-grade one," Duke said. We stared at one another in disbelief, and Alec gave me a look I interpreted as, "So what are you going to do about my education?" As soon as I walked inside the hut, I picked up the phone and called Joan.

After I explained the textbook to Joan she said, "I'm shocked. The elementary school in Corozal seems to be teaching at the same grade level as schools in the U.S." Then she mentioned, "I've heard there are some expat kids on Ambergris Caye following a U.S. Internet curriculum. I think it's called Keystone National High School, something like that. I'll see if I can find the name of someone you can call."

I hung up the phone, faced Alec and Steve, and told them I'd research the Keystone high school program. I could almost feel the anger raging through Steve's body.

"You're screwing up my education and my future," he said, slamming his fist against the dining room table.

Now I realized we'd been conned by the books we'd read about education in Belize. I felt as though we'd made the biggest mistake of our lives. How were we going to educate our high school kids? I had no clue what this Internet high school program was like. Scrambling for something positive to say, I turned to Duke for help.

"You stand a better chance of being accepted into college by being different, not by trying to follow the same path as the masses," Duke said. "Don't you think a college admission staff will find your application more interesting if you say you studied in Belize for two years? They'll see that you've been able to face the challenges of living in a foreign country."

Steve seemed to listen to Duke. "You have so many opportunities here. If you came out with us rather than stay in the hut all the time, I could introduce you to Irina," Duke said. "How many of your friends could ever work in a stem-cell research lab while still in high school?"

"Well, the ROP students can get a job at the hospital." Steve said.

"Yes, but there's a big difference between working as an apprentice in a hospital and being involved with a team of international doctors doing research," Duke said. The discussion ended when Steve ran out of arguments, and we'd managed to calm him down. Had we had this discussion in Orange County, I'm sure he would have run away. I took it as a sign of progress.

Duke and I spent the evening researching Keystone National High School. Though expensive, it started to sound like a good alternative for American kids living abroad. Our boys would have American teachers online to guide them, answer their questions and grade their work. Not only was it an accredited high school, but grades were transferable and accepted by colleges in the States. I began to feel hopeful again.

CHAPTER FIFTEEN

Villas Tropicales

"JUST LEAVE THEM," Duke said. "Sooner or later they'll want to come out."

The boys still refused to come with us to town. Transfixed in front of their computer screens, they instant messaged old friends, scared we might sever their lifeline to "civilization."

Josh missed TV, so he watched Spanish cartoons on the one channel available.

I worried about Duke's work; if he didn't catch up soon, he wouldn't receive a paycheck. With iguanas scurrying along our walls, tropical birds screeching, and Alec and Josh complaining, our hut felt more like a gazebo in the jungle than a law office. I handed Duke a cup of coffee and leaned over his shoulder to look at his computer screen.

"Phil just sent me a blunt e-mail," Duke said.

"Don't tell me he's firing you?"

"He says I'm not billing enough hours since I moved to Belize."

"Want me to get the kids out of your hair for a day? I could take them to Ambergris Caye. We could take a look at the house you liked." Duke reached for my hand and squeezed it.

"Let me call Sandy and make sure she can show it to you," Duke said. "I know you'll like it."

Duke had been right about the kids' reaction to Consejo Shores. None of us cared for the hut, there were no other kids to play with, and Evelyn said we could break the lease. So I was excited about taking them to the beautiful island.

When Duke got off the phone, he told me that Sandy suggested I take Josh to the Island Academy, a private, American-run school. "They have classes up to eighth grade," he said. He asked Sandy what she recommended for Steve and Alec, and, echoing Joan, she mentioned Keystone National High School.

"Sandy's going to give you the name of a parent whose son is starting the curriculum this fall," Duke said. It seemed like things were finally coming together.

Duke dropped us off at the tiny airport at the edge of Corozal Town, which was just as well, as I would have missed it. It sat at the top of a steep gravel driveway. As I stepped inside, the cozy airport lounge reminded me of someone's living room. We all felt more comfortable in the airport than at home. It had a TV, two new wicker, floral-fabric couches and a decent-size coffee table. I felt pampered with cool air from the air-conditioner blowing onto my clammy body. All I needed now was a delicious cup of coffee, and I could easily have spent the entire day perusing the U.S. tabloids left by tourists. I could not purchase magazines or books in Corozal stores.

It felt good to be part of a crowd. I enjoyed watching locals head up to the Tropic Air counter, buy their plane ticket and a beer from the same airline employee, and then relax for a few minutes of CNN before takeoff. No more than eight could fit on the wicker couches, the right number to fill a puddle-jumper flight.

My boys came alive for the first time in days. We all were eager to see the beach house. *And was Steve thinking about flirting with some cute girls on the tourist island?*

The boys had never flown on a propeller plane before, so as soon as they announced our flight to San Pedro, Steve led the way. We boarded the Cessna from the rear steps. With only a few rows of single seats on either side of the center aisle, the boys sat together on the bench in the back, and the pilot casually climbed into the cockpit using a small step-ladder like the one I'd left behind in my California kitchen. We taxied to the end of a skinny dirt runway, then nearly scraped the treetops as we took to the air with our underpowered lawn-mower engine. Alec grabbed his seat cushion with both hands. Within seconds, we were over the Caribbean, and I noticed parallel lines extending for miles along the seabed. I learned that dredgers—barges used to remove sand from the shallow waters—had formed these lines. All four of us had our faces glued to the oval windows, counting manatees and dolphins.

Twenty minutes later we stood on Main Street in San Pedro amid a cacophony of golf carts, bicycles and rusty Toyota taxis driving with-out any obvious adherence to rules of the road. Nothing had changed since Duke and I visited a year ago, except for the roads. Instead of dust swirling with each footstep, a sludgy mixture stuck to our flip-flops, a legacy from tropical morning showers.

Sandy's directions were simple enough: "Exit the Tropic Air gate and turn right. Pass the Island Supermarket, and you'll see the Island Academy on your left. Go to the yellow building. That's the office."

It sounded so simple. Yet, out of habit, I stopped someone to ask for directions.

The school looked adorable. The property was surrounded by a white picket fence. Inside the boundary were small cottages, each painted in bright Caribbean colors. The translucent sea with catamarans and other boats bobbing up and down made this an idyllic setting, especially for a school. The beach served as the playground. We stood there for several minutes, captivated by the possibility of living here, then entered the yellow cottage.

A slender, elegantly dressed Belizean woman greeted us. Sandy had informed her of our visit, and her office looked just as perfect as she did.

"Mrs. Marsh, I'm Jasmine," she said, showing off gleaming white teeth that contrasted dramatically with the olive tone of her skin. Her silky, black tresses could have graced a hair commercial, so I wasn't surprised to learn that Jasmine had been crowned "Miss Belize" a few years previously.

"So you must be Josh," she said, shaking his hand. I was impressed that Sandy had given her the name of my youngest son. "Miss Charlene is our fifth-grade teacher, and she's wonderful" Jasmine's air-conditioned office, mixed with her charm, made it easy for me to pull out a pen and checkbook to pay for the first month's tuition. Though I knew this was taking a risk, not yet having seen the house, my gut told me this was where my family belonged. The vibes were intoxicating and made Consejo Shores seem like prison in contrast.

"You'll love it here," Jasmine said.

"Oh, I'm just curious about the high school on the island," I said, fumbling with the checkbook. "What's it like?"

Jasmine paused and cleared her throat. Not a good sign. "Well, how should I put this?" she said, her face turning a lighter shade of olive. "Most of our parents either send their high school children to a private school in Belize City, where they stay with a host family during the week, or they follow an Internet high school curriculum."

"Why?" I asked, hoping to convince Alec and Steve that the Internet program offered a great curriculum.

"Both the online curriculum and the high school in Belize City offer a higher standard than on the island."

After leaving the Island Academy, the boys kicked off their flip-flops and ran into the warm Caribbean, splashing water with each stride. "Look at the catamarans," Steve said, pointing to six of them moored in a row. "Would you and Dad let me get a sailboat?"

"If we move here, we'd probably look at a secondhand one, if it's cheap enough," I said. It felt good to have my Steve back.

"Let's move," Josh said. "I like it better than Consejo Shores."

"I prefer California," Alec said.

I ignored Alec's comment and pointed to a couple of guys windsurfing.

Sandy's real estate office sat on the beach, and on one side of her front door was sand, on the other, tile.

"So glad to meet you," Sandy said, leaning over her desk. "What handsome boys," she added, shaking their hands. "Let me call my boat captain, and we'll go take a look at the house." Sandy's accent was British; it took me by surprise. "By the way, what did you think of the Island Academy?" she asked. "My daughter goes there. It's a great school."

I told her it seemed perfect for Josh.

"Don't worry about Steve and Alec," she said. "I know several kids on the island who follow the Keystone program. I can put you in touch with Sharon Powell. Her son will start ninth grade like Alec."

"I'd love to talk to her," I said, feeling more and more like our life in Belize was falling into place.

We followed Sandy onto the dock, and the boys jumped into the boat. I remembered that the nicer homes were located north of San Pedro. The one Duke had picked out was five miles north of town.

When we arrived at *Villas Tropicales,* the name of the development, Sandy pointed out the "flats" to the kids. "There's really good fly fishing right here, guys." I kept staring at the never-ending seagrass, not realizing at the time that so much grass in front of their house would be paradise for most fly fishermen. I wanted us to be able to swim and snorkel, and it looked like the seagrass would get in the way. Gratefully, I saw a small, dredged area by the end of the pier where I could swim in some clear Caribbean water.

Villas Tropicales consisted of four almost identical two-story villas. Two were oceanfront, and two sat behind a rectangular saltwater pool. The one for sale happened to be right in front, with its own stretch of beach and palm trees.

I fell in love with the view before setting foot inside the house, a two-story villa with Italian limestone tile on the exterior walls, plus wood trim. It felt so right for the five of us. I watched my boys run around the property playing soccer with a coconut and wetting their feet in the pool. I wanted this house more than anything.

Sandy introduced me to Jill, a fiftyish, tanned expat.

"Jill's the listing agent for the property," Sandy said. I shook Jill's limp hand.

"I already showed this villa to Duke a few weeks ago," she said.

Why was she being so rude?

"Yes, I know, and I wanted to see it with my boys," I said.

Duke had pointed out some flaws he wanted me to focus on, like the dry spots on the exterior wood that craved a coat of sealant. After careful observation, I finally reached the top of the staircase, where Jill stood tapping her fingers on the railing. *Did she think I was wasting her time inspecting the house?* It was months later when I realized that American expats who ran businesses on the island—especially those who had lived here for many years—no longer offered the kind of customer service Americans are used to receiving. They had developed the "Belizean island mentality," quite normal—and a sign they had adapted.

Once inside the villa, I couldn't believe the stunning, panoramic views of the Caribbean. If I could wake up to this view every morning, that would be *my paradise.*

Unfussy and tropical best describes the décor of the open living room, dining room and kitchen. Never in my life had I seen such beautiful tile: slices of rusty-red fossilized coral, with shells embedded in it. A spectacular mahogany vaulted ceiling embraced the open space, and a silent fan circulated ocean breezes, keeping the upstairs cool. I stepped outside the large glass doors opening up to a veranda, where a couple of hammocks overlooked the sea. I could already see Duke and myself swaying in the breeze, knowing we'd made the right decision to get away from the rat race and start to really live life.

The boys dashed around the house picking their rooms. Steve was in heaven when he discovered what would be his room, or perhaps I should call it his "suite." Identical to the master suite, except for its azure bathroom tile versus sunshine yellow tile, it had a small coral patio leading to the beach. Alec and Josh would share a room, something I knew Alec would complain about.

Jill waited for us outside on a lounge chair, and when I asked her about the pool and maintenance of the property, she pointed to a small shack in the back, bordering the unkempt jungle and dirt road. "Juan and his wife, Teresa, live there and take care of the property," she said. "They also have a four-year-old boy." I wanted to meet them, but they were on vacation.

"Can we catch lobster?" Steve asked Sandy on the boat ride back to San Pedro.

"What about spear fishing?" Alec asked. This was my happiest moment since moving to Belize.

Once in town, I treated the boys to lunch in a tourist restaurant on the beach, and their faces beamed when the waitress brought their American-style hamburgers and fries. "These fries taste just like MacDonald's," Josh said, splattering extra ketchup on top.

"Do we have time to check out the rest of town?" Steve asked.

"Yes, if we rent a golf cart," I said.

"Can I drive?" Steve begged.

We found Cholo's on Front Street and rented an electric golf cart. Steve kept bugging me to drive, and I finally caved in. As I had expected, the second his hands grabbed the steering wheel, he turned into a NASCAR driver. Fortunately, electric golf carts don't accelerate very fast, so within seconds, he had all of us in hysterics. It felt so good to hear my boys laugh.

We made it to Tropic Air five minutes before our puddle jumper headed back to Corozal. As our plane landed and taxied toward its parking spot, Duke waved from his truck.

"I love the villa," I said, skipping toward Duke. "Let's buy it. The boys are so much happier in San Pedro, and I already signed Josh up for school."

"I knew you'd want that house."

Back home, Duke called Sandy and made an offer.

Now we had to wait and see.

CHAPTER SIXTEEN

Smiling Again

SATURDAY WAS BARBECUE CHICKEN DAY in Corozal, and Duke knew the mom and pop shacks in town where chickens ran freely, waiting for "slaughter" day. We drove by a large red-and-white tent with several guys barbecuing underneath. They appeared to be the top chefs in town, so I asked Duke to stop the truck. I coughed my way through a white fog of smoking chicken skins and found a chef. "I'd like four pieces of chicken," I said, rubbing my eyes.

"Sorry, ma'am, these chickens are pre-ordered," the cook replied, beads of sweat streaming down his forehead. Silly me had cut in front of everyone without noticing the tickets in their hands. They probably thought, here comes another rude gringa who thinks she's entitled to cut in line. "I just sold my last two orders," he added.

Disappointed, we toured Corozal's streets. I stuck my head out the window, scanning for grills. "There's one," I said pointing to a shack by the Miranda sign.

"Not that one." Duke cringed. "I got so sick from their chicken." I noticed a couple of shriveled chicken skins toasted to a crisp on the grill.

"There's a local takeout on Fifth Street," Duke said. "Order whatever they have." He parked on the side of the road, and I walked inside a gray-tiled restaurant with plastic tables, chairs and vinyl tablecloths. The smell of deep-fried food greeted me at the entrance, where a man and a girl I presumed was his daughter sat perched on bar stools. A chalkboard listed at least ten items, but I had learned that menus never reflected what was available on that day. The chalk letters had faded, so it was best to ask.

"Chicken, rice and beans, and tamales," the father said, swatting a fly off his nose.

"Okay, I'll take three orders of each." In five quick minutes — unusual for Belize — he handed me two plastic bags with three Styrofoam boxes in each. The total came to only $12.

Duke drove back to our hut; the boys waited by the front door, like baby birds waiting for Mom and Dad to feed them. They each grabbed a Styrofoam box and polished off every grain of rice. Always hungry, they no longer complained about the local food.

My kitchen was impossible to keep clean. I had to boil water to wash the dishes. I kept all dry food in containers. Forget *Ziplocs;* I had purchased some expensive *Ziplocs* in Corozal and quickly realized they made no difference. Ants, cockroaches, mice, rats, iguanas, scorpions and other critters helped themselves to everything inside the bags.

Now, with fifteen hard plastic containers stacked on a flimsy, crooked shelf above our stove, I was forced to open each one until I found what I was looking for. I'd thought about labeling them, but sticky labels and Sharpie pens didn't exist in Corozal.

One evening, I was looking for the penne pasta container, and the shelf collapsed. All fifteen containers landed on the floor, with rice and pasta spilling on the counter. I scooped the pasta into a pan of boiling water and, after five seconds, a swarm of small black things floated on the surface. They were fleas, so I ladled them off the surface. This was all the pasta I had left, and everyone was starving. Duke and I rinsed the pasta with bottled water, trying our best to unglue the fleas, one by one. Thankfully the tomato sauce and ground pepper camouflaged the residual fleas, and the kids never complained. Hunger did wonders to lower my standards.

A traveling colony of leafcutter ants on my wooden kitchen counter kept me entertained as I waited for water to boil to melt the grease off our dinner plates. After washing each plate, I'd rinse them off with our cold, stinky well water; however, the kitchen faucet acted like a sprinkler head and soaked my shorts after each meal. I no longer cared.

The boys started coming with us to town. They were hungry and wanted more food. The best way to discover where to shop was to ask the expats. Lydia recommended Chuck, the butcher.

Chuck and his wife greeted us with a friendly, "Good morning," and his two young daughters giggled and blushed when they saw Steve and his brothers follow me to the counter. Stores always kept their front doors open, inviting flies and street dust inside. Chuck's felt slightly different than the average store: a little more like the Louis Vuitton of butchers. Unlike other butchers, Chuck had a refrigerated display case where his meat was neatly arranged. Though I counted three flies on the ground beef, this was nothing compared with other butchers. Chuck's meat didn't reek like the giant freezers in Corozal supermarkets. With sporadic electricity and no generators to keep the freezers running, meats would freeze and then thaw out several times a week. It often required a pickaxe to remove chicken pieces wrapped in plastic Saran wrap, which was glued to sticky pools of meat juice.

At least Chuck's meat looked fresh, and his family offered the best in Belizean customer service. If you asked Chuck for steaks, he'd sharpen the thick blade on his butcher's knife, hold the slab of beef in the air and move his knife until you signaled the thickness you wanted. What a change from the paper-thin frozen steaks in the supermarkets. Chuck did the same with his slab of bacon. Alec loved bacon and couldn't wait to get back to our hut so I could fry it.

Eggs were a different story; they were fertilized. Every egg I cracked open represented an embryo in a different stage of development, perfect had I been home-schooling my kids in biology. One morning, I cracked an egg that felt rather heavy. A feather popped out, and five seconds after my scream, all five of us gathered around the frying pan. The chick was dead, and Alec refused to eat eggs from that day on.

Without a garbage disposer or a dishwasher, the kids learned to finish whatever they put on their plates. Scooping leftover oatmeal or scrambled eggs out of the sink with their bare hands was pretty gross. The rain was our friend, as it offered a dishwasher alternative. We arranged our dirty plates next to the glassless kitchen window, and the raindrops pooled on our lopsided kitchen counters, rinsing the dishes clean. Just a dab of Palmolive and, *voilà*.

We had just started watching a DVD one evening when a sudden rainstorm added a cozy touch. With all our goodies from Chuck the butcher, I couldn't wait to make a special dinner.

"Does anyone know how the oven works?" I asked.

"No," Duke said. "I've never used it." Unlike my California oven, this one used gas, so I opened the oven door to figure out where to stick a match to light it. Just as my eyes reached mid-shelf, a huge rat made direct eye contact with me. I quickly shut the oven door, yelling, "There's a rat in the oven!" The boys immediately thought of Cookie, our suburban rat terrier, and opened the door to see whether she knew what rat terriers had been bred for. All five of us stood behind Cookie waiting for some entertainment. She placed her front paws on the open oven door and wagged her tail; not quite the reaction we'd expected. She finally attempted to jump inside the oven just as the rat ran into a hole in the wall. I made mashed potatoes instead of baked potatoes for dinner.

"Don't you think these steaks taste better than the ones we get in California?" I asked everyone.

"Definitely," Steve replied.

Either our taste buds had intensified or we appreciated food more because it required effort to hunt for it.

CHAPTER SEVENTEEN

Going Local

I FORCED MYSELF TO DRIVE Duke's truck to Corozal. There was no reason for Duke to waste precious time chauffeuring me around like he would an old lady when he should be working.

I attacked the seven-mile dirt road alone. After a mini-course on how to drive like a Belizean, Duke instructed me to copy them. "If you need to stop on the left, veer across the street to the other side and park. No need to do a U-turn," he said.

Corozal didn't have traffic, at least not what we call "traffic" in Los Angeles; however, it did have unusual conditions, such as stray dogs, shoeless kids walking in the middle of the road, swerving bicyclists and suicidal drivers. After I had completed a few round trips, the dogs became more predictable than the people. A skinny mutt always hung out at the end of the seven-mile road. The poor thing was furless, her skin oozing infection, and I realized that she must have been hit by several cars because both hips were dislocated.

Less than a month before, I had stepped inside an upscale pet store in Newport Beach, California, where they sold an assortment of jewelry for dogs; the cheapest necklace cost $175. They even displayed cashmere sweaters for dogs on baby-size hangers, with designer labels and wash instructions. There was also a glass case with rows of refrigerated dog treats, each one decorated with frosting and a handwritten, cutesy message.

How could we treat our dogs in California better than children in Belize?

No wonder the local vet's office in Corozal always looked empty. I couldn't imagine anyone but members of the expat community taking their dogs there. Strays infested with worms and parasites had to fend for themselves. I felt stupid asking for chew sticks to clean Cookie's teeth when many local kids didn't own a toothbrush.

Still shaking from my drive to Corozal, I dried my wet palms on my shorts and stopped at our bank. As I climbed the cement steps, an armed guard opened the door, blasting me with Arctic air. Now I stood freezing in my skimpy shorts and tank top, embarrassed beside the female bank clerks in their conservative uniforms. They reminded me of my teenage years in a strict British boarding school.

"Morning, ma'am," the guard said, wearing a gun on his belt and a smile on his face. "Can I help you?"

"Yes, I'm looking for Mr. Williams," I said.

"This way, ma'am, I'll get him for you." I paused in front of Mr. Williams' door with arms wrapped around my stomach. My clammy skin had turned into a layer of frost, and the strong smell of bleach on the freshly mopped tile made me feel sick. *Was this a bank or a hospital?*

Mr. Williams poked his head around the door. "I'll be right there."

Looking at him, dressed as though he'd had an official luncheon with the prime minister, I couldn't help but reflect on the diverse environments inside and outside this bank.

"How can I help you, ma'am?" the manager asked.

"I need to add my name to my husband's account and deposit a U.S. check," I said, handing him our bank account booklet.

"Yes, Mrs. Marsh, is your husband here to sign, too?"

"No, he's at home, but he called you to say I'd be over." Mr. Williams gestured for me to follow him into his office and proceeded with the paperwork. When I asked to withdraw $250, he frowned. "Sorry. I need your husband's signature."

"But this is our joint account, and both of us have endorsed the check I'm depositing," I protested.

"Sorry, Mrs. Marsh. Your husband has to come over and sign."

Duke warned me not to argue in Belize. "Accept their rules," he said. Duke explained that everyone gossips and, if you upset one person, everyone would soon find out.

I thanked him, trying hard not to say what was on my mind, and continued with my errands.

Our life in Consejo Shores appeared to be settling into some sort of routine. Knowing that escrow on our new house seemed to be moving right along made it easier to put up with the hut.

It was time to find out more about the Internet school for Steve and Alec. Sandy gave me Sharon's number. Her son, Matt, would be starting ninth grade along with Alec.

"We'd love to have your boys join Matt at our house," Sharon said. "My husband finished a room addition with six workstations, so there's plenty of space."

She said not to worry about getting the textbooks; her sister in Texas would send my boys' books to her along with Matt's. All we had to do was register our boys for the online classes, order the books and have them shipped to her sister's mailing address. I felt so much happier now that we had a specific plan and a "classroom" in San Pedro for our boys to study their high school curriculum.

Duke was right. The kids came out of their cocoon, exploring the jungle surrounding our hut and swimming in the bay. Perhaps the lack of TV, shopping and entertainment had started to create the change in them we'd hoped for. Our boys even agreed to a dishwashing schedule, without complaint. We had so few plates and cutlery, we had to hand wash them after each meal.

Once the kids realized it was impossible to stop the bugs from excreting on our floors, a miracle happened. Their wet towels and dirty clothes ended up in the laundry hamper. Of course, I kept quiet about the bug poop inside the laundry hamper. As hard as I tried in the beginning, I could never quite get the floors clean, despite my daily sweeping and mopping. Dust kept blowing inside our glassless windows. But since no one visited me or my hut, the "perfection" habit I'd absorbed in Orange County no longer mattered. I now had time to enjoy my family, and talk to them about things other than school, schedules and rules.

While checking e-mails at my desk, I heard Duke's alarmed voice.

"What happened, Alec?" I heard him say. I dashed into the living room.

"I think Steve did something to Alec," Duke said. "Leave him alone for a few minutes; he's crying."

How could I ignore Alec? I had to see what happened. I entered his room and found Alec crouched in the corner, sobbing.

"What happened?" I said placing my arm around his shoulder, wanting nothing more than to cradle him like a baby and make it all better.

"Did Steve do something to you?" I knew they'd been swimming in the bay and wasn't sure whether Steve had pushed him off the pier or said something hurtful. I knew Alec was having a tougher time adapting to Belize than his brothers. He'd always hated change, and I wondered how long it would take him to feel settled, if ever, in a country so different from where he was born and raised. It wouldn't take much teasing on Steve's part to throw him off.

"I want to go back home," Alec bawled. "It's Steve's fault we're here."

Seeing my six-foot-two, gangly-limbed teenager break down made me feel like the worst mother ever. I sat on the floor next to him, took his hand in mine and stroked it. *If only I could tell him we were going back to California. But I couldn't. Our adventure had just started, and we couldn't give up now.*

I forced myself to remain firm. Watching Alec cry made me question the reasons Duke and I had for escaping Orange County. I admit that living in Orange County for more than twenty years had influenced my own values, especially when it came to the attitude that looks were all-important and aging was intolerable. I hated the media's undue influence on the culture of conformity, as far as people's clothes and cars — basically everything surrounding us. I always felt it was impossible to escape mentally unless I escaped physically.

Here in Belize, I hoped we would finally understand that it's OK to be yourself. You don't have to "fit in" and value the wrong things, whether you're a kid or an adult. I also hoped we would learn the difference between wants and needs, something I felt Belize could teach us. *But was I being a hypocrite?* Besides, had Alec ever been a difficult child? Had he ever acted like the entitled kids in Orange County? Not really; in fact, not at all.

I tried explaining to Alec that it takes awhile to adapt to a new place and that I was proud of him, but my words sounded phony, even to me. As I left him whimpering on the floor, I could almost feel my heart tearing apart. I begged Duke to go talk to him. He returned only seconds later. "Alec won't talk," he said.

I stormed out to see what Steve had done to upset Alec. With snorkel and fins in hand, Steve wandered slowly toward our hut. I knew he'd waited for things to cool down on purpose.

"He's such a baby," Steve said, as soon as he saw me.

"What did you do to him?"

"Nothing."

"You'd better tell me."

"I just borrowed his mask. He's such a baby."

I knew he wasn't telling me the truth, so I asked Steve one more time to explain what happened.

"He fell in the mangroves," Steve said.

"You pushed him, right?"

"We were just play fighting."

Barracudas and crocodiles were known to live around the mangroves, so Alec probably got scared.

"Would you stop bugging Alec?" I said, forcefully.

"Such a baby," I heard him repeat under his breath. We climbed the steps into the hut, and, as I sank into the ugly couch, I thought about our house in California. I suddenly missed the comforts we'd left behind. We could never afford to move back. Alec didn't know that, and I refused to crush his hope of one day going "home."

Suddenly, a gust of air hit my face as Alec charged past me. He kicked the front door open and escaped without his shoes.

"Leave him," Duke ordered when he saw me getting ready to follow. "Sometimes kids need to be alone."

Twenty minutes went by, and Alec still had not returned. *Where was he hiding? In the jungle?* The afternoon sun was slanting through the hut. I couldn't wait any longer. "We have to go look for him," I said.

We jumped in the truck and took off. I spotted Naomi, the only kid in our neighborhood.

"Have you seen Alec?"

"Yes. He walked across the street," she said, pointing in the opposite direction.

We found him at the end of the road, walking aimlessly.

"Please get in the car; it's getting dark," I pleaded. He ignored us. "Alec, please get in the car." He refused.

Duke turned his truck around and drove back slowly toward our hut.

Through the rearview mirror, I watched Alec trudge along, shoulders hunched. He kept his eyes on the ground. At least he was heading toward the hut and not in the opposite direction.

I started cooking dinner and listened for the spring on the front door to squeak. When Alec walked in, he headed straight for the shower. I left him alone, relieved to have him back.

An hour later, we sat down to dinner, and Alec became quiet again. I sensed his pain and frustration at being stuck in a place he disliked. I felt torn between the guilt of Duke working a job he hated in order to support us in Orange County and the guilt of Alec suffering in Belize where he did not belong.

Although Steve seemed to be showing signs of improvement, I felt as though Alec, my "good child," was suffering. *Had I sacrificed one son for the sake of another?*

CHAPTER EIGHTEEN

Fired

DUKE WAS FIRED. I had feared this would happen, as Duke barely had time to work, what with me and the kids, and the critters in our hut. Even so, we didn't think it would happen this soon.

"I think Phil's jealous," Duke said. "I'm sure he'd love to be living in the Caribbean, getting paid U.S. wages."

"What about our legal transcription business?" I asked.

"I need Phil to send me some files."

"Are you crazy? He's not going to send you files after he's fired you," I exploded.

"I've been terminated, not fired," Duke said, pausing to sip his coffee. "Besides, I need him to recommend me to other law firms."

"You honestly think Phil's going to send you business? You never told me you were relying on Phil to get our transcription business going." My voice shook the palm-thatched ceiling. "We're in shit trouble now. We're buying a house, and you get fired! What do *you* plan on doing about it?"

Duke gave me his *look* — the one that showed I'd crossed the line. I knew what was coming next, something he'd done several times during our marriage in California; he stormed off. Now I felt stranded in the hut.

Two hours later, Duke walked through the front door.

"You think that's the solution?" I yelled. "Walking out?"

"Drop it," he shouted back.

From now on, we would be living entirely off our savings, which was scary considering we were in the midst of purchasing a house. I felt as though our future had become one huge question mark.

Duke returned to his computer, seemingly calm and confident. With a heavy sigh, I sat on the couch and waited. I stared at his back, fully aware that he had no intention of turning around to face me. The need to brainstorm with him was almost a physical ache. *Surely Duke had a backup plan in mind?*

Since he wouldn't talk, I began questioning why I'd married him. Because he was kind, intelligent, creative, and I admired him. Then I said to myself, "He's worked hard for sixteen years as a workers' compensation attorney. Surely he deserves some time off." *But how much time?* I decided two months off was about right. After all, I asked myself, what was I scared of? That Duke would turn into a lazy beach bum? *Yes, that was what I feared the most.* I'd noticed a fair number of American expats did nothing all day except smoke and drink.

"I think I should go look at boats today," Duke announced, a few days after he'd been fired. "Sandy e-mailed me. Our house purchase is coming along, and the guy she works with has a boat for sale." Boats were essential for daily transportation on Ambergris Caye, especially when you didn't live close to town.

"It's a 26-foot skiff. Chris wants me to come take a look at it," Duke said.

Duke flew over to San Pedro with Alec to take a look at the *Island Rider*. It had a ninety horsepower, four-stroke Honda engine, the same engine you'd find in a Honda Civic. The boat was practically brand new, and Chris convinced Duke that this was exactly what we needed. Duke took it out for a test drive and bought it right away.

"It's so cool, Mom," Alec said, when I picked them up at the airport. "We can go fishing in the boat." He was beaming.

"But we're not even sure if the house is ours yet, are we?" I asked.

"Sandy said they've accepted our offer," said Duke. "We've got an attorney doing the paperwork, and the deal should close in two to three weeks."

To me it all sounded a little crazy, to be spending our savings on a house and a boat without any idea of when we'd have an income. But Duke wasn't a procrastinator.

"I sat next to the pilot on the plane," Alec said, glowing with pride.

Thrilled to see him excited for once, I asked, "How was it?"

"He makes it look easy."

"Do you want to take flying lessons?"

"Not really."

The boys and I decided to swim before dinner. Duke was exhausted and sunburned from driving our new boat, so he took a nap.

As we put on our snorkels and masks, black clouds rolled in. Thunder resonated, so we ran back to the hut. The sun disappeared within minutes, yet not a single drop of water fell. As the winds picked up, the kids grew agitated. Duke woke up, and we all helped him move the furniture toward the middle of our living room. This was how we kept our couch dry with no glass in the windows. "Turn off your computers," Duke shouted.

That evening, our hut would have made the perfect setting for a horror movie — howling winds, deafening thunder, lightning so close the entire hut glowed and then the arrival of rain that fell sideways. Even the curtains cooperated with the eerie atmosphere by refusing to hang straight.

We huddled together with our flickering candle and talked.

"Should we change the name of the boat?" Duke asked.

"That's bad luck, isn't it?" Steve said. Upon reconsideration, he added, "It'd be neat to give it a pirate name."

"We could put a pirate flag on it," Josh chimed in.

For now, we decided to keep it as the *Island Rider* until we could come up with something better.

The following morning we had the usual post-storm invasion of mosquitoes and dock flies. We now had a morning routine. I cooked breakfast, and we talked while eating. No need to rush as we didn't have appointments or schedules. I didn't even have to plan entertainment for the kids. In Orange County, I felt pressure to keep the kids busy, especially during the long summer vacations. Theme parks, movies, fun zones, camp and eating out cost a fortune, and my boys and their friends took it for granted. I dreaded those long summer vacations, and every year was the same.

Duke suggested we snorkel in front of Casablanca Hotel, and this time, Steve agreed to come along. Duke had started a competitive treasure hunt without realizing it. Since his latest find, an antique glass bottle from the 1700s, the boys and I were eager to prove we could also find buried treasure from shipwrecks.

Casablanca Hotel had its own protected cove by the entrance of the River Hondo, where numerous artifacts lay scattered on the seabed. "This one is probably an old ink bottle," said Duke, extending his arm for all of us to admire the item. This bottle had writing on it, *FRS. Cleaver London*. Duke couldn't wait to get back to the hut and Google it.

We ordered lunch on the pier, where we compared our loot.

"Is this Mayan pottery?" I asked Duke. A rusty clay color, it certainly looked old.

"Probably," he said.

"This reminds me of the formal plates I used to eat roast beef and Yorkshire pudding on in England," I said, holding a chunk of white and blue porcelain.

"It's probably from a sunken British ship," Duke said.

The kids found this fascinating, and Steve displayed two bottles he hoped were ancient relics. Unfortunately, they were modern beer bottles turned white from barnacles. Josh and Alec picked up anything they could find on the shallow seabed.

By now, we were used to Belizean customer service. Rather than get frustrated by the one-hour wait for hamburgers, I started viewing it as a gift. More time for us to interact. As we finished our last bite, the usual afternoon thunderstorm rolled in.

Both Duke and I were restless during the night. I couldn't stop thinking about Duke losing his job and wondering: *Did we do the right thing? Should we have sold our house in California? Will the kids get as good an education over the Internet as they would going to a school in the U.S.? Will Duke get his transcription business for attorneys up and running? Will we make enough money at it? Will we be using up all of our savings to live on Ambergris Caye?*

I nudged Duke. "Are you thinking the same as I am?"

"Probably not."

"Why aren't you sleeping?"

"I'm physically tired, but not mentally."

After two hours of tossing, I finally fell asleep, but the sound of my own whimpering soon woke me. I'd had one of the worst nightmares of my entire life.

I was back in California, shocked by how much things had changed in just one month. New buildings had sprouted up, more people were on the freeways than before: Basically, it was chaos. I drove a small, white rental car and entered the Interstate 5 freeway at about sixty miles per hour. I spotted a police car in front of me and slammed on the brakes, but too late. I smashed into the police car and saw myself flying above all the other cars and dying.

I didn't feel any pain, but I could hear the radio announcing a terrible accident on the southbound 5 freeway, stopping all traffic. I kept thinking, *Why don't they say my name? Why don't they announce that I just moved to Belize and that my family's dreams have been shattered?* I wanted to talk to Duke again. I could hear him, but he couldn't hear me. I told him how sorry I was not to be with him to make our dream happen, and that I loved him so much. I asked if he would stay in Belize or move back to California. I knew the kids would want to move back. Then Duke answered me. He said in a loud, clear voice, "I'm going to continue with our dream."

After waking up exhausted, I found Duke sipping coffee at his computer desk.

"I got so mad at you during my nightmare," I said, accusingly.

"Why?" he said.

"Didn't you hear me speak to you? Didn't you hear me whimper?"

"No."

I explained my nightmare, careful not to leave out a single detail. Duke did his best to soothe my fears. "Sonia, you've always been a worrier. Everything will work out," he said.

CHAPTER NINETEEN

Alec's Birthday

"HAPPY BIRTHDAY TO YOU," I sang cheerfully as Alec stumbled into the living room, half-asleep. I sauntered over and squeezed his pencil-thin body.

"I'm sorry we don't have a present for you. There's nothing you'd want in Corozal, but Dad has an idea." I turned toward Duke. It's your turn, I signaled.

"How about we visit some Mayan ruins? You know the Mayans settled in Belize about 3,000 years ago. Lamanai is close by," Duke said.

"I want to be with my friends," Alec moaned. "This place sucks. It's all because of Steve we're here." He then turned around and stormed to his room.

I thought things were getting better with Alec, but evidently not. He still longed to be with his friends.

I took a deep breath and tapped on his door. "Let's talk."

Alec followed me to my room, and I raised the mosquito net so we could both lie down on my bed. I chose my words carefully, first acknowledging his desire to be with Jeff and Jake, then suggesting they could visit us in our new island house. I reached for Alec's hand and noticed his breathing relax. We remained silent for a while.

"I think you'll like Lamanai," I said. "We might see crocodiles along the river if we're lucky." Alec perked up as much as I could expect. "Come, let's make pancakes for breakfast."

I mixed pancake batter using powdered milk from Mexico. The aroma of sizzling pancakes attracted the boys like humming birds to nectar.

"We're going to Lamanai today," I said digging into my pancakes.

"Do we have to?" Josh whined.

"I'm not going," Steve snapped.

After a few minutes, a yelling match erupted between Duke and Steve.

"Stay in the hut," Duke snarled. "You'll only make things miserable for us."

Josh and Alec dragged their feet down the steps and climbed into the bed of Duke's truck. We still only had two beach chairs for them to sit on, but with our lowered standards of luxury, they accepted them. Duke drove to Orange Walk Town, about an hour south of Consejo Shores, and parked on a gravel lot next to the New River Bridge. Our tour boat was docked underneath the bridge, where two English backpacking students waited for the tour to start. I was upset that Steve had missed yet another opportunity to interact with young people.

Alec and Josh sat together behind Tony, our Belizean tour guide. Duke and I parked ourselves on the bench behind them. Tony's boat tore down the murky green New River, stopping abruptly whenever he felt the need to give us an update. Our first stop was to observe a Mennonite community.

Six identical-looking blonde boys with hypnotic, light-blue eyes fished and swam in the river next to a man who looked just like them. They wore burlap-colored overalls and white shirts, and they swam fully clothed.

Tony told us about the morelet crocodiles living in the river; this didn't seem to bother the man or the kids. I still couldn't fathom why the Mennonites had picked Belize, an environment so foreign to their physical complexions. I could easily visualize them in the rolling green pastures and temperate climates of Austria, Germany or Switzerland, but not in the hot, balmy climate of Belize with its crocodiles, howler monkeys, jaguars and jungles.

Tony slowed his boat down to point out a baby crocodile basking in the sun on a gutted tree trunk. He announced the exact location of the crocodile before we turned the river bend. Josh believed it was real, but it reminded me of the crocodiles on Disneyland's Jungle Cruise ride.

Familiar with every nook and cranny along the shoreline, Tony stopped the boat, then grabbed a long wooden stick that he poked inside a cave. A family of bats swarmed above our heads like a miniature black cloud. I was sorry he had disturbed them for our sake. Great egrets, with their long, elegant necks, waddled along the river bank.

When the boat docked at Lamanai, all we could think about was food. The long boat ride and lack of snacks made us long for lunch. We helped Tony carry giant coolers up the steep, dirt path toward some picnic tables. All of us, including Alec and Josh, collapsed on the wooden benches in the heart of the jungle. The lush canopy blocked most of the sun's rays, giving us the eerie, cool feeling of an eclipse. Inside nature's giant dome, insects and howler monkeys screeched, their unfamiliar sounds echoing within.

After lunch, Alec started exploring, and I was grateful to see him interested in this unique environment. Tony pointed toward the main Mayan temple, built in 100 BC. We followed a narrow path in the jungle and reached an open expanse where the sun's rays hit us full blast. There stood a majestic old temple, 112 feet in height. "Dad, want to climb to the top?" Alec asked.

"Sure," he said. "Want to come, Josh?" he asked. Knowing my fear of heights, he didn't ask me.

"I'll stay with Mom," Josh said.

It felt good to see Alec and Duke doing something together. I watched them climb the steps sideways, as the uneven, stone stairs were too narrow for their feet.

Josh and I focused on specks of fur hidden inside the foliage. Boisterous howler monkeys were frolicking in the tallest of trees, and it felt both strange and rewarding to be this close to wilderness.

Although not your typical teenage birthday gift, I knew Lamanai would remain ingrained in Alec's mind forever. During our drive home, Duke planned to have a *talk* with Steve.

"I can't believe he refused to come," Duke said, his voice filled with disappointment. "This was such an educational experience for our kids."

After a quick shower, Duke approached Steve's room. I stood by the door and listened. "If you don't want to participate in our adventure in Belize," Duke said, "and you just want to continue instant messaging Tina until 3 A.M. every night, we can send you to military high school in the U.S."

Steve's eyes unglued from his monitor, and he stared at Duke in disbelief. Duke knew he'd struck a chord, as military school had come up before our move and Steve had protested.

"You'll get the education you want, and you won't make life miserable for us," Duke continued. "We want you to be part of the family, but every time we ask you to come with us you say no. We're tired of your lack of interest in experiencing life here."

Steve remained unusually quiet. I noticed his eyes moisten and tears forming. I'd grown a hard shell, but I still longed to hug and comfort him the way I did Alec. I feared being rejected, though.

"Give him time to think about it," Duke said, knowing I felt bad for him. "If he cries, that's OK; he needs to figure this out for himself."

The following morning, Steve stepped into the kitchen, dressed and energized. "What's for breakfast?" he said, reminding me of a furnace that finally got its pilot light lit. "I have an idea," he continued, before I had time to respond. "I want to make my own spear to catch a crocodile. Alec, want to come?" he said.

I beamed with joy, not from the project itself, but from the change in his disposition. "Alec, let's go look for wood. Dad, can I use your machete?" Steve asked, wolfing down the last of his scrambled eggs.

We knew he wouldn't kill a crocodile; we just wanted him outside, even if that meant having a Robinson Crusoe moment. Duke handed him the machete, and an hour later, Steve and Alec returned with an eight-foot-long, slender trunk, perfect for a spear.

"You should have seen the looks we got from a couple of expats," Steve said.

"Where they mad at you?" I asked.

"No, just surprised to see two white kids cutting down a tree." Steve peeled off the bark and let it dry in the sun.

"We'll see if he finishes his project," Duke whispered when they left.

"We'll see if he's changed," I replied.

CHAPTER TWENTY

Island House

"I CAN'T BELIEVE IT," Duke said, slamming his coffee cup down, hurling a wave of coffee onto his keyboard. "Sandy e-mailed me that Jill won't give us the key."

"Why not? I asked. We'd all been counting the days until our move.

"Jill says she wants us to send our final payment first."

"So they get our money, but we don't have any proof that we own the house?"

"Exactly."

"That's crazy," I said. Duke knew how much I had looked forward to celebrating our seventeenth anniversary in our new villa. I'd saved a bottle of champagne just for that occasion, so I continued packing and mopping floors, as if we were still on schedule to move the following day.

"Happy Anniversary," Duke said, waking me up at 4:30 A.M. I rolled over and came face to face with a scorpion, five inches from my nose. "Thanks for the scorpion," I joked, pretending this was his gift to me, since we rarely exchanged presents.

"You really are a magnet for scorpions and jellyfish," Duke said reaching for the plastic bug catcher we kept underneath our bed. We didn't kill most bugs, except for the cockroaches I sprayed. Since most bugs were oversized, and therefore not easy to squish, we'd adopted a catch and release program.

"Why don't you make coffee, and I'll check e-mails," Duke said. "Hopefully, there'll be some good news from Sandy or Jill."

"Any luck?" I asked, bringing our coffees over to his computer.

"Nothing. I'll call Sandy again around nine."

The kids woke up earlier than usual. "We're still moving today, right?" Josh and Alec asked as soon as they saw Duke at his computer.

"Not sure yet," Duke replied.

Our phone rang at 8:30. I picked up.

"Congratulations!" Sandy said, "You're now the owners of a beautiful home on Ambergris Caye."

"Thanks," I replied, stunned by the fact that we now owned a beachfront villa.

"So, are we moving?" the kids asked, standing next to me.

"Yes, the house is now officially ours," I said.

"My suitcases are ready," Steve said, standing by the front door.

"Put them in the truck," Duke replied.

Everything was packed in the same ten Walmart suitcases we'd arrived in only five weeks ago.

"What about our computers?" Alec asked.

"I'll have to come back and get the satellite dish and our computers later," Duke said. Cookie's ears and tail went down when she saw our suitcases and her dog crate heading out the front door. The boys wasted no time finding their seats in the truck, as if scared we might not have room for them. I looked forward to relaxing in the cozy airport lounge while Duke dropped the truck off at an expat's house in Corozal. We weren't sure whether we should sell the truck. We had no need for it on the island, but it was comforting to know we had transportation on the mainland if we had to escape a hurricane.

Duke took a cab back to the airport, and fifteen minutes later we boarded the small Cessna. The belly of the plane scraped the short palm trees at the end of the runway. "Did you hear that?" Duke said turning toward the boys. "I bet it's the extra weight from our suitcases." Cookie sat on Duke's lap during the flight, with the pilot's permission. Her wet nose made streaks on the oval window as she stared at the Caribbean. She'd become the perfect frequent flyer dog.

We soon landed in San Pedro, and the boys each grabbed a suitcase and schlepped it out the narrow gate, where a row of rusty old Toyota taxis awaited customers. Two drivers raced forward and piled our suitcases into every crevice of their vehicles. We squeezed our butts onto wiggly benches, our legs resting on the suitcases in front of us. Duke asked our driver if he knew of a private boat that could take us to Villas Tropicales.

"My brother Miguel has boat," the driver said. "I call him right now." He pulled his cell phone out of his pocket and called while driving. I loved the way everyone knew one another here on the island. No reservations were required, and you improvised as you went along.

"Miguel said he pick you up on beach in ten minutes." One taxi followed the other through Middle Street, then turned sharp right and dumped our suitcases on the sandy beach. Small waves lapped dangerously close to our belongings. None of us spoke, hypnotized by the beauty of this island. The turquoise sea met the horizon and gradually blended into a perfect blue sky. We stood there, stunned, and let the movie unfold in front of our eyes. Fast boats, sailboats and kite surfers kept us entertained. Tourists drove golf carts on the beach trail, while kids played soccer with a coconut. Even stray dogs entertained us, having formed two distinct gangs protecting their territories.

Our kids must have been starving, but they didn't complain once about the heat or their hunger. A skiff headed straight toward us. Miguel and his boat *Victoria* pulled up close to shore. "How are we supposed to get on the boat, Duke?" I asked.

"Take your flip-flops off, grab a suitcase and walk to the boat."

Steve lifted his suitcase above his head, flexing his biceps. Josh dropped his heavy suitcase in the water. "Here, take Cookie," I said, lifting his soggy suitcase out of the shallow water.

Victoria had surpassed her maximum permitted load, but locals appeared immune to rules and regulations. The boys pyramided their way on top of the suitcases, and off we headed to Villas Tropicales. Poor *Victoria* battled her way up north with her two-stroke engine sputtering and coughing like a heavy smoker trying to run a marathon. Duke pointed to three figures standing at the end of our pier. "That must be Juan, Teresa and their son," Duke said. They greeted us as we pulled up in the boat, and Juan wasted no time lifting our suitcases into his wheelbarrow. "Are we supposed to tip Juan?" I whispered in Duke's ear.

"Maybe the first time but not on a daily basis," Duke said. "Remember, we live here now."

I followed Teresa, the sweet, twenty-year-old mom to Little Juan, now four. The moment she unlocked the door, a whiff of frangipani escaped from the recently mopped glistening tiles.

"I cleaned and put fresh sheets on your beds," she said. Little Juan peeked from behind his mother's legs, looking up at my boys, then hid behind her leg again. I felt awkward, like a tourist renting Villa One, instead of its new owner.

We'd purchased the villa *as is*: fully furnished, with kitchenware, linens and even pictures on the walls. Now the problem was food; how and where would we get it? As if reading my mind, Teresa lifted a foil-covered plate off the kitchen counter and said, "I made you some fry jacks. I hope you like." The deep-fried, triangular shaped doughnuts were still warm, and my boys devoured them like starving hyenas.

Red hibiscus flowers filled our living room and bedrooms. They were plucked from bushes scattered around the property. I thanked Teresa for making us feel welcome in our new home.

While Duke and I admired our view of the Caribbean and the coral reef that seemed so close, the boys inspected their rooms and the pool. Alec and Josh shared the upstairs bedroom and, within seconds, an argument erupted. "I want my own room," Alec complained. "Me, too," Josh whined.

Duke shut them up by offering to put a plywood divider in the middle. "You realize you'll both get tiny rooms that way."

"That's better than sharing with Josh," Alec replied.

Steve seemed happy to have his own bedroom downstairs, even though it was next to ours. We had separate doors opening onto a coral-tiled patio and the beach. All four villas, including ours, were designed as rental properties, thus the self-contained downstairs suites with double sink and large, romantic open showers.

A large freezer blocked part of the hallway between Steve's room and ours. Rust stains covered the lid, probably as a result of the salty sea breezes. From now on, all of our grocery shopping would be done by boat. With three growing boys, food and water were our main priority. The freezer would help us stock up on meat; however, vegetables would have to be purchased on Wednesdays and Saturdays, when the local vegetable store in San Pedro received its deliveries.

Salt, pepper and leftover canola oil were the only food items I found in our kitchen. I panicked about dinner and asked Juan where we could find food. He pointed north to the closest restaurant: a ten-minute walk along the beach.

All five of us marched single file and barefoot, carrying our flip-flops in our hands, along the water's edge to Emerald Resort. August was the middle of hurricane season in Belize, so we had the entire restaurant to ourselves. "Can I have a hamburger and fries?" Alec asked. "I know it's expensive, but I've only had two since we moved here."

"Me, too," Josh exclaimed, and Steve chimed in as well.

"Of course," I said, happy to see my boys perking up.

"Look, they even have salads here," I said, excited to eat lettuce for the first time in five weeks.

All three boys devoured their hamburgers and fries, and Josh started licking his plate clean.

As we strolled home, our bellies full, the boys pointed toward the dark sky.

"Look at all the stars," Alec said. "They're amazing."

"Hey, I just saw a shooting star," Steve said, pointing.

We all stopped and stared at the sky. During that moment, I felt we had found the paradise I was looking for. And for the first time in years, we seemed closer as we enjoyed our new lifestyle.

With a positive shift in our moods, even Steve showed interest in his new island life. Six weeks ago, he would never have volunteered to do anything with Duke, and now they were exploring the brush area behind our house.

"Look, I found a piece of tin that we can use to make a lobster shade," Steve said, excited by his discovery. Determined to trap lobsters for dinner, Duke and Steve put on masks and fins, and placed the sheet of tin on the shallow seabed. They hoped lobsters would hide underneath, making it easy to grab them for dinner. It sounded simple and logical to me.

The tide was out, and the sea looked dirty with loose strands of seagrass floating around, so I decided to swim in the pool next to our house. Josh and Alec splashed me like happy fish.

"The water's salty," I said. "It reminds me of the pool I used to swim in as a kid in Denmark."

"Juan pumps water into it from the sea," Alec said.

The boys wasted no time mingling with Juan and his son. They craved attention from guys closer to them in age, so I was delighted they'd become friends.

"I can't open my eyes. It stings," Josh said.

A red-tailed hawk swooped over our heads, only two feet above us. Thinking we were being attacked, I ducked underwater with my sunglasses on. The hawk landed on the other side of the pool and gazed in our direction with a majestic air. Cookie spotted the hawk from our balcony and torpedoed down the steps barking, the hair on her spine and tail rising.

"Steve," I yelled. "Grab Cookie, she's going crazy."

"The hawk's going to eat Cookie," Josh hollered. "Get her, Steve!"

Steve sprung out of his room and grabbed Cookie.

"Let's name him Hank," Josh suggested.

"Have you seen Hank today?" was our first question of the day when we woke up. For the next two weeks, Hank showed up on schedule, every day, by our pool.

CHAPTER TWENTY-ONE

Settling In

"WE ONLY HAVE ONE INCH of water left," Duke said, handing me the long wooden ruler he used to measure the water level in our cistern.

"How much does it hold?" I asked, holding the flashlight so Duke could crawl out of the musty-smelling, cave-like space underneath our house.

"Up to thirty-six inches, when it's full."

Each villa at Villas Tropicales was built on top of a large circular concrete cistern, used to store rainwater collected from the villa's roof and gutters.

"How come we have no water left?" I asked. "We've barely used any."

"Teresa said the guys we bought our house from invited a bunch of their friends over last week. They probably took long showers and used up all the water," Duke said, brushing the dust off his clothes from rubbing against the walls.

I was about to suggest we call Jill and ask the previous owners to cough up some cash for us to buy water when I spotted Juan outside our storage room, unraveling a garden hose on the sand.

"Mr. Henry won't be coming for another two months," Juan said. "We can pump water out of his cistern."

"Isn't that stealing?" I whispered in Duke's ear. He shrugged.

The hose throbbed as water flowed from Mr. Henry's cistern into ours, and after one hour of pumping, I was eager to stick the ruler back in to measure our water level. Opening the latch to the cistern door, I poked my head through, but couldn't see a thing. My voice echoed in this dark, moldy chamber as Duke handed me a flashlight and the wooden ruler. The water level barely reached the three-inch line. How could that be? I'd hoped for at least eighteen inches of water.

As though feeling sorry for us, the skies released the first raindrops on the island in months, right after Juan finished reeling in the hose. Duke and I changed into our swimsuits and inspected the gutters around the perimeter of our house. We found one major leak where the gutter had split apart. Rainwater gushed out like a powerful waterfall, digging a trough in the sand below. Having spotted the leak, Juan was already on the top rung of his ladder reconnecting the gutter. We needed to collect every cup of roof water we could get. I never imagined myself getting hysterical over lost water, but I did.

A giant umbrella crawled on the sand like a crab toward us. Underneath, Little Juan's tiny frame was completely concealed until he tipped it to one side and revealed his adorable, mocha-colored face. Little Juan had big chestnut eyes, with the thickest eyelashes I had ever seen.

"Is Alec there?" he asked in perfect English. Alec had become his older brother, and although he hadn't spoken a word of English three days ago, Juan managed to mimic everything he heard.

When the rain stopped, which happened way too soon, I asked whether anyone wanted to ride bikes to town. "I need some exercise," I said. No one wanted to come along, and I knew it was because of Eric's visit. Eric was the guy we'd hired to install the satellite dish, and the boys were suffering from Internet withdrawal.

We needed food, so I borrowed Juan's beach cruiser and headed off to San Pedro. "Stick to the beach path, not the back road," Duke hollered from the balcony.

"Why?" I asked

"Just stick to the beach," he repeated.

I followed the narrow trail along the water's edge and headed south toward town. Most beachfront properties had already been snatched by affluent gringos looking for their own slice of paradise.

A few minutes south of Villas Tropicales, I saw some construction guys napping underneath the coconut palms. Those who weren't asleep eyed me and whistled, making me feel uncomfortable. I pedaled as fast as I could to get past them, wondering whether the island was safe, especially for my boys.

As I paralleled the water's edge, I rode past plastic bottles, shoes, Styrofoam boxes and even syringes, washed ashore by the never-ending cycle of ripples from the reef. The sun-baked trash formed two-foot mounds of debris mixed with rotting sea grass, the perfect breeding ground for flies. I'd witnessed Belizeans tossing their beer and soda bottles straight into the sea or onto land, yet Belize continued to have a reputation for being eco-friendly — or so the guidebooks claimed. I was already thinking of ways to clean it up. Perhaps I could organize a crew of high school students to pick up trash in exchange for free textbooks. Belize offered free education to every child but charged a hefty fee for textbooks. Often parents couldn't afford the books, so kids would ask expats and tourists for money to buy them.

I got off my bike and pushed it onto the hand-drawn ferry at Boca del Rio. Rusty Toyota taxis sped past me on Middle Street, arms emerging from open windows as their drivers gestured and waved to passersby. Drivers yakked to relatives and friends in several dialects, including Creole and Spanish, facing backward to talk as they continued driving. I had to be ready to brake at any moment.

I decided to check out some grocery stores. Prices in the tourist sector were double those of the local mom and pop stores. I now knew where

I'd be shopping. As I rode past Castillo's hardware shop, I witnessed my first street fight. A Rasta guy with dusty dreadlocks bolted out of the store, chased by a guy with a baseball bat who was yelling, "Foooock Yuuuu," right behind me.

I jumped off my bike and hid inside a grocery store across the street. Within seconds, locals had formed a crowd and were enjoying the entertainment. A few minutes later, Juan appeared. *How did he know I was inside the store?* I wondered whether he came to check on my safety, as I'd left home more than four hours ago.

"What's going on outside?" I asked.

"Just two guys fighting. I'll catch up with you later," he said, and left. Now I worried even more about the safety of my boys when they started school. *Did the locals pick fights with the expats, too?*

On my way back to the ferry, I found the only bakery in town: La Popular Bakery. It was way past lunchtime, and I'd forgotten to eat. The pastries looked like they were made from the same dough as the bread, and they were bland. I was excited when I spied my first loaf of brown bread since moving to Belize — until I realized it was white bread with food coloring. Healthy multigrain bread didn't exist here, and I missed it. I stuffed a mango tart in my mouth and washed it down with a bottle of water. I started thinking about the fancy dog treats in the expensive Orange County pet store, wondering whether they had more flavor than La Popular's pastries.

Feeling energized, I peeked inside Oscar's, looking forward to joining a gym again. With torn posters of bodybuilders stapled to the walls and even the ceiling, it had a certain rustic charm. Uneven wooden shutters opened up to the Caribbean breezes and turquoise sea. I knew Steve, Duke and I would probably join Oscar's gym as soon as we had the *Island Rider* to take us there.

It didn't take long to bond with Juan, Teresa and Little Juan; they became our second family. They showered us with kindness, and Teresa always baked extra johnnycakes for breakfast and brought them over, still warm from her oven. I invited them over for an American steak dinner with baked potato and salad.

"We never eat steak," Teresa said.

"Why, are you vegetarian?" I asked.

"No, too expensive."

During dinner, Teresa chewed each piece of meat for a good five minutes before swallowing. It took her one hour to eat her T-bone steak, and I wondered whether she was being polite to finish it. Little Juan had never seen a green salad before, and with his small hand cupped over his mouth, he whispered in Teresa's ear in Spanish, "Why do they eat leaves from trees?" Juan translated it for us, and we all laughed, recognizing the differences between cultures.

Juan and Teresa spoke Spanish at home, and yet their English was good. Juan summarized their short life together. Juan was only twenty-one and Teresa twenty. They had married at seventeen and sixteen, "in order to have sex," Teresa said. "Sex isn't allowed unless you are married," she continued, not at all embarrassed in front of my kids. "Nine months after our wedding, Little Juan arrived," she added.

"What about high school?" I asked.

"I quit school at twelve to work in sugar cane fields," Juan said. "I work from five in morning to five in afternoon, seven days a week." My boys turned quiet.

"I got paid $75, which I give my dad to pay for food." He paused, took a sip of water and continued. "I have eleven brothers and sisters."

Teresa also quit school at twelve because her parents couldn't afford the books.

My boys liked Juan and listened to every word he said. No lecture in the world could have been more effective than Juan's story in teaching my boys gratitude and how privileged they were to get an education.

Juan was extremely proud of his job as caretaker of Villas Tropicales. He made a lot of money by Belizean standards, and the four homeowners in the development paid for his one-bedroom house and electricity through our homeowners' fees.

Juan's days started at seven, raking sea grass off the beach for a couple of hours. He'd fill one wheelbarrow after another and dump the contents on the jungle side of the back road. It wasn't a fun job, but he worked hard.

I knew this would be a good learning experience for my boys.

CHAPTER TWENTY-TWO

Materialism in Belize

I ACCEPTED AN INVITATION to our first party on the island. I figured we needed to socialize. So when Christie, a Canadian woman I'd met in town, mentioned that teenagers and kids would be there, I couldn't say no.

"I'm not going," Steve said half an hour before we had to leave.

"There are other kids, including a 15-year-old girl," I said.

"I don't want to go," he repeated, then headed straight to the shower to get cleaned up.

We started our trek along the beach toward Christie's house. After twenty-five minutes of fast walking, we noticed the houses looking more and more Americanized. The kids *oohed* and *aahed* at these 4,000-square-foot mansions. I could smell the money. We trotted past the Royal Star Resort, a beautiful golden-yellow, luxury resort. We'd heard that famous people such as Clint Eastwood and Dr. Phil had stayed here. A snobby feel blanketed the resort. Unsmiling European guests sunbathed until dusk, and I could hear German, French and Italian spoken as we traipsed past them.

Christie's place was hard to find. Her instructions were as follows: "After the Royal Star Resort, continue past the house with the seawall and palapa huts, and mine is the two-story house. I'll hang something on the balcony so you can find it."

"Look, there's a stuffed bunny on the balcony," Josh yelled.

"That's got to be it," I said.

"Hello, anyone home?" I shouted. The house wasn't very impressive, but we had no idea what type of house we were supposed to be looking for, except that it was two stories. A shirtless guy appeared on the balcony.

"We're looking for Christie," Duke said, craning his neck to look up.

"I don't know Christie," he replied with a British accent. "Try the next house."

We continued along the beach, and our boys spotted teenagers on a boat dock. Christie had informed me that her friend Joanna had a fifteen-year-old daughter who would be waiting with a couple of boys.

"Hi, I'm Emily," a cute teenage girl said, her eyes glued invitingly on Steve. "You're Christie's friends, right?" she asked.

"Yes, where's her house?" Duke asked.

"It's back there," Emily said pointing to a two-story house with a towel draped on the balcony.

Christie heard our voices. "Hi, guys! Did you have trouble finding it?"

"Yes, I worried we'd passed it," I said. "I didn't realize you were this far north from us."

"Come inside," she said.

We walked up a flimsy staircase — definitely custom architecture — in an exclusive cluster of six upscale homes. For a second, I thought I was in Laguna Beach, California.

"Welcome," Christie said, meeting us at the top of the stairs. The décor was stunning, nothing we'd dreamed of finding on this island. The furniture, lighting, fabrics and marble were all imported from Guatemala, Europe and the U.S.

A massive mahogany dining table with a ruby-red velvet runner sat in the middle of the dining room overlooking the Caribbean. Elegant crystal glasses were lined up on an antique silver tray, waiting to be filled. A silver bucket with chilled white wine caught my eye, as did several bottles of Cabernet.

"Can I get you a glass of white or red?" Christie offered.

"I'd love a glass of white wine," I said.

"Help yourselves to cheese and appetizers." The spread was amazing. Duke and I felt like hungry teenagers in front of free food.

"Let me introduce you to my friend Joanna and her sister," Christie said, holding my forearm and leading me to the balcony. I shook hands with a well-dressed, subtly perfumed Italian woman. She reminded me of a young version of Sophia Loren.

"Joanna and her husband, Pierre, own the Royal Star Resort," Christie said. "You passed it on the beach on your way up here."

"Oh, it's gorgeous," I said, intimidated by Joanna's wealthy air. I felt out of place, bordering on nauseated. I had nothing against Joanna, but this was the life we wanted to escape.

Joanna's French husband, Pierre, evaluated whether Duke and I were worthy of his time with a quick head-to-toe scan. I realized we had flunked the test when he turned his back and started talking to someone else. It bothered me that he would judge us on our lack of designer clothes, so I tapped Pierre on the shoulder and proceeded to speak to him in fluent French. But he'd already made up his mind. Duke and I were not *rich enough* to purchase one of his properties — one of the three remaining houses for sale in this exclusive development — so he turned his back again and chatted with a well-dressed couple from South America.

Steve and Alec appeared to be having a better time than Duke and I were. Emily was driving them around the beach in her own all-terrain vehicle. When Joanna and Pierre invited Christie's guests to tour their newly finished house, we discovered our boys inside Emily's penthouse suite. She had the whole upstairs — the size of our entire house — to herself.

We were then led into Joanna's relaxation room. A flat-screen TV stretching eight feet high took up the entire wall. Opposite the TV was a Jacuzzi tub where Joanna could soak while watching a wall-size movie. Everything was imported and looked expensive. Had I known we'd be back in the heart of Orange County materialism, I'd have declined the invitation. The atmosphere was cold and phony.

On our walk home Alec said, "Mom, why can't we buy a house like theirs? At least I'd have my own room."

"That's not why we moved to Belize," I reminded him. It took a couple of days for Alec and Josh to quit talking about the house. Steve never even mentioned it.

Our boat, the *Island Rider,* was finally ready for pickup. Caesar would deliver it to our dock because Duke had no experience driving a motorboat. All five of us, plus Juan and his family, sprinted to our pier when we heard the engine.

After several experimental maneuvers, Duke succeeded in turning the boat around so it headed south instead of north. Months went by before Duke got his captain's license, after the laws changed on the island.

"Go faster, Dad," Steve yelled. We headed to San Pedro to buy three inexpensive computer desks at our local Mennonite store. Duke babysat the *Island Rider* at the Texaco boat dock in town while Steve and I jogged to the store and bought three desks for $60 each. Five Belizean men drinking Belikin beers inside the store pulled three desks down from a tall stack. After paying them, I lifted a desk and balanced it on top of my head. The guys stared disapprovingly, but refused to help.

"Your son is coming back to help?" one of the men asked, squirming in his chair.

"Yes, but I can carry one myself," I said, hoping he'd be a gentleman and volunteer to carry it for me. But no, he took another swig of beer and continued his card game. After we loaded all three desks onboard, it took Duke five attempts to get the boat turned around. It wasn't easy with so many other boats heading to the Texaco boat dock for gas.

That evening, we sat underneath the palapa umbrella by the pool. Alec and Josh were chasing Little Juan on the beach, while Steve fished at the end of our pier. Duke and I sipped our drinks, enjoying the present moment. This was our home, this was our paradise, and our new life was just beginning.

CHAPTER TWENTY-THREE

Island Routine

JOSH'S FIRST DAY OF SCHOOL happened to fall on my forty-seventh birthday. Josh always complained about school, even in the U.S. This time, however, I couldn't blame him. He was starting a new school in a new country.

I made pancakes from scratch, hoping to distract him with food. After inspecting the ingredients, I noticed that the flour looked white, but not the sugar. A cockroach had bitten a hole in the bag, and ants were pacing along the shelf into the sugar. I scooped the sugarcoated ants into the sink and, with a wooden spoon, stirred powdered milk and water into a mixing bowl.

"You making pancakes?" Josh asked, stumbling up the three steps from his bedroom into our open living room.

"Yes, plus it's my birthday. Come give me a hug."

"Steve and Alec are so lucky," Josh mumbled, heading towards me, arms outstretched.

"Why?"

"They don't start school till next week."

"Yes, but you get to make new friends. Remember to wear your uniform today; no flip-flops."

None of our boys had ever attended private school. Josh had to adhere to a prim and proper dress code — polo shirt, khaki shorts and closed-toe shoes — while Steve and Alec continued dressing tribal, half-nude and shoeless.

The smell of banana pancakes sizzling in butter wafted through the house, and out of nowhere, Little Juan boomeranged into our living room, still wearing his Spiderman pajamas.

"You like pancakes?" Josh asked.

"Is it fryjacks?"

"No, pancakes. Here, taste." Josh stabbed a piece dripping with syrup and shoved it in Little Juan's open mouth.

"Yumm. I like pancakes," Little Juan said. I cooked an extra one for him while he blasted across the living room, leaping from coffee table to couch.

"No, Juan," I said. "You don't jump on furniture."

He slid down the staircase to Steve's room and, before I knew it, Steve and Alec were sprawled on the couch being entertained by Little Juan.

"How much sugar have you had today?" Steve asked.

"What you say?" Little Juan roared. He continued to race around the room, pointing his toy car at the boys and making pretend gun-shooting noises, until they tackled him.

"Josh, get dressed," I said. "We're leaving in fifteen minutes."

Josh frowned. "Can't I stay here and play?" he pleaded.

"No," Duke said. "It's time to get ready for school."

I grabbed the camera, waited until Josh was seated in the *Island Rider*, and snapped photos of him, paparazzi style. He clutched his backpack with clenched fists, and his face looked like he'd been forced to sit on a scorpion. I could not get him to smile for a single photo.

During our fifteen-minute boat ride, we spotted dolphins for the first time. Duke slowed the boat and veered toward them. Within seconds, two dolphins were swimming alongside the *Island Rider*.

"This is better than Sea World," I said, attempting to get a smile out of Josh.

"How cool is that on your first day of school?" asked Duke.

Josh tried his best to stay grumpy.

As we approached the Island Academy, Duke slowed the boat to a crawl so Josh and I could jump off the bow onto a boat dock.

We had arrived twenty minutes early. I walked Josh to the bright yellow cottage with the fifth-/sixth-grade combo classroom. Each grade had a different colored cottage. With only forty-five students in the entire school, the four brightly painted cottages on the property resembled a resort rather than a school. We knew we were early, so we tiptoed up the wooden steps, opened the front door and were greeted by a blast of cold air on our faces. All nine students diverted their attention from teacher Charlene onto Josh.

"Welcome to our classroom, Josh," teacher Charlene said, shaking his hand. "This is your desk," she pointed to the one empty one. "Raul, can you show Josh his cubby?" she continued. I followed them into the hallway.

"Am I late?" Josh whispered. "I'm the last one here."

I also wondered if we were late. *Did we do something wrong?* I'd never seen kids in the U.S. so eager to get to school.

"Don't worry," I said. "We'll pick you up at four. Love you."

Duke took the *Island Rider* back home while I explored town. Right across from the Island Academy was the largest supermarket on the island. I enjoyed cooling off in the store while looking at U.S. food items we hadn't bought in months. Jiffy peanut butter, Doritos chips and Breyers ice cream. I knew I couldn't buy ice cream; it would melt the second I stepped outside.

After the cashier scanned the bag of Doritos I'd put in my shopping basket — a surprise treat for the boys — she looked behind me to see whether anyone was listening. Apparently the coast was clear. "Be careful who you do business with on the island," she whispered. "You can't trust people here."

*How did she know I lived here and wasn't a tourist shopping? Had I
already acquired the scruffy expat look? Were my clothes already stained
and outdated?*

My throat felt scratchy, and I wondered why she was telling me
this. *Did she think we were going to start a retail business that would
compete with hers?* Duke's warning kept playing in my head about being
careful what I disclosed to others. So I told her we were planning on
starting an Internet business with U.S. clients, so she wouldn't see us
as a threat.

"Oh, good," she said. "That way you won't have to deal with the
locals." She'd succeeded in ruffling my feathers. I didn't understand why
she was so mistrustful of the locals, and felt that I was getting my first
taste of island politics.

As soon as the supermarket doors opened, I stepped back into a
mixture of heat: the kind you'd expect from Death Valley combined
with a steaming hot tub. As it was my birthday, I stopped at Best Fine
Wines, the only gourmet shop on the island that sold imported wine and
cheeses from France. Christie had purchased everything she'd served at
her party from Best Fine Wines, so I treated myself to a very expensive
bottle of sparkling wine to celebrate my day, plus a slice of overpriced
Roquefort cheese. I knew there wouldn't be any presents waiting for
me at home.

Holding my *chic* paper bag from Best Fine Wines, I strolled along
the beach to get away from the bustle of golf carts, taxis and bikes on
Front Street. The next *Island Ferry* was scheduled for 11 A.M., so I collapsed on the wooden step in the shade, thinking about how much our
lives had changed in just two months. Curiosity led me to the end of
the boat dock, where some locals had gathered. They were pointing at
something in the distance, and when I saw what they were looking at,
my heart skipped a beat. A boat had capsized and six men holding long
poles were attempting to flip it over. "Oh, my God, Duke must have
lost control of the *Island Rider*," I thought, straining my eyes to see if a
Cubs baseball cap was floating in the water.

"Mario, what happened to the boat?" I asked. Mario was one of the *Island Ferry's* boat captains.

"It's a drug boat from Colombia," he said.

"Does this happen often?" I asked.

"Yes, lots of drug smuggling from Colombia to Mexico." After years of living in my safe Orange County neighborhood, I suddenly felt vulnerable. When I reached home, I hurried upstairs to tell Duke about the capsized boat. He'd seen it on his way home, but he wasn't thrilled to hear that I'd immediately thought it might be him.

"Shows how much you trust my driving," he said.

At 3:30 P.M., we headed back to town to pick Josh up from school. I planned on waiting outside his classroom when the bell rang at 4 P.M. At 4:01, Josh stomped out the door and ran far away from the other kids. When I caught up with him, he said, "I hate this school, and I hate Belize. I want to go back to California."

"What happened?" I asked as we stepped into the boat. Josh refused to talk.

"Just leave him alone," Duke said. "Everything's new, that's all."

It took two weeks for Josh to calm down about school. He complained about the long hours and homework, which made us realize he was finally getting some instruction. California public schools did not offer much assistance to children, and with fewer students in his classroom, he was finally getting his teacher's attention. Josh mentioned playing soccer with Raul and Pedro, his Belizean friends, during recess. He also liked the school cafeteria. A cook prepared every meal from scratch; even the pizza dough on Fridays was homemade. Nothing was frozen and defrosted, as it had been in his Orange County school.

His Canadian teacher, Miss Charlene, was brilliant. I sensed she loved her job. With her soothing voice, calm disposition and classical music playing before school started, kids were motivated to show up before the bell.

One morning we offered Juan and Teresa a boat ride to town on the *Island Rider*. They brought their bikes on the boat so they could ride the five-mile trail home. On the way to San Pedro, I bragged to Teresa that I'd become an expert at bargain shopping.

"I found a store that's even cheaper than SuperBuy."

"Where?" Teresa asked.

"It's Dahlia's on the river side, right by La Popular Bakery."

Duke docked the boat, and Teresa followed me inside. She picked up canned items, turning them upside down to see the handwritten price on the bottom. "You're right, Miss Sonia. Condensed milk is cheaper, and so is rice and flour." I'd forgotten how much Teresa and Juan relied on non-perishables; they only shopped once every two weeks, on payday.

Juan rolled their bikes over from our boat and locked them to a pole outside Dahlia's. When he entered the store, I noticed his interest in a small watercolor paint set. "I like to paint," he said.

"Do you have paints?" I asked.

"No, but I save for some."

I bought the paints as soon as he and Teresa left the store. Later that day, Alec and Josh walked over to Juan's hut with the present, along with a small blank canvas. "What did he say?" I asked when they returned.

"He's going to paint something right away," Alec said.

As I lit the gas stove, ready to boil water for spaghetti, I heard, "Miss Sonia," in Teresa's high-pitched voice. I opened the front door. "Oh, you busy?" she said.

"Getting ready to make dinner. Why?"

"This is for you." She handed me a small black plastic bag. "For your birthday. Juan said you like shells." I pulled out a triple strand of shells, each one a different length, and hugged Teresa.

"Can you clasp it around my neck, please?" I lifted my hair up and headed straight to the mirror above the couch in our living room. The splash of cream-colored shells complemented my tan.

"Thanks, Teresa, this is beautiful. Tell Juan I'd like to see his painting when it's done."

"He finished it," she said.

"Already?"

"Yes. I get Little Juan to bring over for you to see."

After dinner, we heard the familiar sound of Little Juan's feet scampering up the steps at lightning speed. He wore his Spiderman pajamas day and night, and we'd given him two nicknames: "Spiderman Juan" and "Monkey Boy." He could climb anything like a monkey, using both hands and feet. He liked to climb the palapa umbrella by the pool and dangle from his feet. Even with all the blood in his body rushing into his head, he just kept dangling.

"Look, guys," he said in his newly acquired American accent. "My dad painted this." We stared at the small canvas. "Look, guys," he repeated, climbing onto a chair so all five of us could admire the picture. "There's a sun and water."

"Very nice," I said, aware this was a proud "show and tell" moment.

"Hey, Juan," Josh blurted. "Sure you didn't paint it?"

"Josh," I snarled, frowning. Turning back to Juan, I said, "Tell your dad he painted a beautiful sunrise. If he wants to paint more, I have some special paper."

"I go tell him now," Little Juan said. Spreading his arms like wings, he let out a piercing, "Spiderman!" as he flew down the steps, the canvas in hand.

CHAPTER TWENTY-FOUR

Internet School

STEVE AND ALEC WERE EAGER to check out their Internet classroom at Sharon and George's house in San Pedro. Alec, in particular, was anxious to meet their son, Matt, who also would be studying the ninth-grade curriculum offered by Keystone National High School.

Both wore swim trunks to school, soaking up the sun's early-morning rays as the *Island Rider* headed for San Pedro. As usual, Duke swerved around some aggressive Belizean boat drivers on the way to town. Many young drivers appeared to enjoy intimidating the gringos, heading straight toward our boat on a collision course, then swerving at the last possible second. I now realized boat driving would take more guts than driving Duke's truck in Consejo Shores.

"That's the kind of sailboat I'd like to get," Steve said, pointing at *Sailaway,* a damaged wooden sailboat with a ripped pirate flag.

"It's in pretty bad shape," I said. "Looks abandoned."

"I'd love to fix it up."

I smiled, relieved that Steve was showing interest in something other than a girlfriend.

Duke docked the *Island Rider* at the Xanadu Resort south of town. Sharon had said we could leave our boat at the resort for a couple of hours. We followed a narrow, sandy path through a patch of overflowing sea grape vines and hibiscus bushes. As we strolled through a tunnel of tropical lush vegetation with splashes of yellow, red, orange and purple, we heard birds squawking.

"Are those parrots?" I asked.

"Mom, look, they're camouflaged in the tree," Alec said. "That's so cool." I loved the way Alec relaxed as soon as animals and birds surrounded him. Since our safari trip to Kenya and Tanzania, when Alec was only six, we assumed he'd study something related to biology and animals when he grew up.

Steve and Alec ran ahead. I forced them to put their T-shirts on to meet Sharon, George and their son, Matt. Our serene path merged into Coconut Drive, where the obnoxious sound of golf carts and busy taxis took over. This part of town was new to us, and I could smell stews simmering inside the local mom and pop restaurants. Though still early in the day, chickens were already grilling on street-side barbecues, making the boys hungry.

"How'd you like some cow foot soup?" Duke asked, reading the lunch menu on a small chalkboard.

"I'm hungry, but not for that," Steve said.

"You just had breakfast," I said.

"I'm always hungry."

"We'd better head to George's or we'll be late," Duke said.

We found Sharon and George's two-story house at a busy intersection on Coconut Drive. George, a tall, bony man, had long gray hair pulled back in a straggly ponytail. Waving his cigarette, he gestured for us to come upstairs. Matt waited at the top of the stairs. Like Alec, he was tall for fourteen and seemed eager to meet his new classmates. Alec paid more attention to the parrots in the cage on the front porch than to Matt.

"This one's mine," Matt said. "Want to hold him? He's the friendly one. My dad's parrot bites." Alec wasn't sure whether to smile, but as soon as Matt placed his parrot on Alec's shoulder, his face glowed.

"Come on in and meet Sharon," George said. I scanned the freezing living room with its lace curtains, antique furniture and wall-mounted grandfather clock. *Where was I?* This reminded me of my aunt's old house in Denmark, not a house in Belize.

Sharon was a large, curvy woman, her face covered in thick foundation, black eyeliner and red lipstick. When she welcomed us, I couldn't place her accent, so I asked her where she was from.

"I'm from Dallas, Texas," she said. "Come with me; I'll show you the house." Meanwhile, George offered Duke a Belikin beer.

"A little too early for a beer," Duke said.

"I have a full-time maid who can fix a hot lunch for the boys when they start school," Sharon said. Her kitchen had new stainless steel appliances and all the amenities of a comfortable U.S. house. We strolled back to the living room, chatting as though our mouths were on treadmills, and realized that the guys were gone. "George must be downstairs showing off the classroom he built."

We headed down the outside cement staircase, and I worried that Sharon's makeup would melt. She was explaining how George, a contractor, had converted the downstairs office into six computer workstations, each with a shelf for the kids to keep their textbooks. "We hope to add three more students soon," she said. "We'd love to turn this into a hybrid high school, and I've already researched the legal aspects of running this as an accredited U.S. Internet high school."

When I walked into the classroom, Steve and Alec were busy selecting their desks. Sharon continued talking. "The Keystone curriculum allows our boys to transfer grades to any U.S. high school or university. My goal is to offer the SAT exams here so our kids won't have to fly to the U.S. to take them." I was impressed.

Sharon told me she wanted Matt to finish high school on the island, then move to the U.S. for college. "He loves it here," she said. "He was born here, and all his friends are here. He's crazy about fishing on his boat. I know he'd miss the island." Her observations were proof that kids can get used to any place and miss what they're used to. The location, per se, didn't matter.

While Matt took the boys to see his boat, George wanted to discuss costs. Duke almost backed out of the deal when George suggested we pay him extra to watch over our kids. George wasn't a teacher, and Duke refused to pay him for supervising the kids. Sharon interrupted, sensing Duke's frustration. "I found a certified teacher from New York who's looking for part-time work," she said.

"Would she be willing to monitor the kids' work, making sure they're doing their assignments?" Duke asked.

"Yes. She used to teach art at the Island Academy," she said. "She's married to a Belizean and has an eight-month-old baby."

"That sounds great. When can she start?" I asked.

"Next Monday. That's when I thought we should start the program."

We'd already pre-paid for one year of Internet school, and Sharon had received Steve's eleventh-grade and Alec and Matt's ninth-grade books, so we agreed.

"You'll really like Kimberly," Sharon said.

Duke and I felt better now that we knew a professional teacher would be monitoring the boys' work.

As we headed back to the *Island Rider,* the boys asked for lunch. We stopped at the restaurant serving cow-foot soup, and all four of us ordered the stewed chicken. We sat in the screened porch area with its mustard-yellow, vinyl tablecloths, watching golf carts whiz past on Coconut Drive.

"I can't stand Matt," Alec said.

"Why not?" I asked.

"I can tell he's going to be disruptive. He's hyper, like Josh," he continued.

"I'm sure Kimberly will tell him to be quiet if he's not paying attention."

"Who's Kimberly?" Steve asked.

"She's the young art teacher from New York who's going to be monitoring your work," Duke explained.

"Great," Steve said. "So we get an art teacher when we need help with chemistry, physics and math."

"Yes," I replied. "You'll get the help you need from your online teachers."

I never knew rain could hurt. Each raindrop felt like a scalpel jabbing my face, and the pain grew more intense when drops hit my eyelids. We were totally unprepared. Without raincoats, head protection or even backpacks, the boys' first boat trip to start Internet school seemed surreal. Instead of crying, we tried joking that we were being attacked by Belizean rain. I had to keep my eyes closed the whole way, while poor Duke wore sunglasses and continued driving the boat full-speed with dark clouds above.

By the time we reached the Island Academy, Josh was soaked. "You're going to be freezing when you get into the air-conditioned classroom." I said, wishing I had a dry towel to wipe him off. Josh jumped off, and Duke continued south to Xanadu pier, where Steve and Alec leaped onto the pier. The wooden slats on the pier were slippery, but they managed to grasp the surface with their bare toes. Duke and I headed back home.

Despite the rainstorm, our water supply was so low that our pump started hiccupping and burping whenever we turned on a faucet. Now we only flushed the toilets when absolutely necessary. "I think we're going to have to buy water," Duke said.

"You said that's too expensive."

"I'll call Bill and see how much he charges."

Bill could only deliver 500 gallons by boat and charged $100 just to deliver. The water was extra.

"Let's pray for rain instead," Duke said. We rationed our water and allowed sponge bathing only. I never told Duke I stole two gallons of our drinking water to wash my hair. Several days later, our prayers were answered and we received one hour's worth of steady rain. This only added a couple of inches to our cistern, but it was enough for me to do laundry without feeling guilty. I never imagined I would feel guilty about doing laundry.

Funny how much we'd changed in nine weeks.

CHAPTER TWENTY-FIVE

Oscar's Gym

DUKE SEEMED PERFECTLY CONTENT to remain in the house and read books, but I needed social interaction. After nine weeks, I wanted friends.

I rode my bike along the sand, five miles to town, and decided to try Oscar's gym.

Two bikes and one golf cart were parked in front of the gym. I could hear voices inside, despite the reggae music blaring from the speakers. I pushed open the squeaky, spring-loaded door of the gym, and two women turned around and stared at me for so long that I grew self-conscious. They ignored the older guy who was demonstrating various exercises. I had been a personal trainer in the past, so I could tell this man had no clue what he was talking about.

I sat on the bench, kicked my flip-flops off and dug into my backpack for my workout gloves and gym shoes. I couldn't wait to get my strength back — after all, I'd been a gym addict in Orange County for twenty-two years.

As I picked up the twenty-five pound dumbbells and started my bicep curls, both women gasped. I worried about the skinny woman, who made Twiggy seem fat.

"Nice to see other women at the gym," I said, hoping to stop the disturbing glances. "Do you live here?" I asked.

"Yes, do you?" the emaciated woman asked me, as though hoping for a "yes."

"I just moved here a month ago," I said.

"Well, this is our first time working out," the fleshier woman said. After shaking hands, I found out they were U.S. expats.

"I had a personal trainer when I lived in Denver, four years ago," Jennie, the skinny one, said.

Should I tell them I used to be a personal trainer? Suddenly I realized this might be a way for me to make some money, something Duke and I hadn't talked about since he was fired.

"If you're interested in training, let me know," I said. "I'm a certified trainer."

"I might be," Jennie said. "It depends on how much you charge."

I asked her for her phone number and said I had to check the going rate on the island first.

As soon as I got home, I called the only other gym on the island — the fancy one — pretending to inquire about personal training for myself. Seventeen dollars per hour seemed to be the going rate, so I called Jennie. She immediately said she was interested.

The following morning, a little nervous, I hurried to our boat a few minutes early.

A man sprinted toward me along our pier, panting. "We can't get the *Island Ferry* to pick us up. They don't answer the phone."

"They don't answer before eight," I said. "You have to call Emerald Resort, and they can page them."

He carried a heavy-looking backpack, and sweat trickled down his forehead and dripped off the tip of his nose. Feeling sorry for him I asked, "Where you going?"

"Scuba diving with Amigos del Mar. There are four of us, and we have to be there by nine."

"You can come with us to town," I said.

His frown disappeared and, within seconds, all four of them surged into our boat, as though worried I might change my mind.

Duke and the boys jumped in, and we enjoyed hearing about San Francisco, where they were from. They were renting Maureen's villa, which was next to ours.

I had noticed a definite change in my boys since our move; they now engaged in conversations with strangers. I guessed they missed social interaction as much as I did. After we dropped Scott and his three friends off, it was my turn to jump off the bow before Duke continued home.

As I entered the gym, my nostrils caught a pungent whiff of urine by the dumbbell rack. Even the outhouse in the back didn't smell this bad. Jennie arrived promptly at nine, chained her bike to the bike rack and bounced in, ready for her first training session. It felt weird to be training someone for money in a stinky gym with rusty dumbbells and a leg press that didn't look like it had been greased or maintained since Arnold Schwarzenegger's youth.

Jennie and I got along really well. Only a few years apart, we chit-chatted the whole time, and it felt good to have a friend. She signed up for ten personal training sessions.

Beaming with pride, I bragged to Duke that I'd succeeded in getting a job.

"So what are *you* going to do?" I asked, a little frustrated with Duke for not looking for work. I'd given him two months to do nothing, but we were now beyond the two-month period. *Was I being unreasonable?*

"I'm happy for you," Duke said, ignoring my question.

He placed his book on the coffee table and headed for the door. "I have to secure our boat," Duke said, "There's a storm heading toward us."

I watched him wade towards the boat with mask and tools in hand. He looked relaxed, happy with his new life. I started thinking about all those endless commutes in L.A. traffic, and noticed how much trimmer and healthier he now looked. He worked on securing the *Island Rider* for several hours, adding extra lines and attaching them to cinder blocks in the shallow waters. I worried that his pale skin would burn. But Duke hadn't burned once since moving to Belize, and he'd already spent more time outdoors here than he spent in an entire year in California. "It must have something to do with the ozone layer," Duke joked.

What I loved about our new life was the adventure that Belize brought. Every day offered something new and different: a change in the sea, the clouds, the winds, the stars, the lightning, the thunder, the moon, the fish, the iguanas, the insects and the birds. Nature spoke to me, entertained me and made me fearful because I was at its mercy.

This time we wanted to be prepared in advance for a storm, so Duke called Castillo's hardware store to see whether we could pick up some sheets of plywood. Our windows had wooden shutters but not our glass patio doors. We needed eight large sheets of plywood to prevent the glass from shattering.

"Sorry, no plywood till next Wednesday," the assistant said.

What good was that?

"Duke, we need to get more organized," I said.

In order to get my mind off this storm turning into a hurricane, I baked a carrot cake. It was Scott's birthday. I sent Josh over to deliver the cake, which he did without complaining. Whenever someone rented one of the villas, Duke and I introduced ourselves. Even Alec started coming out of his cocoon and initiated conversations with the visitors. We craved interaction with other Americans, and I liked to catch up on what was happening in the U.S.

I heard the patter of Josh's bare feet climbing the wooden steps. His freckled face and bright blue eyes were beaming as he told us about the free video games Scott had promised him. Scott worked for a video game company in San Francisco.

"How long you think before I can play them?" he asked.

"Scott has to get back to his office first," Duke said.

"Mom, Scott said thanks for the cake, and no one has baked him a cake since he was in third grade."

It felt good to do something kind for someone you barely knew.

CHAPTER TWENTY-SIX

Marital De-Stress

AFTER THE STORM, the weather calmed down, but not me. Jennie warned me this was just the beginning. "Hurricane season gets worse," she said. The uncertainty surrounding the storms played havoc with my emotions, and I started resenting Duke for his lack of desire to work. It scared me, as I had not anticipated this would happen to us.

After our daily commute by boat to school, I lashed out at Duke, aware that my comments would sting. "I'm wondering if we made the right decision to sell our house and move here," I said. Waiting for Duke's comeback, I busied myself with the coffee pot, rinsing it in the kitchen sink. Duke reached for the jar of peanut butter, scooped several spoonfuls into his mouth, and then crashed on the rattan couch for another full-day reading marathon. This felt like *déjà-vu*. One of our reasons we moved to Belize was for Duke to de-stress and get healthy, but sometimes I wondered whether he had gone too far in the opposite direction. There were moments when I no longer felt close to him and started to question our marriage.

Duke did what I half expected him to do: He ignored me. He'd heard me bring up doubts about our decision to move several times before. He probably dismissed it as PMS, not realizing how angry and resentful I'd grown toward his laziness. I figured he'd run out of books to read, as there were no bookstores on the island. But when he'd gone through his stash of sci-fi books, he started rereading them. I had a vision of him turning into a bum like so many expats who spent their days doing nothing. Perhaps I should be grateful that Duke drank coffee and read books at home, unlike other expats who spent their days sitting on a stool at JD's beach bar drinking their first Belikin beer at 9 A.M. and their last beer at midnight. *What happened to the idea of us starting a business, making a living instead of living off our savings? After all, I thought we'd decided to spend the rest of our lives here.*

We had nothing left in California, and with monthly association fees of six hundred dollars, our savings were diminishing faster than expected.

My resentment increased as days turned into weeks. I already had my first personal training client, Jennie. *Why wasn't Duke contacting other law firms in California as potential clients for the legal transcription business he claimed he wanted to start?*

"Duke, I'm going to the Chamber of Commerce meeting in town. I think you should come. It's important for us to meet local business owners and learn how things work."

"I'm not in the mood," Duke said. *What was he thinking? We didn't have a job, we didn't know what type of business to start, and networking could only help us.*

"You really piss me off," I shouted. "Don't tell me you're going to sit on your butt all day and read another book?" That's when Duke stormed off; only this time, he left in our boat. *What was going on in his head?* Now I was scared.

I took the *Island Ferry* to town and attended the meeting, where I met fourteen other expats. Sitting next to the Island Coffee couple, who had started roasting coffee beans on the island, it saddened me that Duke hadn't shown any interest in attending the meeting. I felt as though the burden of starting a business rested on my shoulders alone, and I grew more and more confused about how long Duke planned for us to live off our savings.

What should I do? Relax like him? But I kept hearing my mother's voice, "Sonia, do something! Don't just sit there!" *Had I become my mother?*

Things between us grew more uncomfortable, and that evening, I snapped. "When you lose respect for the person you live with, then love goes."

"And you've lost respect for me?" Duke asked. I kept quiet for as long as I could stand it, then blurted out my growing resentment toward him. I was brutal, and I knew it. If Duke had dared to say to me what I said to him, I'd probably have walked out the door for good. In my mind, I was right, however, and therefore justified in what I said. Duke couldn't accuse me of being lazy. I was the one thinking ahead and networking.

It was dark outside, and there was nowhere for him to escape to cool off. We were stuck; when we got mad, we couldn't get away from one another. I imagined Duke trying to flee by boat in the middle of the night, hitting rocks and shredding the propeller. So instead of remaining bitter enemies for days, we were forced to talk.

"I'm sorry, Duke. I went overboard," I said, reaching for his hand on the couch. "Let's talk in our room."

Duke followed me downstairs, and we both sat on the bed, leaning back with our heads resting on pillows. "I know you want me to contact other law firms," he said. "But quite frankly, the legal transcription business cannot work here."

"Why not?" I asked, surprised it had taken Duke this long to talk about it.

"You know the electricity shuts off, storms block the Internet and their definition of literacy isn't the same as ours. No U.S. company would put up with how unreliable we'd be."

I wished Duke had told me all this earlier. I might have backed off a little.

The kids heard us arguing, and during dinner that evening, all three boys brainstormed about potential businesses we could start.

"How about a paintball business?" Alec said.

"Or laser tag," Josh added.

Was this really happening? I could not believe Alec and Josh were offering advice. I remembered an offhand comment I'd made to Duke: "The mayor said she wants new businesses to keep teenagers busy on the island."

Now I realized my boys listened to everything we said. They felt insecure when Duke and I argued and wanted peace at home.

CHAPTER TWENTY-SEVEN

Alec Meltdown

ALEC STORMED INTO HIS ROOM. I found him face down, arms curled around the pillow covering his head.

"I want to go back to California," he whimpered.

I felt so guilty. He was terribly homesick, missing his best friends Jeff and Jake. I now realized how naïve I'd been to expect my boys to adapt. *Had we been unfair to Alec?* But then again, how could we have found a place that suited each one of our boys? They were all so different.

As Duke walked past his door, I gestured for him to come inside. He leaned against Alec's doorframe. "Tell Alec what you told me the other day," I said. Duke squirmed and clammed up. Duke didn't like dealing with the kids' complaints about our move to Belize, so I took charge as usual.

"Alec, you know we moved to Belize because Dad's job was killing him."

"So change jobs," Alec answered, his voice muffled under the pillow.

I turned toward Duke, hoping he'd respond to Alec's comment, but he'd already disappeared.

"It's impossible to live in Orange County without a good salary. Owning a house, cars and fixing things costs a lot," I said.

"Well, don't fix things till you can afford to," Alec replied, sounding way more mature than his fourteen years.

"That's easy to say, Alec, but some things you're forced to fix. Remember the deck we changed last year? That cost thousands of dollars, but we had to do it. The termites were eating the wood, and our homeowners' association kept sending us notices to fix it." Alec kept quiet, and I had no clue what to say to make it all better.

Leaving Alec on his bed, I ran downstairs to hide in my bedroom. I felt trapped and missed having a close friend to confide in. The one person who could help me was Duke, but he no longer seemed to understand my frustration and fears. *What was going on with him? What had changed? Why wasn't he listening?*

After calming down, I made myself a cup of tea and heard voices outside. From the upstairs patio, I could see Steve and Alec fishing. I was pleased to see them engaged in creating their own entertainment and settled in the hammock to enjoy the moment. The fun soon ended when Alec raised his voice and smashed his fishing pole on Steve's back. Steve spun around and punched Alec's chest, causing him to fly into the air and land flat on his back in the sea grass below. Alec turned wild with anger, something I'd never seen before, as he trudged through the slimy seabed toward shore. He spotted me on the patio and howled, "I hate Steve."

I felt my throat constrict, and all I could say was, "What happened?"

He pushed past me and dashed downstairs, his shorts dripping seawater on the tile.

"I'm going to smash his computer." I witnessed a different teenager inside my son: one who exploded with aggression.

"Tell me what happened!" I repeated, trying to stay calm as I followed Alec, who was clearly intent on destroying Steve's computer. As he picked up the computer, I saw tears streaming down his cheeks and Duke's firm voice behind me saying, "Alec, that would be hurting us, not Steve." I left Duke alone with Alec and headed out to our boat dock. Steve strode toward our house, head high and chest thrust forward. *Why was he overly aggressive?* There was no way Alec would smash a fishing pole on Steve's back without being provoked.

That evening, we had a family meeting. Steve claimed that I always favored Alec. This time, Duke took charge and spoke in his lawyer's voice, which generally got results. As usual, Steve mimicked Duke's authoritative manner, which I found unnerving. We never found out the real reason for their fight, but I knew Alec blamed Steve for our move.

Without television, Juan to go fishing with or Little Juan to bug them before and after school, our boys were bored. Juan and his family had left for their two-week vacation on the mainland. Meanwhile, Juan's uncle, Alviro, a fifty-five-year-old Belizean, took over the daily duties of raking the beach, but he wasn't company.

"What time is Juan coming back tomorrow?" Alec asked Alviro.

"He come on 9 o'clock boat."

A warm smile lit up Alec's face. I had not realized how close my boys had grown to Juan and his son until they were gone.

After three months without cable, the kids and I reached the point where we wanted to watch TV. We had grown tired of watching the same DVDs. I thought we could live without it, but I missed world news and shows such as *Survivor* and *American Idol*.

Betty, who owned the villa behind ours, had a cable box in her empty villa. I e-mailed her to ask whether we could use her box to find out what the reception was like on Ambergris Caye. She agreed. "I can't wait to watch *MythBusters*," Alec said, glowing for the first time in two weeks. "It starts at 8 P.M. Can I watch?"

"Of course you can," I replied. All day, Alec acted like a little kid waiting for Christmas to open his presents. At 6 P.M., Steve started watching the movie *Armageddon*. "That's a great movie; let's watch," Steve said.

"That's fine, but don't forget Alec's program at eight," I said.

"Mom, we all know he wants to watch *MythBusters*." I was proud that Steve wasn't going to argue about it.

At eight sharp, Duke switched the channel so Alec could watch his program. A commercial came on, so Duke hit the remote to continue watching *Armageddon*. "Dad, I want to watch my show now," Alec begged.

"But it's a commercial," Duke replied.

"I know, Dad, but I want to see the beginning of my show and we might miss it."

"There's nothing important at the beginning," Duke replied.

I knew I had to say something.

"Alec loves *MythBusters*; let him watch it."

"We can watch this now. There's a commercial on the other channel," Duke repeated. I couldn't believe Duke was acting this way. I sided with Alec, empathizing with his enthusiasm for the show. Now Duke wanted to take control of the remote.

"I've warned you several times tonight," Duke said. "Since you guys are fighting over the television, I'm taking the box back to Betty's. No more TV, period."

"You can't do that." I screamed hysterically. "That's totally unfair. You're the one fighting over the remote, not them." Duke stormed out of the house, cable box in hand, and I followed, feeling heartbroken for Alec.

"Duke, stop it right now." I commanded. "That's cruel to Alec. You know how much he looked forward to seeing *MythBusters*." Duke ignored my request and continued his fast trot into Betty's house, where he left the TV cable box.

Why was he doing this? I wasn't quite sure, but the kids and I had noticed Duke's moods shifting. He no longer seemed as kind and friendly as he used to be. He'd become even more introverted than before. Maybe he worried about how to support us, maybe depression had set in, or perhaps things weren't going the way he'd planned.

I thought he expected too much from the kids. It was tough for a teenage son — especially one such as Alec, who was sensitive, worried about his education and had such close buddies in California — to just forget his past life and gladly accept a completely different one. But Duke seemed to expect more.

Duke and I were the ones who'd made the decision to move to Belize, not the kids. I agreed with Duke that we couldn't give in to the kids' complaints, but we also couldn't ignore their feelings. My approach was so different from Duke's. Alec frequently said, "I feel trapped. I need to go back and see my friends."

"I understand you want to see your friends," I'd reply, "but..."

"No, Mom, you don't understand, I *need,* not want, but *need* to see my friends. I've already been trying to adapt. I've tried fishing and many other things, but I've also tried to cover up my feelings. I just can't do it any longer," Alec said, sobbing on my bed later that evening. I felt so torn and so alone trying to comfort Alec. I thought Duke's approach was too harsh.

That night, I cried myself to sleep and woke up several times whimpering. My eyes felt raw the following morning. I believed this incident had scarred Alec, or perhaps it had scarred me more than I thought possible. *What was happening to us?*

CHAPTER TWENTY-EIGHT

Socializing

L IFE GOT ROSIER WHEN WE BEGAN socializing with more expats.
One of the best meeting places in town was the Veggie House
on Wednesday afternoons, right after the weekly delivery of fresh vegetables and fruits from the mainland. Expats crowded inside, making
sure they got their fresh lettuce, broccoli, mushrooms and, on rare
occasions, strawberries.

"You must be Sonia," a stranger said, dropping her basket on the
stone floor to shake my hand. I stared at the perfect mangoes, plump
tomatoes and bags of fancy imported lettuce in her basket, hoping she'd
left some on the shelves for me. "I'm Annette, Meghan's mom," she said.
I'd heard of Meghan — the only girl following the same Internet program as Steve, Alec and Matt. I knew that Sharon had tried her best to
encourage Meghan to join our boys' classroom, but Meghan preferred
to study at home.

"I hear you're also from California?" Annette said.

"Yes, Orange County."

"We used to live in Seal Beach. We'd love to have you over for lunch next Saturday. Meghan's been dying to meet some California boys, and they're the same age."

I didn't hesitate one second before saying yes. We needed expat friends, especially those with kids.

Annette gave directions on how to get to her place by boat. "Look for the Pepto Bismol-colored resort south of town. My husband, Rick, will meet you at the boat dock at noon."

When I told the boys about being invited to Meghan's, they didn't object. I think they looked forward to something to do.

It took us forever to get there. Duke had never driven the *Island Rider* this far south and worried about hitting rock formations in the shallow waters. Annette had not exaggerated; the resort was actually neon pink, a color I'd never seen on any building in my life. As we approached the pier, a thin, tanned man directed us to where we could dock our boat.

Rick fit the California middle-aged surfer dude image. He had thick, wavy, sandy-brown hair tucked behind his ears and a rope-like necklace with a coin pendant.

"Sorry we're late," I said as Rick helped me off the boat.

"Sonia, you're no longer in Orange County," he said. "No one is late in Belize."

"Hi, guys," he said, beaming at my boys. "Want to take the WaveRunner out for a spin? I'm selling it." What a fantastic sales pitch to deliver to three active boys.

"Look, there's the teacher from my school," Josh said, pointing to a lanky young girl heading our way. Her posture was ruler straight, and she wore jeans and a white, long-sleeved, breezy tunic. There was a Bohemian, mystical air about her, and when she got close, I noticed that her porcelain skin matched her linen tunic.

"This is Meghan," Rick said. Despite not wearing a hint of makeup, she looked older than fourteen. "Josh, you've probably seen Meghan at school. She volunteers at the Island Academy." Josh nodded.

"Lunch is ready," Meghan announced.

We followed Rick and his daughter along a dirt path meandering through thick bushes and overgrown palms. Everyone except Rick remained quiet during this hellish walk. The humidity felt thick under the canopy, and mosquitoes gnawed away at our bare skin. I now understood why Meghan wore long sleeves and long pants. After a ten-minute jungle hike, we were drenched.

Ginger, a lab mutt, greeted us at the bottom of their cement staircase, where she licked the salty sweat off our hands. "She's still a puppy," Meghan said.

Rick explained with pride that he'd built this two-story house. He and his family lived upstairs and rented the downstairs, for income.

After climbing a steep, narrow staircase, we reached a small landing with a peek-a-boo view of the Caribbean. Only the hint of an ocean breeze blew through gaps in the tree canopy. Annette opened the front door of her home, and a gush of arctic air froze my sweat into mini-icicles. Though comfortable, the living room was somber, lacking windows. That, combined with early American, dark oak furniture and lace-covered tables, made me forget we were on a tropical island.

After one beer, Rick started cracking jokes, mostly making fun of American TV shows. He knew how to connect with teenagers, and both Steve and Alec spoke more words over lunch than I'd heard since we left California. Rick showed them a book, *How to Smoke Fish,* and explained the step-by-step process to Steve. He gave us samples of his home-smoked snapper jerky. "Here, try this," he said. The kids asked for another taste. Back in California, I could never get them to eat fish, except for breaded fish sticks, which hardly deserve to be called "fish." Steve was eager to make his own fish jerky after listening to Rick explain his method of digging a deep hole in the sand to smoke the snapper.

After lunch, Rick brought out his tools and demonstrated how he made jewelry out of Belizean and Guatemalan coins. "I set up a table on the beach and sell my jewelry to the cruise ship tourists when they come to the island," he said.

I left the guys in the dining room and followed Annette into the kitchen. I craved a one-on-one female chat, and I envied the close relationship she had with Rick. What was their secret? She told me Rick loved making his coin jewelry. "He doesn't make much money, but at least he's doing something he enjoys," she said. It hit me that I wanted the same for Duke. If only we could find something he enjoyed to make a living. *After all, wasn't that why we'd left Orange County?* We still had enough money in our savings; I just didn't want it to dry up. Perhaps I was holding on to my Orange County insecurities about money, scared that we would soon run out. In reality, we were living on much less here than in Orange County. If we could find something to do that covered our daily living expenses, I'd feel more secure.

After that Saturday with Rick, I noticed a more positive attitude at home. Instead of complaining, the kids and I slowly embraced the island. Now I questioned whether the U.S. had brainwashed me into believing that life was about making money, that if we slowed down and focused on enjoying daily life, we were failures.

It didn't help when our kids said, "Shouldn't you and Dad get a job? You're just sitting at home doing nothing."

In one way they were right, but part of me disagreed. I decided to call this a time of reflection, of discovering our passion and turning it into our life. Annette gave me the best piece of advice. "Try to divorce yourself from your kids' comments. You'll see how enlightening that can be."

If only Duke and I could come up with a business we both loved. *But what were we passionate about?* All we cared about was to make enough to eat and enjoy life's small pleasures. We no longer wanted anything fancy or expensive. *Was that so wrong?*

The smell of onions wafting downstairs woke me up. I found Steve standing over a frying pan, stirring green peppers and onions into his scrambled eggs. I guess he felt the need to make his own seventeenth birthday breakfast. Duke walked in, mumbled "Happy Birthday" and

headed straight for the coffee pot. All we had to offer Steve was a home-made card, a fishing lure and a pirate flag. Our choices on the island were limited. We knew Steve wanted an old sailboat, but we'd told him it cost too much. I could tell he longed for us to change our minds.

I started baking a cake for Steve but didn't have the right ingredients. These were the moments when I missed the civilized world. Back home, I could jump in my car and buy what I needed, but nothing was fast or easy here. As usual, I improvised and substituted homemade servings of flan for a birthday cake. I stuck one leftover candle in the middle of Steve's flan, and we sang "Happy Birthday."

Steve's eyes opened wide when he saw the steaks I had purchased at Angelo's meat shop in town. They were thicker than usual, but nothing more than a tease. I didn't have mushrooms and garlic to pile on top, nor wine for a sauce to give them flavor. They ended up tasteless, just like the nonexistent birthday cake. I suddenly yearned for my local Trader Joe's in California and its famous "Two buck Chuck," a decent wine for only $1.99. We could buy wine in San Pedro, but I hated spending $15 for a vinegary Chilean wine.

I longed for a friend who could listen to me bitch and moan, but calls to the U.S. were expensive, and I didn't want my friends to think Duke and I had given up on Belize or that we regretted our decision to move here.

Waiting for day to turn into bedtime had become my only goal on Steve's birthday, and that saddened me. Back in Orange County, I complained about not having enough *time*. Now time was plentiful, and I still complained. *What was wrong with me?*

The following morning, during my training session with Jennie, I spewed out all my anger, guilt and resentment. "It was Steve's birthday yesterday, and we couldn't do anything special," I said, realizing how stupid I sounded. That was just a symptom, not the real reason I was unhappy.

"Sometimes I feel trapped where we live," I said. "I feel unsettled, and Duke's behavior scares me." Jennie listened. Although she didn't have a solution to my problems, I felt better once I had expressed my feelings

After the gym, I rode my bike along the beach toward town, inspecting all the local businesses along the way. I noticed the abundance of dive shops on practically every pier and suddenly came up with a unique business idea that might work. I thought about having a small coffee shop at the end of a pier in the center of town — sort of like a drive-through Starbucks for boats. I was quite proud of my idea. I thought it could be successful because dive boats and tour boats left San Pedro early in the morning. What tourist didn't need his latte or coffee to start the day? Our coffee shop would not only be the first decent one in town, but also we would become pioneers in the boat-through coffee business.

I couldn't wait to tell Duke about my idea and was pleasantly surprised when he said, "I saw a pier for sale north of the *Island Ferry*."

"Which one?" I asked.

"In front of the new condos they're building. It needs lots of repairs, but we could do it."

I perked up. It felt like Duke was back to his normal self, and we had a brief bonding moment. The following morning, Duke investigated who owned the pier and learned that it was Martin, a local Belizean. Once home, he dialed Martin's number and made an appointment to meet him that afternoon at the pier.

I felt calm again, for the first time in weeks. Amazing how, when I focused on money, I could feel the same stress on a Caribbean island as I had in Orange County.

Martin arrived thirty minutes late, giving us ample time to count the wooden planks that needed replacing and to check the support structure for damage from previous hurricanes. Martin, an easygoing, dark-skinned Creole, gave us the impression that opening a coffee shop at the end of his pier would be no problem.

"What about permits?" Duke asked.

"No problem," he said. "This is existing pier, not new one."

With repairs, we figured the pier would cost around $100,000, not including construction of a small coffee shop.

The San Pedro Town Board supposedly issued work permits to expats like us who entered Belize under the QRP program. Their only requirement was for us to employ local Belizeans. But we still hadn't received our QRP cards. The six-week waiting period had now turned into nine months!

Duke and I agreed that the pier idea was a huge financial risk. We would have to spend every last penny we owned — and what if we couldn't make a profit? We had no idea whether boats would stop and get coffee. Sadly, my one glimmer of hope for a business turned out to be a potential failure.

Duke reverted to his 40-hour, relaxed reading week with renewed gusto. My resentment toward him grew, and I had no more desire for intimacy with Duke than I had toward an iguana. This, of course, set off a vicious cycle, making it more and more unbearable for us to be around one another.

One night, Duke decided to avoid me by going to bed ridiculously early, then waking me up in the middle of the night saying he felt sick.

"What's wrong with you?" I asked with little compassion.

"My eyes are infected and I have trouble breathing," he replied. I could hear wheezing from his chest, which brought back bad memories of a pleurisy episode he'd once had in Orange County. That episode resulted in a visit to the emergency room in the middle of the night. *Is this to punish me and make me feel like I caused your sickness?* Duke had made it clear that he was angry at my constant nagging. He even said, "You make me sick," which was completely out of character. I was scared. *What am I going to do if you need the emergency room at night? How will I get you to the airport?*

The following morning I told Duke he should go see a doctor.

"If I need a doctor, I'll go to one," he replied. The boys felt the hostility between us.

"What's wrong with you, Mom? You're constantly nagging and on our case," Steve said. It finally hit me that I was part of the problem; perhaps it wasn't all Duke's fault.

That's when I decided to stop nagging Duke about a job and start enjoying myself. After all, what was the purpose of our move to Belize? Was it to continue experiencing the stress we'd had in Orange County? Or was it to get away from all the things we didn't like about our life in Orange County and focus on family? It seemed ironic that it took Steve to point this out to me.

I felt suddenly lighter after I'd made the decision to change my attitude. It didn't take long for a smile to replace Duke's frown, and for the first time in weeks, he got off the couch, put on his trunks and swam out to place markers in the shallow water. "Now we can go out for dinner and not have to worry about hitting rocks when it's dark," he said.

Duke was thrilled when I suggested we try scuba diving, something I still feared after getting certified before leaving California.

We packed our gear, jumped in the boat, and I forced myself to just do it. I flipped backward off our boat into the water, holding my mask and regulator, and was surprised to end up the right way. We never dove deeper than thirty feet, the maximum depth on our side of the reef. "Did you see the three bat rays?" Duke asked me as we climbed back onto the boat. "There was a huge one, about five feet across, and two smaller ones."

"No, I didn't see a single one. I was too busy checking my gauges." *Why did I focus on sticking to the rules of the PADI book instead of enjoying the experience?* It was as though my dive master were grading my performance. I was mad at myself for not sharing Duke's enthusiasm for diving, especially as I'd always considered myself a good swimmer. In fact, swimming was what had attracted me to Duke when I responded to the ad he'd placed in the singles magazine nineteen years prior. When we first dated, we often met at the local YMCA. I admired his butterfly stroke, something I'd never been able to figure out myself. Now, if only I could relax while scuba diving, I might enjoy it.

CHAPTER TWENTY-NINE

Belizean Orthodontist

ALEC NEEDED BRACES, so I called Dr. Milo's office in Belize City to set up a consultation. A bit nervous, I awaited his recommendation on how to get rid of large gaps on either side of Alec's front teeth. Alec was missing his lateral incisors; they just didn't exist, so his canines bordered his front teeth.

Back in Orange County, one orthodontist had recommended implants, while another suggested pushing Alec's teeth forward to close the gap.

The implant orthodontist asked, "What's the closest U.S. city to Belize?"

"Houston," I replied.

"If I were you, I'd fly Alec to Houston for his braces," he said. "You need someone with the right training; and if anyone suggests pulling a single tooth out to fix the problem, stay away from them," he advised. "Let me give you a referral."

Leaving Alec trapped in the reclining dentist's chair, he returned a few minutes later with a directory of orthodontists, the schools they attended and their credentials. Before he had time to flip to the Houston section, I asked him if there were any orthodontists in Belize. "Well, there's only one in here," he said, finger scrolling down the page. "He's in Belize City."

"Does it say what his credentials are?" I asked.

"Er, well, er, it does state that he uses the same metal braces and wires we use here in the U.S.," he said.

"Can you give me his name? It would be so much more convenient than Houston."

He scribbled Dr. Milo's name on a piece of paper, handed it to me and said, "Good luck." While his assistant undid the blue paper bib hooked around Alec's neck, I asked her what she'd do in our situation.

"My husband's Mexican," she said, closing the door. "I know some great Mexican orthodontists. Most train in the States, anyway, so I'd probably go with the Belizean orthodontist." She added, "You do realize you'd have to fly to Houston every month for a couple of years for adjustments?" I thought about the cost of flights back to the States, which helped me decide.

On the morning of Alec's consultation, we dropped Josh off at school and headed straight to Tropic Air. I pushed open the tinted glass door of the prefab terminal and stepped inside the refreshingly cool waiting room. Duke headed for the uniformed woman sitting behind a tall Formica counter, who greeted him with a warm smile and a polite, "Good morning, sir," He purchased three roundtrip tickets to Belize City Municipal Airport, while I headed straight for the free coffee.

A teenage kid, wearing beige slacks and a well-ironed beige shirt, waited politely behind me while I stirred creamer into my coffee. I smiled as I edged my way between him and the couch. I squeezed my rear between Duke and Alec on the hard plaid couches facing the television set. The young man sat facing us. "Is he the pilot?" I asked Duke, turning my head so the teen wouldn't hear me. "He looks awfully young."

"That's 'cause we're getting older," Duke said.

As soon as they announced our flight's departure, the teen — he was indeed our pilot — bolted out the door, jogged a hundred yards to some metal steps and crawled into the front left seat. A Belizean staff member stood at the exit, collecting our green, laminated boarding passes.

The plane's tiny tires reminded me of the tires on Alec's old bicycle in California — except they looked even more worn out. *Were they safe?*

During the fifteen-minute flight, I pressed my forehead against the oval window, examining every carved channel and dune formation on the sea floor from 1,000 feet above. As we flew over Caye Caulker — the second most populated island after Ambergris Caye — Duke pointed out a two-story house right below us, on the beach.

"That's the house I wanted us to buy. Remember the one I e-mailed you photos of and said we could start a bed-and-breakfast business?"

"I wish we'd bought it," I said. "We could have had a bed-and-breakfast business going by now." Duke had discovered the house after moving to Consejo Shores and realizing the hut wouldn't work out in the long run. He'd hesitated because Caye Caulker was tiny. It had a population of only 1,000, compared with 11,000 on Ambergris Caye.

At the time, we had worried about the lack of schools. We didn't know Steve and Alec would be following an Internet curriculum. As for Josh, it turned out that one of Josh's teachers lived on Caye Caulker, and Josh could have taken the water taxi to the Island Academy with that teacher. That being the case, perhaps we could have made it work. "I wonder if it's still for sale," I said. "That was such a great price."

I shifted in my seat, looking back as the island grew smaller. Our teenage pilot landed as smoothly as could be expected on the narrow gravel runway, which ran parallel to the beach. I'd expected a larger airport than San Pedro's, but it was the same size. We deplaned and walked straight out to the road, where a huddle of taxi drivers waited for customers. Gilbert, a large Belizean Garifuna from Dangriga, offered a special rate to be our taxi driver for the day. We followed him to a dark green Isuzu Rodeo. His car looked shiny and luxurious, but these days it didn't take much to impress me.

"So where are we going?" Gilbert asked.

"To Dr. Milo," Duke said. "Do you need the address?"

"Oh, no, I take people there all the time."

It only took five minutes to get there. "Can you pick us up in 45 minutes?" Duke asked.

"I wait in car," he replied. As we paid him by the hour, he preferred to stay put.

Dr. Milo's waiting room looked normal and smelled sweet, like most Belizean floor-cleaning products. The décor was minimalist: no coffee table, no magazines, no water dispenser; just plain, white tile and white walls, with one tired poster depicting a smiling Belizean kid with metal braces.

A receptionist greeted us warmly, and I felt like the office had been opened just for us. She led us to an examination room, where she asked Alec to lie on an antique, foot-pedaled dental chair. I clutched my large envelope from California, with state-of-the-art X-rays, including panoramic X-rays; detailed mathematical calculations of Alec's jaw line in relation to his nose; and, of course, his cosmetic profile. All of these were taken a few days before we left the U.S., and I couldn't wait to see Dr. Milo's reaction to such advanced technology.

We waited ten minutes, with a radio blaring from two speakers attached to opposite corners of the room. Apparently, the prime minister of Taiwan was on an official visit to Belize. The radio crackled irritatingly, making it difficult to hear anything but cheering crowds and the monotone voice of the announcer.

Dr. Milo, dressed in khaki pants and a polo shirt, strolled in as though he'd been paged straight from home. After a brief handshake with each one of us, he proceeded to say something, but all I could hear was the president of Belize's speech on the radio.

"Sorry, Dr. Milo," I said. "Could we turn the radio off, please?"

"Of course," he said, smiling. "But today is a very important day for Belize. We have an official visit from the prime minister of Taiwan."

He left the room and I felt guilty about my request, but when Dr. Milo returned, he continued listening to the radio, just a tad lower in volume.

"Here, Dr. Milo, I brought Alec's recent X-rays so we don't have to retake them." He took one out and held it above his head toward the dangling light bulb in the middle of the ceiling. *Where was the light panel that you clip X-rays onto?*

"I shall need to make molds of Alec's teeth before I can come up with a diagnosis," he said, not even bothering to check the envelope.

"Our California orthodontist said these X-rays are so advanced, there's no need for molds." I said. "Can you give us an idea of how you propose to fix Alec's lack-of-incisor problem?" I continued.

Duke gave me his *how dare you* look?

"We can pull out a couple of teeth," Dr. Milo said. Alec flinched in his seat.

"Can't you file the teeth to get extra space instead of pulling teeth out?" I asked, giving Dr. Milo one last chance to redeem himself. "Well, slenderizing is an option," he said. "But if you file too much off, you risk damage to the enamel, and then there's the possibility of an infection. Once again, I can't make a diagnosis until after I do some calculations using the mold."

I wasn't happy with his answers, and Duke kept frowning and repeating, "Sonia, he needs to do the molds first." I felt torn. Should I believe Dr. Milo or the California orthodontist?

"Let's think about it," I said to Dr. Milo, not allowing him to proceed with the molds.

As soon as we were seated inside the taxi, Duke said, "What a complete waste of time."

"But, Duke, I really didn't feel the guy was competent."

Duke insisted we should at least have let him do the molds because that was how he was used to doing it.

"But Alec didn't feel comfortable with him, either, did you Alec?" I said, looking for backup.

"Not really," Alec said. "He wanted to do everything the orthodontist in California said not to do."

"See, Duke. I told you so."

"So where would you like to go now?" Gilbert asked, waiting for us to quit arguing.

"We need to buy some school uniform polo shirts for our son. Do you know where to go?" Duke asked.

Gilbert knew exactly where to take us and weaved in and out of lanes, disregarding traffic rules. He then stopped in the middle of the road, amid all the cars honking at him, and pointed to the right. "Here's the famous swing bridge," he said.

"What's special about it?" I asked, wondering if this might be the Eiffel Tower of Belize.

"It swings open at 5:30 P.M. every day to let the larger boats through," he said.

"I'd like to see that," Alec reflected.

Gilbert dropped us off in front of a fairly large department store in the heart of Belize City. Store attendants greeted us in uniform. "Can I help you find something?" one after another asked. *Had I stepped into a Belizean Nordstrom?*

The layout of the store was unusual. Washers and stoves were lined up between the shoe department and the pharmacy. I asked one of the attendants where the restroom was located. She led the way and asked me to pay "one dollah" to use the toilet.

"I only have a five-dollar bill," I said, as I followed her to a door in the back. She pulled a key out of her pocket and took my money. "I'll bring the change," she said.

I felt like I was in a secret part of the store, a place that few people had access to.

She didn't come back, so I returned to the main part of the store and couldn't find her. Eventually, I spotted her at the cash register and hated myself for doubting that I'd ever get my money back.

Meanwhile, Duke and Alec bought a couple of polo shirts for Josh to wear at the Island Academy, and then Gilbert drove us back to the airport.

Now I had no idea how we would get braces for Alec.

CHAPTER THIRTY

More Like Home

"Can Juan come with us? He wants to buy a WaveRunner," said Alec, out of breath after sprinting back from his chat with Juan. Since the day Alec took Rick's WaveRunner out for a spin, his desire to get his own had intensified. He brought it up daily, which made me wonder whether he'd pushed Juan to get one first.

"Sure, we can take him," I said, relieved to see him bubbly for a change. Alec sat next to Juan on the way to school. I could hear him quizzing Juan about the WaveRunner, adding, "Can you check if there's another one in good shape, at a good price?"

After dropping the boys off, we took Juan to the back lagoon. Duke slowed the *Island Rider* to a crawl, respecting the no-wake-zone. Most Belizean drivers sped through, unconcerned about the disappearing mangroves and erosion of the lagoon.

Juan instructed Duke to pull up at a shack where a bunch of secondhand WaveRunners — most of them past their prime — sat in a junkyard. "Hey, Juan," I said, "ask the guy if he has one in good shape that's cheap for Alec." Duke didn't think we should spend money on a

WaveRunner, but the kids needed something to do on weekends and I figured this might encourage Steve and Alec to go to town and play basketball with some local kids.

"Did Juan get it?" Alec asked as soon as we picked him up from school.

"Wait and see," I replied teasingly. Juan heard our boat arrive and ran over to show off his new toy. Though it was an older, slower model, both Alec and Steve were eager to try it out. We sat on the wooden pier while they took turns. "Why can't I try?" Josh whined.

"I'll take you," Steve volunteered.

It felt good to see Steve interacting with his brothers.

Josh jumped on the back seat and, after several minutes turning in circles, they returned.

"What happened to your hand?" I shrieked, watching blood gush out.

"I must have cut it," Steve said, acting as though it were no big deal.

"Duke, does he need stitches?" I hollered, afraid to look. "Where the hell are we going to find a doctor at this time of day?" I was panicking, while Duke was calmly inspecting Steve's hand.

"Don't worry. The cut isn't deep; it just looks that way," Duke said.

The following morning, Duke dropped me off in town for groceries. As I turned the corner, my eyes locked on a sign that stopped me cold. I saw the familiar, dark green umbrellas of Starbucks fronting a brand new sign that read "Sandbucks."

"I can't believe it," I muttered. "Someone just opened a coffee shop in town and *stole* my idea." I felt betrayed, and I stepped inside to do some detective work. The place was empty and the décor uninviting. I knew tourists would complain about the lack of air-conditioning. The place had a nice granite countertop and a few large stainless steel thermoses behind the counter, but they couldn't compare to the expensive Bunn coffee machines Starbucks used in the U.S.

"Hi, what can I get you?" an attractive young Belizean woman asked me. "Our drinks menu is on the board," she said, turning and pointing a freshly painted red fingernail at the sign above her head. "We also make great sandwiches."

Surprised — and envious that this was her place, not mine — I said, "Are you the owner?"

"Yes, together with my boyfriend, Cory," she said, flashing a row of perfect white teeth. "I'm Nellie." She extended her limp hand over the counter to shake mine.

"Well, congratulations on your store."

"Thanks. We're so excited."

"Do you serve Island Coffee?" I asked.

"Yes, of course." Nellie pushed the spout on the stainless steel thermos, and I saw a thread-like stream of translucent coffee trickling into the cup. She had to pump the handle a good twenty times to fill it up. Just by looking at it, I knew it would be old and cold. Before I had time to stir cream in, Nellie asked, "How does it taste?"

I took a quick sip. "Very good," I lied. She reminded me of a little girl in a new dress, asking, "Mommy, how do I look?" I couldn't hurt her feelings.

After a quick stop at SuperBuy, I hurried home on the *Island Ferry*. "You'll never guess what just opened in town," I blurted from the top of the stairs through the screened window.

"What?" Duke asked.

"Sandbucks. Is that legal? They have the same green colors and all."

"This is Belize," Duke said, helping me with the grocery bags. "Aren't you glad we decided not to invest all of our money on a coffee shop?" He sounded proud that we'd procrastinated long enough for someone else to do it first. *How could he not be more concerned?* The coffee shop was the closest we'd come to agreeing on a business we could build together.

"Now they'll be making all the money," I said, disheartened. "It's a crappy location," I went on, trying to make myself feel better. "I don't know why they didn't put it on the beach."

I needed to work off my frustration, so I grabbed Cookie's leash and took her for a walk on the beach. Mitch, an expat, drove by in his gas-powered golf cart, then slammed on his brakes.

"Haven't seen you in a while," he said.

"You were gone, weren't you?"

"Yeah, back to Florida. I'm building so many luxury homes right now."

A successful contractor, Mitch hopped between his job in Florida and Ambergris Caye, where he'd almost finished building a 4,000-square-foot Mediterranean retirement villa for himself and his wife. Mitch knew San Pedro better than most expats, and I managed to lure him to our house by offering him an ice-cold beer.

Duke heard us talking as we climbed the wooden staircase and opened the front door. While I headed to the fridge and pulled out two beers, Duke quizzed Mitch on his successful lobster-catching technique. As the guys snapped off their bottle caps and gulped down several mouthfuls, I said, "So Mitch, Duke and I are still looking for a business to start; any suggestions?"

"There's a job you can do right here," he said, without pausing to think.

"What?" I asked, leaning in closer.

"We could use a great property manager up north. The ones in town are too far to check up on all the new houses being built."

Duke and I glanced at one another, and suddenly I felt giddy at the prospect of a fantastic opportunity.

"You guys would be awesome," Mitch continued. "You could walk along the beach to check on the houses."

"Have another beer," I said.

As soon as Mitch left, I researched the Internet for anything I could find on property management. How I wished I could jump in my car and head to my local Barnes & Noble or to the library. I needed a *Property Management for Dummies*-type book. Ordering online was out of the question, as merchants wouldn't ship to a P.O. Box in Belize.

Thankfully, Duke seemed equally enthusiastic about Mitch's business proposition. With his prior background in real estate and law, property management seemed like a good fit. He could deal with the legal aspects, and I could network and promote our business. We sat at our computers for hours, Duke developing contracts while I studied the basics of property management.

"Duke, why don't we make a website? You're good at that," I said.

"I've already started one. What do you think of 'Northcaye'?"

"I like it," I said, happy to see that my "Dukie" was back.

"We'll offer tourists information and advice, like which stores are cheaper, where to find good deals, and then have a separate section on property management."

Things started coming together, not only in the business, but also in our lives. Steve interacted more with his brothers, Duke and I felt close again, and Little Juan helped our family in so many ways. The boys adopted him as their little brother, expecting him to wake them up in the mornings before school, disappointed if he didn't show up on our boat dock to greet them when they returned home. Josh often asked whether we could buy a small toy for Little Juan.

Whenever Teresa cleaned a villa, we knew someone was arriving.

"Who's coming this time?" I asked.

"Miss Betty," she replied. "She come alone for a week."

"What time is she getting here?"

"I think six o'clock."

After three months at Villas Tropicales, we'd finally meet one of the other owners. "We should buy Betty a bottle of wine and some fresh coffee, and I'll bake some peanut butter cookies as a welcome gift," I said to Duke as we headed to town on our boat to pick up the boys.

I wrote Betty a note. "Welcome back to Paradise. Hope you enjoy the wine, cookies and coffee. Your new neighbors, Sonia, Duke and boys."

The following evening, Betty invited us over for wine and cheese.

"What are we having for dinner?" Steve asked as I squeezed my nearly empty tube of lip gloss, the only makeup I wore these days.

"Well, Steve, I have steaks in the fridge. It'd be nice if you cooked dinner for us tonight."

In Orange County, the kids would have asked for pizza money, but not here. They had adapted to life with fewer conveniences.

Duke and I climbed Betty's wooden staircase. I knocked on the door, and a smiling, gray-haired woman in her late fifties welcomed us inside. It took me a few seconds to take in her stunning décor. Betty had exquisite taste; walls were painted in warm yellow tones, unlike our plain white — bordering on dirty-white — walls. A set of three handwoven Guatemalan straw baskets — small, medium and large — were arranged on a shelf, and a bright orange, yellow and green tapestry draped the wall behind them. I envied her paintings, something we sorely needed in our house. Hers tied in with her warm color scheme and gave her house a polished look.

"Thank you so much for the goodies. How sweet of you, especially as I arrived after the stores closed," she said, leading us to her rattan green couch overlooking the Caribbean. A selection of imported cheeses and a bottle of red wine sat atop a thick mahogany coffee table. *What a treat!* We spent the evening talking about our backgrounds and the four villas at Villas Tropicales. Betty, who lived in Ohio, came down to check on her villa three times a year. She made sure it looked perfect so she could rent it to tourists for a hefty fee. Even her towels were monogrammed with the name of her villa. It soon became obvious that Betty relied a great deal on Teresa and Juan as caretakers, and she showered them with expensive gifts whenever she visited. She said the other two villa owners did the same. Now I understood why Teresa had asked me to purchase a sewing machine for her. Did she really expect us to compete with the other homeowners? This was something we were both unable and unwilling to do.

After a pleasant evening, we returned to our house. Steve had two dinner plates with steak and a baked potato wrapped tightly in foil so the ants and other bugs wouldn't get to it on the kitchen counter. "I guess he really wants a sailboat," I said to Duke.

Several months of pleading had finally paid off for Alec and Josh. Duke divided their tiny room into two even smaller rooms with floor-to-ceiling plywood. We separated the bunk beds and barely squeezed them in sideways. Thankfully, the vaulted ceiling gave the narrow space a less claustrophobic feel. I promised the boys I would either paint the plywood or staple fabric to it. When Steve offered to help Duke cut and install the plywood, I knew something was up. "Mom, can you find out who owns *Sailaway* when you go to town? Please?"

"Come with me, and we'll ask at JD's Bar." I replied.

"I'm helping Dad. Please, can you ask around?"

"I'll ask," I promised him.

I took the *Island Ferry* into town and headed to JD's, along the beach. It was a local hangout where many alcoholic expats spent their lives. Since *Sailaway* was anchored in front of JD's, someone would know about it.

"Who owns *Sailaway?*" I asked the Belizean bartender.

"Heather knows the owner; follow me," he said.

I loved the way locals had time to help. Heather's house was right next to the bar.

"Watch out for the dogs," the bartender warned me. Two fierce-looking boxers approached the gate. "Wait," he said. "Let me go first." I never used to be scared of dogs, but there were so many guard dogs on the island that I'd grown apprehensive. A massive boxer approached my legs and started sniffing them. I knew he smelled Cookie; I hoped he liked expat dogs.

The bartender tapped on Heather's screened door. No one came. He tried again, this time opening the door. I heard loud snoring, which soon turned into pig-like snorts. "Sorry to disturb you," he said. "I have someone here who wants to ask you a question."

Heather hauled her large body off the couch and hobbled over. On a scale of one to ten, ten being the ugliest, Heather was a twenty. She had a gray bushy mustache, iced-tea-colored teeth, liver spots and hanging warts splattered on her face. Her hair was a tangled, greasy mess, and I couldn't imagine her being married to the expat guy who walked in the door as we spoke. It was only 10:30 A.M., and she reeked of booze.

"Sorry to disturb you," I said, "but my seventeen-year-old son is extremely interested in the boat *Sailaway* and I was wondering if the owner is selling it?"

"They've had it for sale on and off," she said in a raspy smoker's voice. "They're in Australia until January, but I can give you their e-mail address."

"That would be great," I said.

When I returned, Steve and Duke had finished installing the plywood divider. I pulled out the e-mail address, and Steve's face beamed.

Juan had succeeded in negotiating a good deal on a used WaveRunner for Alec. We soon learned that locals got a better price than expats. "Did you get the WaveRunner?" Alec asked when we picked him up at the Belikin boat dock after school.

"You'll see," I said, giving away the answer with my smile. Alec's face glowed when he saw the personal watercraft sitting at the end of our boat dock. He flung his schoolbooks on the pier and took it for a spin. As he bounced on the waves, enjoying an engine that was faster and louder than Juan's, Alec couldn't stop grinning. He loved it, and he let everyone, including Juan, take turns riding it. Steve attached his boogie board to the back, managing to stand on this flimsy piece of Styrofoam for a good twenty seconds before falling into the warm sea.

Since leaving Orange County, my boys had become more creative and relied on one another for entertainment. I could see them growing close as time went on.

CHAPTER THIRTY-ONE

Parental Approval

I JUMPED OFF OUR BOAT, missed the pier and landed feet first in the shallow warm waters of the Caribbean. How could this happen on such an important day? I wanted to look my best for my dad and his wife, visiting from Paris.

Dad had no burning desire to visit Belize other than to assure himself that his only daughter hadn't "gone native." Like most people, Dad thought we were crazy to move to Belize with our kids at an age where their education mattered more than ever for college.

A tourist spotted me in the water and sprinted to my rescue. "Here, grab my hands," he said, dangling them over the pier. I reached up, held on tight, then wrapped my legs around a slimy, submerged pillar.

"Watch out, Sonia!" Duke yelled.

The winds were stronger than usual, making it difficult to maneuver our boat, and Duke's shout alerted me that the propeller was dangerously close to my back. I let go of the man's hands and hid underneath the pier for fear of becoming shark bait. "There goes my flip-flop," I cried, watching it float away.

I treasured my brand new flip-flops, especially as I'd splurged at the expensive tourist shop in town. These days, twenty dollars for flip-flops seemed on a par with buying a Louis Vuitton bag. After rescuing my shoe, it dawned on me that I could wade to the beach and get out the easy way.

Back on dry land, I assessed the damage. My tank top and shorts were soaked and now see-through. There was no way I could take the shortcut through the Seabreeze Hotel, exposing myself to tourists. Instead, I followed the dusty path flanking the Roman Catholic school, hoping those five extra minutes of breeze would dry my clothes.

Despite my mishap, I still managed to show up fifteen minutes before Dad and Jill's puddle jumper was due to land. Inside the Tropic Air terminal, I finally felt like a local, recognizing other faces. One in particular caught my eye. "Hi, Dad," I shrieked, running up to kiss his flushed cheek. "Where's Jill?" I asked, feeling his tense body.

"She didn't make the flight," he said, pulling away from my hug.

"What do you mean?" I asked, worried about some medical problem.

"Those bloody American rules," he said, tapping his fingers on the counter. "The U.S. changed their passport rules a week before our flight, and no one bothered to call us."

"What rules?"

"They want all passports to have bar codes," he said mopping his brow with a white cotton handkerchief. "Jill's passport was renewed, but it doesn't have a bar code. They have too many stupid rules."

For a 79-year-old man who'd been on three different flights in two days, he seemed wide awake, almost like he'd overdosed on caffeine.

"How long does it take to get your suitcases in this country?" he snapped.

Only three suitcases remained on the rusty wheelbarrow, and they weren't his.

"They've lost my suitcase," Dad shouted. "They put me on an earlier flight, and now those idiots have lost my bag," he continued.

"It'll be here in a few minutes," I said. "They put you on an earlier flight, and your bags will be on the next one."

Now I felt depressed. I'd made such an effort to get everything ready for Dad and Jill, including negotiating a free week in Betty's gorgeous villa so they could have their own TV, kitchen and refrigerator. What would I do with my dad for one whole week? He hated being outdoors in the heat and humidity, exposing his milky white legs for the world to see.

Ten minutes later, Dad's suitcase appeared on the metal wheelbarrow. I carried it out to the dusty street, waiting for a taxi driver to approach us. Usually drivers fought for customers, but today was different; they ignored us — except for one dark-skinned Creole, who'd obviously smoked too much of the local weed.

"This place reminds me of when we lived in Nigeria," Dad said. "It even has the same smells." I took this as an insult. Dad had spent seventeen years in Nigeria, and I lived there for six. I knew what he meant, and it upset me.

The Creole driver took us along the unpaved road to David's pier, where Duke sat waiting in the boat. "Sonia, you OK?" Duke asked. "I was so worried when you fell off the pier." By now, I'd forgotten the incident.

"I'm OK," I said. "It's what happened to Jill that pisses me off." Dad explained the whole story on our boat ride home.

"Never again will I go through the U.S. to come visit you," Dad said. "They fingerprinted me as if I were a criminal." I could taste what the French disliked about the Americans. Dad had become so French since he married Jill after Mom passed away. It always took him a few days to readjust to his British side, the side I knew from my childhood.

The boys greeted Papa Don at the end of the pier and offered to carry his bags to Betty's house. A barefooted Steve showed off his muscles lifting the heavy suitcase over his head, while Alec carried Papa Don's leather briefcase, which my Dad feared might get dropped in the water. "Careful, all my important papers are in it," he said. Little Juan joined us, as he always did, acting as though Papa Don were his own grandpa. Little Juan's antics finally earned a smile from my dad.

I kept waiting for Dad to comment on our beautiful view and how we'd found paradise, but he said nothing. I'd splurged on two expensive bottles of wine and filet mignon from Angelo's to impress Dad, but he took it for granted. During dinner, the whole conversation revolved around politics, and Dad's hostility towards the Americans. "Why didn't Bush go after Bin Ladin instead of Saddam Hussein?" Dad said. Then he attacked Dick Cheney and the Halliburton scandal. My heart was aching. After saying, "Goodnight," I fell apart and burst into tears. Alec and Josh walked Papa Don to Betty's and helped him get settled. Dad said he couldn't wait to catch up on CNN news. His hunger for world news never ceased to amaze me.

Duke put his arms around me. "You'll feel better in the morning," he said.

Duke was right. I did feel better after a good night's sleep. As I made coffee, I watched Dad sitting on the wooden bench at the end of our pier, staring at the calm, turquoise sea. I had no desire to go out and talk to him right away. Instead, I drank coffee and wrote in my journal. "Sit there, I don't care," I started writing. "You were so mean last night, attacking us. How would you like it if I criticized the French?" Then I realized it wasn't about us. It was about Jill not being here. Dad was mad at the strict new U.S. security regulations invoked after 9/11.

After fifteen minutes, I was calm again and headed out to see him. We met halfway along the pier. I gave Dad a hug, and he asked, "Has Duke thought of a job while you're living here?"

"We're still deciding," I mumbled, growing tense again. I knew Dad was concerned about our finances, but it still made me angry that, in his eyes, we were failures for moving to Belize and not conforming to what "society" expected of us.

As soon as I had time alone with Duke, I said, "See, I told you Dad would ask what we're going to do for a living. Now you understand why I was in such a hurry to get a job going."

"Sonia, we're here to do what we need and want to do, not to please others."

"Why don't you tell my dad that?" I barked back.

After the first couple of days, Dad appeared to relax a little and fell into the groove of Caribbean life. Without Jill, he had no desire to visit the famous Mayan ruins of Lamanai or Altun'Ha. Had Jill been here, they would have packed their weeklong stay with a bunch of tours, as they always did on vacation. But Dad preferred to follow our daily routine: taking the boat to school, walking along the smelly back street to the gym and stopping at Monkey Bites or the Belize Yacht Club for breakfast before returning home.

On the third night, I decided we should invite Dad to one of the nicer restaurants on the island.

"Let's try Mariposa," I said.

"I guess," Duke replied, understandably not thrilled about maneuvering the *Island Rider* around sharp coral heads in the dark. The locals had a sixth sense and knew which spots to avoid, but people like us relied on flashlights and kept to a snail's pace to avoid slicing open the bottom of our boat. There were no lighted markers on the water, so we had to memorize the exact location of each clump of coral.

Everyone piled inside the boat except me. "Don't untie the ropes yet," Duke shouted. "Pull the boat forward; get inside now!" Duke ordered the boys and me as if we were in the Marines, adding a thick layer of tension to a supposedly pleasant evening out. My dad kept his mouth shut while the rest of us offered suggestions that Duke couldn't handle.

"Duke, this is the Mariposa pier," I said, pointing to it, as he continued heading south.

"Don't tell me where it is," Duke snapped — shortly before he realized he had to make a U-turn.

We tied our boat up at the Mariposa dock, tiptoed around some broken planks and continued up a small stretch of beach. Charla, the owner, greeted us at the front door. It felt like we were entering someone's home. Why was this place empty? Either we were too early or the place had bad food. I felt uncomfortable as she seated us at a large oval table in the middle of an English country cottage with Indonesian artifacts. With Dad sitting next to me, I forgot I was in Belize.

The cuisine was described as Indonesian-French fusion, but we had no idea what to expect. Most of us ordered the Indonesian chicken sate, although the T-bone steak sounded tempting. Belize was not known for steaks, and if you saw a Belizean cow, you'd understand why; they looked anorexic. Although I'd heard that some island restaurants got their meat shipped in from the U.S., I still hesitated to order the T-bone.

Mariposa had its own winery, which used imported grape juice. After purchasing a bottle at the local supermarket, Duke and I preferred to order a rum and Coke. We warned my Dad — a connoisseur of fine wines — but he decided to order a bottle of their house wine. As Dad insisted on paying, I didn't dare complain. "Let's try their house white as an aperitif," Dad said.

"2003 was a good year for nail polish remover," I whispered in Duke's ear. To my amazement, Dad ordered a second bottle of wine.

"Maybe their red tastes better than their white," Dad said. With Charla hovering, I kept my mouth shut. When the check arrived, Dad picked it up and asked Duke whether the price was correct.

"This is almost as much as a four-star restaurant in Paris," he commented.

"I know, Dad," I said. "That's why we rarely eat out." Duke and I agreed the meal didn't come close to a mediocre Indonesian restaurant or steakhouse in the U.S. However, the longer we lived on the island, the less picky we grew.

Dad and I walked Cookie along the beach the following morning before taking the boys to school. "I'm so happy Steve has finally become interested in his future," I said. "He's studying hard and getting good grades." Dad mumbled something. I knew he thought we were robbing our kids of a decent education, but he kept his thoughts to himself.

"He's changed so much since California," I continued, hoping for some positive feedback. "He's no longer focused on girlfriends," I added.

Since the conversation wasn't going anywhere, I stopped.

"Let's go to Caye Caulker today," I suggested, feeling guilty that I hadn't taken Dad to see anything special. He said he wasn't interested in going on tours without Jill; but still, we had to do at least one touristy thing, didn't we?

Dad didn't say much when he followed us to our gym every morning. He walked slowly, hunched over, trying to keep pace with Duke, but without the stamina. I slowed down and walked next to him, embarrassed by the stench of rotting piles of trash on either side of the dirt road. I tried ignoring the foul odor, but I knew what Dad was thinking. *How can my daughter live in such a filthy third-world country? Why did they sell their beautiful home in California? What happened to them?* Just then we walked past trash floating in a mosquito-infested swamp. I felt like puking, but pretended it didn't exist.

During our last breakfast together, I could tell Dad was relieved to be returning to Paris. "You must be boiling," I said as Dad walked into our living room wearing his long woolen pants, socks and a long-sleeved shirt.

"I'm cool, actually," he replied.

"Why don't you change into your winter clothes in Houston?" I said, suffering by proxy from the layers of clothing he wore. "As long as I don't get wet on the boat, I'll be fine," Dad said.

We carried Dad's suitcase and carefully loaded his briefcase and bags into the *Island Rider*. I covered them with an old beach towel to avoid the salt spray. Dad climbed into the boat, grasping my hand for support, and took the middle position on the front bench. He wrapped two towels around himself and tucked them underneath and behind, so they'd stay in place. From a distance, he looked like a mummy with a baseball cap on. I'd never seem him wear a baseball cap in my entire life, but he explained, almost apologetically, that this was to stop his hair from blowing in the wind and protect his nose from developing another cancerous mole.

Duke started the engine, inching his way with caution, tiptoeing around each choppy wave. The breeze picked up, and Dad released one arm from underneath the towel to grab the brim of his cap. As Duke turned the boat south, I heard the sound of a large wave slapping Dad's face. He cringed and grabbed the edge of the towel to wipe the salty warm water off his cheek and sunglasses. I suffered his pain during this twelve-minute boat ride. He just couldn't relax. Whatever happened to the man who loved taking his motorboat out every weekend and splashing with me in the waves off Tarkwa Bay when we lived in Nigeria? My dad was the outdoor man in those days, *or was I mistaken?* Not once did Dad ever comment upon the beauty of the turquoise Caribbean. All he focused on were the stench, the primitiveness and, I suppose, how selfish we were to impose this lifestyle on our children.

As with everything in life, it depended on your choice of focus. If you chose to concentrate on the discomfort of the ride, your hair blowing in the wind, the spray of the seawater and the trash, then you'd miss the beauty of nature surrounding you. Even darkness was stunning in this part of the world, the abundance of constellations, shooting stars and the clarity of a sky that seemed almost fake after living in a city.

Of all the days for this to happen, Duke could not find a single spot in town to dock the *Island Rider*. Instead, we were forced to head further south and catch a cab to the airport. Dad grew more agitated, and I sensed that the last thing he wanted was to spend one more day on the island. I had accepted island time, knowing that our casual San Pedro airport let you board even if you arrived two minutes before departure.

We arrived 28 minutes early, and I hoped Dad would relax. I longed for his approval. I needed to hear him say, "I admire you both for what you're doing, especially for Steve. Things will work out." That would have lifted a heavy burden off my shoulders. I would have felt less inclined to nag Duke to death about getting a job. Dad's approval meant so much to me, perhaps because I am an only child. Had Mom been alive, she would have been more accepting.

"Will those holding a red boarding pass for Belize International please proceed to Gate A." Dad jumped off his seat and started heading toward the gate without looking back.

"Dad, you have a green boarding pass," I said, getting him out of the wrong line.

"We'll be calling the green boarding passes in a few minutes," the Tropic Air lady announced.

Eight minutes before departure, passengers climbed the metal steps from the rear of the Cessna. Dad picked a seat next to the wing facing me and waved. I waited until his plane took off. I had all the time in the world. The propellers started turning, the engine noise grew louder and his plane didn't move for a couple of minutes, waiting for another Cessna to land before it could use the runway.

I stared at him through the oval window, and tears flowed down my cheeks like salty waterfalls. I felt a surge of heat inside my heart; I loved my dad. The first time I saw Dad cry was in 1971, when I was fourteen. It was the day I left Paris for boarding school in England. Dad had taken me to Le Bourget airport alone. Mom was too heartbroken. I didn't think dads could cry, but I remembered how he tried to hide his tears. Ironically, Dad was 47 when I left home, the age I had now reached, and this time it was me crying about Dad leaving.

CHAPTER THIRTY-TWO

Shopping Gringo Style

After running out of food every other day, I finally learned how to stock up gringo style.

It had never occurred to me that *hunting down* food and getting enough of it to feed my hungry sons would become a full-time job. This was something I'd taken for granted in the U.S., and now I worried that my boys weren't getting enough nutrition to stay healthy — especially Alec, who seemed to be growing skinnier by the day.

Jennie advised me to call Raul, her taxi driver. "For $12.50 per hour, he'll drive you to each store in town," she said. "He'll even help load groceries into your boat."

I pulled out my Belizean cell phone. Never sure whether a call would go through, I was always happy to hear a voice at the other end.

"Raul? I'm a friend of Jennie's. Are you free to take me around town grocery shopping?"

"Sure, where are you?" he asked.

"Outside Moncho's by the airport."

"Give me eight minutes," he replied.

Raul showed up in a burnt sienna van — the same model all taxi drivers in San Pedro drove. I never understood how every burnt sienna Toyota van ended up in San Pedro. In the U.S., most would have been crushed and used for scrap metal.

I soon learned to tell Raul's taxi from the other taxis by his happy face bobbing in and out of the car whenever he drove past a relative or friend. He rarely showed up alone; most of the time another passenger, or a family member, sat in the front passenger seat, forcing me to take the back bench. He'd drop that person off somewhere while I tagged along.

Raul made shopping in bulk so much easier. He even gave me a few tips, such as where to buy chicken for less money, although that meant stocking up on 25 pounds of chicken breasts at a time. Duke rarely came with me. He preferred to wait for my call, then drive the boat over to Dahlia's dock. All three of us carried cardboard boxes filled with canned goods, pasta, peanut butter, laundry detergent, meat, vegetables and fruits, and loaded them onto our boat.

Our freezer and cabinets were finally stocked with ground beef and chicken, and canned goods lined the shelves. The kids complained less about starving to death, even though we rarely purchased American snacks such as cookies or chips; these were too expensive, so the boys filled up on mangoes, bananas, homemade peanut butter cookies and carrot cake.

Despite Raul's help, shopping was exhausting, as we often had to go to three stores to find everything I needed.

One day Raul showed up late. I called him from the gym. "You coming, Raul?"

"On my way," he said, sounding less perky than usual.

Twenty minutes later he honked his horn.

"Sorry, Sonia. Today's my birthday, and I have a hangover," he said.

"Happy Birthday, Raul. How old are you?"

"Thirty," he said, looking more like forty.

"I really could use some *sopa de lima,*" he told me. "Mind if we stop?"

Locals loved their chicken-lime soup with rice: the best cure for hangovers.

"Drop me off at Super Buy," I said.

When Raul returned, I asked him whether he knew of a dentist. It was time for my family's annual teeth cleaning.

"Yes, Doctor Afonso. He's on Middle Street. Want me to drive you there?"

"Sure," I said. "Does he do braces, too?"

"Yes, I know kids who go to him. He's good," Raul said.

I made an appointment for Duke the following Thursday, the only day Doctor Afonso worked on the island. Apparently, he'd catch the puddle jumper over from Belize City on Thursday mornings. I couldn't wait to hear what Duke thought of him before I made appointments for the rest of us, including Alec.

After our usual stops at the Veggie House and the butcher, I called Duke to meet us at the boat dock.

"They didn't have milk today," I said. It was so frustrating not to get what we needed. I checked three different stores for non-fat powdered milk, and all I could find was powdered whole milk. Forget fresh milk; that was a luxury. The boys hated powdered whole milk, so we all had to be patient until the store stocked non-fat milk again.

The following Thursday, Duke was the guinea pig at Doctor Afonso's dental office.

"Was he good?" I asked.

"Yes. I actually got a better cleaning with him than I've ever had back home."

"Think he can take care of braces for Alec?" I asked.

"He said he trained as an orthodontist in the U.S."

We were looking for convenience and a good price, so when Doctor Afonso told Duke he could get the same braces shipped from the U.S. for half price in Belize, I plucked up the courage to get my teeth cleaned.

I arrived early and was greeted promptly by the receptionist.

"Good morning, Mrs. Marsh. Sorry, but Dr. Afonso isn't coming here today," she said.

"Why didn't you call to cancel?"

"Sorry, but Dr. Afonso didn't let us know he wasn't coming until this morning. We have no water, and the electricity is being cut off."

"Oh, OK," I said, wondering why she hadn't told me that first. This excuse would not have seemed plausible in the U.S., but I'd become far more accepting in Belize. I also knew not to argue with the locals, as I didn't want to get a reputation for being "the bitchy expat." Everyone knew everyone on the island. I rescheduled for the following week, and also made an appointment for Alec to come along.

The following Thursday, Duke dropped us off at the Texaco dock, and Alec and I headed to our appointment. I decided to go first. "Sorry, Doctor Afonso," I said. "I don't mean to sound rude, but I worry about AIDS and want to make sure everything is sterilized before it goes in my mouth." I felt awkward and insulting asking him this question, but Doctor Afonso's grin demonstrated he'd heard this concern before.

"Yes, everything is sterilized," he answered, pulling on a fresh pair of latex gloves. After he gave me a thorough exam, the cleaning lasted forty-five minutes. "Sorry, my assistant is not here today," he said. "Sometimes she misses the first flight from Belize City."

I'd grown accustomed to the way things worked in Belize. Had my dentist in Orange County apologized for her assistant not being there, I'd have expected to hear, "My assistant was in a car accident this morning," or something equally serious.

When it was Alec's turn, I went in with him. I grew slightly concerned when Doctor Afonso sprayed the latex gloves he'd worn to clean my teeth with dry air, then placed them on his table. He didn't throw them away.

After taking a look at Alec's teeth, he said, "I need to make molds before I decide how to proceed with braces."

This time Alec and I said, "OK." We no longer felt a need to present our "state of the art" Orange County X-rays to a Belizean orthodontist. We'd learned to do things their way.

CHAPTER THIRTY-THREE

The Bickering Old Ladies

M Y MOTHER-IN-LAW, DOREEN, found a good deal on Continental Airlines and invited herself and her eighty-year-old sister, Mildred, for the Christmas holidays. I had no idea how they would handle two weeks of heat, humidity and bugs. Both had Irish, milky-white complexions. Although they lived in California, their ancestors were from Newfoundland, which has an Arctic climate. They missed seeing our kids, but I dreaded the visit from a couple of old ladies who hated to travel and explore other countries.

Doreen was a workaholic Realtor with one passion other than closing a deal: reading. Mildred, her skinny older sister, was the early riser. She liked Sunday mass, JC Penney and coupon shopping. Duke's mom hated cooking and taking care of live plants; Mildred hated chicken. They had three things in common, though: Both were devout Catholics, staunch Democrats and preferred staying indoors with the drapes closed.

Their initial plan was to stay for one week during the Christmas holidays, which I could have handled. But when Doreen announced,

"We're staying two weeks so we can get cheaper airfares," I was less than thrilled.

We left our villa before sunset to pick up Grandma and Mildred. By five o'clock we had docked our boat at David's pier. In the midst of rush-hour commotion, all of us marched, single file, to Ali-Baba's restaurant, located almost across the road from Tropic Air.

"I'll run over to see if they caught the earlier flight," Duke said. "Order the roast chicken and fries for me." I decided not to order, thinking it was rude not to wait for them. Besides, it was too early for dinner. Five minutes later, Duke walked back to our table alone.

"Let's all order now; the next flight isn't due till six," he said. Forty-five minutes and two drinks later, our cooked-from-scratch meal was served. I had temporarily forgotten that in Belize, the concept of customer service had a different meaning than in the U.S. It often meant: "You're lucky when you're served."

A few minutes before six, Duke ran back to Tropic Air to see if his mom and Mildred had landed, while the kids and I polished off the last morsels on our plates. I heard the restaurant door squeak, and when I looked up, two pale old ladies dressed in black baby-stepped their way toward our table. For one split second, I thought I was at Coco's back home, not Ali-Baba's.

"Hi boys," they said, as though they'd had breakfast with them last weekend. Hasty hugs were exchanged, followed by the sound of purses unzipping. Rehearsed to synchronized perfection, each pulled out three crisp $100 bills and proceeded to distribute one bill to each boy. Apparently, their routine of giving money to my kids as soon as they saw them hadn't changed. Though I'm sure they had the best intentions, it made my boys feel uncomfortable. Besides, there were no electronics stores or malls on the island where they could spend their money. Candy and snacks from the U.S. would have been more appreciated than cash.

Duke left us for fifteen minutes while he caught a taxi to our boat dock to drop off their suitcases. Meanwhile, dressed in long-sleeved black blazers, Doreen and Mildred were turning bright red from the heat of the ovens.

"Is it raining that hard?" I asked Duke, who had returned, his hair and face dripping wet.

"Yes, it's pouring!"

"Doreen needs to eat." Mildred said. "She hasn't had any food all day, and she hasn't taken her insulin shot yet."

Duke's mom was a severe diabetic who neglected her health. When our waiter returned, Duke asked him, "What's the fastest meal we can order? We have to be at the Island Academy by seven."

"The chicken is fast," he replied. That was an exaggeration, but we ordered it for Doreen. Mildred refused to eat chicken ever since a sandwich she ordered at McDonald's turned out to be "bloody and raw," as she described it later. I'd forgotten about her McDonald's experience and realized she'd be a pain to feed since we ate chicken almost every day.

"Can you make a quick hamburger?" I asked.

"Yes," the waiter said. Fifteen minutes later, Mildred nibbled her burger like a mouse. "That's way too much food for me," she muttered. "Can I have a doggie bag?"

"Not here," Duke said.

Duke paid the bill, and off we headed to Josh's Christmas play at the Island Academy. "Mom, put this raincoat on," Duke said, offering both ladies ponchos to protect them from the tropical downpour.

I was mad when Duke and the boys took off jogging to Josh's school, leaving me in charge of Doreen and Mildred. They looked miserable, especially Mildred, hunched over with an oversized plastic hood tenting her permed head, taking toddler steps and squelching in the cement gutter. "My new shoes are getting all muddy," she squealed, as gray sludge flowed into rivulets down Front Street. Taxis, golf carts and trucks weaved in and out of murky puddles, forcing us to remain in the gutter. For $2.50 we could have grabbed a taxi, but Duke coaxed us into walking.

"It's only a block away," he told them. I desperately wanted to catch up with Duke, but stayed behind with Mildred, who was now almost in tears because her leather shoes were soaked.

When we arrived at Josh's school, most seats were already taken, except for one empty bench. Duke grabbed it, and after we sat down, teacher Ernie came up and said, "Please, can you get off the bench? We need it for the students in the play." Mildred refused to get off, and when Duke pulled her up, she stood shaking despite the tropical humidity. "I'll try to get another bench for you," teacher Ernie said.

Once everyone settled down, the Christmas show started, and I looked forward to seeing Josh sing in his first Belizean Christmas play. Initially, it seemed more amateurish than the productions we'd attended at our kids' elementary school in California. But then something struck me. This play wasn't about being perfect; it was about honesty, naiveté and kids being kids. The teachers weren't uptight about having a professional-looking performance. It felt more like a big family performance, where kids laughed when they forgot their lines or a flute squeaked. The lack of pressure was refreshing. The students weren't being asked to emulate precocious kids on television, and they appeared on stage without a trace of makeup. Teachers seemed relaxed, enjoying the play like proud parents, despite the screw-ups.

A couple of the jokes would have been considered inappropriate in the U.S. For example, one kid said, "Omar eats too many fry jacks; that's why he's so fat." I noticed that I no longer cringed, wondering whether some offended parent might sue. It reminded me of an incident at a basketball game in Orange County. Steve, who was about eleven at the time, jumped up to prevent a boy from throwing the ball into the basket. Their bodies slammed together. The other boy fell and insisted that Steve had punched him. The boy's father was adamant that Steve had done it deliberately and called police. The police later called me, asking to speak with my son. Fortunately, the referees straightened everything out, but parental behavior was the main reason I hated attending my

kids' games in the U.S. In Belize, I enjoyed freedom of expression, a
freedom I hadn't had during my twenty-two years in the U.S., where
people had become overly sensitive and "politically correct."

During the show, I kept wondering how we'd make it home by boat
in such a severe rainstorm with Doreen and Mildred aboard. I might have
relaxed had we decided to take the *Island Ferry* home, but tonight Duke
would be our captain. He tended to bark orders and make a boat ride by
night unpleasant for all of us. By nine, the play was over and we helped
the old ladies climb on board the *Island Rider*. Still tethered to the dock,
the boat rocked ever so slightly, and the women had trouble taking seats.

A few minutes after we left David's pier, Duke said, "Hand me the
flashlight. Is that a sailboat in front of us?" He slowed down to a mere
two miles per hour. At this rate, it would take us two hours to get home.

"Are we almost there?" said a little old lady's muffled voice from
underneath her plastic raincoat. I laughed inwardly, although this was
nearly as hellish a boat ride as the time we almost capsized.

The rain slapped our faces. Mildred had her neck tucked into her
chest like a turtle. Doreen, my brave mother-in-law, said this reminded
her of her boating days in Newfoundland as a child. Every ten seconds
I heard, "Are we almost there?" We ignored Mildred because the answer
was too depressing. Suddenly, Duke stopped the boat completely.

"What's wrong?" Doreen asked.

"I'm looking for our channel marker," Duke replied.

"Dad, you've barely left town," Steve said. Duke was paranoid
about hitting rocks and seemed disoriented as the clouds blocked the
moonlight and stars. The rain was unusually cold, although soothing
gusts of warm wind reminded me we were still in the Caribbean.

"Where's the coastline?" I asked Duke, not being able to see a single
light on the beach.

"Dad's almost on top of the reef," Steve replied. My eyes focused
on the water, and I realized we'd drifted several hundred feet starboard,
almost brushing coral heads. No wonder we couldn't see the coast.

"We need to find the marker close to our house," Duke said, continuing to let the boat drift in neutral as he tried to get his bearings.

"Who cares where the marker is? Get closer to shore," I yelled.

Duke took his time pushing the throttle forward, one millimeter at a time. I wanted to yank the damn throttle into full forward motion before the reef sucked us in. Painful rain attacked our faces, and we'd all lost our patience.

Please get us home safely.

"There's the flashing light on our boat dock," Steve said, pointing to a flickering light in the distance. I scrunched up my eyes, trying to squeeze out the rain, and spotted it, too.

"Duke, you see it?"

"Barely," which I knew meant, "No."

"First I have to find our channel marker," Duke said.

"Go toward our house! Stop looking for the marker," Steve shouted, his voice muted by the sound of a train engine right behind us.

"What the hell is that?" I screamed, thinking that another boat had come up right behind us. There was no light, but that didn't strike me as unusual; many locals never turned on their navigation lights. They enjoyed intimidating the gringos.

"It's the bilge pump," Duke said. "It won't stop running."

"Is that serious?" I asked. Duke didn't answer. At this point I no longer cared. The orange light at the end of our boat dock gave me hope.

"Here, Steve, flash the light on the markers," Duke ordered. He'd placed five markers in a row with reflective tape so we could identify our dock at night. Once he recognized those five markers, Duke could breathe again.

"We made it!" I said jokingly to Doreen and Mildred, hoping to lift their spirits. They were not amused as we helped them step first onto the wobbly bow, then onto the uneven planks of our wooden pier. The boys carried their suitcases, and I held onto Mildred and Doreen, our arms interlocked while Josh pointed the flashlight in front of us.

As soon as I walked in the front door, I took out the rum and poured four stiff rum and Cokes. "Here's Steve's room, where you'll be sleeping," I told Doreen and Mildred, now tranquilized by the booze. "Hope you don't mind sharing a room." They didn't smile or say thank you.

All of us splurged on long, hot showers before bed. Duke and I didn't count the number of minutes this time; we figured there was enough rainfall for at least one good shower each.

I slept beautifully, almost forgetting that my mother-in-law and her sister were with us.

The following morning, I crept upstairs trying not to make noise and saw Doreen and Mildred both sitting stiffly on the rattan couch. "Good morning," I said cheerfully.

"I can't sleep with her; she snores," Doreen said, pointing at Mildred.

"She reads all night, and I like to get up early," Mildred countered.

I couldn't believe I had to deal with these bickering sisters. We'd kicked Steve out of his room, forcing him to sleep with his brothers.

I'd offered to reserve two single rooms at the reasonably priced Emerald Resort, a short walk along the beach from our house, but they'd refused. "Don't worry about us; we can sleep on the floor in sleeping bags," Doreen had said before her trip. Now I had to bite my tongue.

"Josh, come help me scramble the eggs," I said, hoping that a home-cooked breakfast would change their mood. I set the table for seven and opened the patio glass windows to let the stunning view of the turquoise Caribbean and the massaging breezes spill into our living room. Mildred picked up her fork, stabbed at a speck of egg, then started babbling. With my eyes shut, it sounded like we'd never left Orange County.

"I go to Carl's Jr., where I can get a 99-cent hamburger," Mildred said. "I always get up at five to do my laundry, eat breakfast and then go to JC Penney and stand in line. The first 350 people get a coupon for fifteen dollars off. I'm always one of the first in line, every weekend."

"Shut up!" I wanted to scream. "You're in the Caribbean now. Why can't you see the beauty of this place?"

After breakfast, Josh invited Grandma to join him in the pool. "The water's real salty, Gramma," he said. "You have to keep your eyes shut or they sting."

Duke helped me clean the breakfast dishes. When we heard Josh splashing in the pool with Little Juan, we peeked outside. Doreen sat on the coral tile bathing her feet inside the salty pool. She seemed relaxed, and she smiled when Josh asked her to throw a plastic ball for Little Juan and him to chase. I changed into my swimsuit and, with goggles around my neck, joined Doreen. "Isn't the water nice and warm?" I said.

"Oh, the saltwater feels good on my big toe," she said. "It's exactly what the doctor ordered," she said.

"What happened to it?" I asked, staring at her black and yellow toenail, an instant turn-off to jumping in the pool. Doreen explained her toenail infection in detail. Her diabetes was the cause, something fairly common, so she claimed. Mildred refused to swim. Instead, she swayed for hours in the hammock on our balcony. Had I known this moment would be the only civil conversation during their entire two-week stay, I might have savored it longer.

CHAPTER THIRTY-FOUR

The Worst Christmas

CHRISTMAS WAS ONLY TWO DAYS AWAY, and Steve twirled a string of lights around the trunk of the tallest palm tree in front of our house. Duke strung small white lights around the wooded perimeter of our upstairs patio, adding a dose of holiday cheer. Meanwhile, Doreen hibernated in her own world.

She'd been giving everyone the silent treatment for days, hardly budging from the armchair in the living room, where she sat and read for hours on end. I had asked Mildred why Doreen was so uncommunicative. "I think she's mad at me for some reason," Mildred had replied. This wasn't unusual behavior for Doreen. She'd bottle up her feelings and ignore her family for days. Her lack of sociability didn't seem to bother Duke and our boys as much as it tormented me.

"Dinner's ready," I said. Doreen closed her paperback, cranked her body upright and headed out the patio door. She selected the corner hardwood chair, plonked herself down and continued reading al fresco for two more hours. I heard a gentle creak as she pushed the glass door open and skirted Duke's computer desk. She tiptoed to the water cooler and poured a glass of water. As she swallowed her pills, I noticed the skin on her arms and legs. It had taken on the texture of bubble wrap. She must have donated two quarts of blood to the hungry mosquitoes that night. "Doreen, that must hurt," I said pointing to the welts.

"No," she said shortly. She meandered her way to her favorite faded armchair in our living room and sank into it.

I signaled Duke to follow me downstairs to our bedroom, and as soon as I slammed our door, I spewed out my anger. "What the hell's wrong with her? What have we done to piss her off? She's making our Christmas miserable." Duke listened without commenting, something he was an expert at. "I cook, and your mom is rude. She doesn't say 'thank you,' and she hasn't invited us out for dinner once," I continued.

Without uttering a single word, Duke crept back upstairs and confronted his mom. "You know, Sonia spends a lot of time preparing meals for us," he said. His tone was soothing, not argumentative.

"I never asked her to," Doreen barked back. "At home I eat steamed veggies. I don't need much, you know," she continued.

"Well, I think we should take her out to dinner." Duke said.

"I never said you two couldn't go out for dinner."

I heard Duke's flip-flops cross the living room tile toward the staircase where I'd been hiding. I made a *tsssk* sound, and he joined me halfway down the stairs. "Why didn't you ask why she's so mad and why she quit talking to Mildred? Why can't she invite us out for a change?" Duke hated confrontation and had given up on his mom years ago.

Christmas morning, Josh knocked on our door at 6 A.M. "Can I open my present?" he asked.

"Are Grandma and Aunt Mildred awake yet?" I asked.

"No," he said.

"We have to wait until they wake up, Josh." He went back to his room, and thirty minutes later, I heard his feet flying down the stairs. "They're up now, can I open my present?"

"Wait till we make coffee," Duke said.

This year we didn't have a Christmas tree and only one present apiece for Josh, Doreen and Mildred. Alec had his WaveRunner. Steve hoped for a sailboat and said he didn't want anything else.

I cut some bamboo branches from the jungle behind Juan's house and decorated them with shiny red and green ornaments I'd purchased from Dahlia's store. Bamboo wasn't Christmas-like, but it would have to do. Josh watched me scoop Folgers coffee into a paper filter. The minute we each had a mug in our hands, he said, "Can I open it now?" It pleased me to see him more excited over this one gift in Belize than over a two-foot stack of presents in California. He couldn't wait to play his new video game.

"Here, Mom, this is for you," Duke said handing Doreen her present.

"I told you not to get me anything," she replied curtly.

Duke had bought a replica of a Mayan vase with inscriptions for Doreen and one for Mildred. "Thank you," Mildred said, wrinkling her nose. Doreen ripped the paper off like a kindergartner and said, "Nice."

The two women sat diagonally across from one another in our living room, still not talking. I wondered how they were coping since they shared the same bed and the same bathroom.

After breakfast, I could not stand another second in their company, so I jumped on my bike and rode to Oscar's gym to release my anger. Lifting heavy weights always helped.

Three hours later I returned, tired and dripping sweat. Since I had to cook Christmas dinner amid this miserable atmosphere, I decided to do it with my favorite music blasting in my ears. No Christmas music here, just dance music to make me happy.

I mixed the flour, sugar and butter to "Beat It" by Michael Jackson and chopped onions to the sounds of "Thriller." Donna Summer and Barry White helped me with the roast turkey, stuffing, mashed potatoes and gravy. I was quite proud of myself. When all seven of us sat down to dinner, Alec asked, "Is this a Belizean turkey?"

"Yes, no hormones injected in this one. I think it's delicious, don't you?" I said.

"Very good." Duke replied on cue.

During dinner, we heard footsteps and giggles approaching, followed by a loud knock on our front door. All of a sudden, three stunning young American girls with perfect smiles showed up singing, "We wish you a Merry Christmas." Steve immediately jumped out of his seat to greet them at the door. They brought so much energy and joy that I was grateful they were renting Betty's villa for a few days. The girls reminded me of bouncy cheerleaders as they handed Steve a plate of cookies with thick white frosting, and red and green sprinkles. I asked them where the cookies were from.

"We brought them with us from home," they said. Josh and Alec landed on the cookies like flies and stuffed their faces. I sensed this reminded them of the California life they missed.

The day after Christmas was our final full day with Doreen and Mildred.

"Would you like to go out for dinner tonight?" Doreen said as we opened the front door.

"Thank you, Doreen, that would be very nice," I said, surprised by her sudden change in attitude. Duke asked her what kind of food she wanted to eat.

"Fish, baked potato and vegetables, without any seasonings," she said. I suggested Capricorn, a popular restaurant catering to tourists. Duke called for reservations, but it had no openings during peak tourist season. We decided to have dinner at Emerald Resort instead. Just before dinner, Duke told me his mom didn't have any money and asked whether he could pay for dinner. She promised she'd pay him back later.

Duke took off with Mildred and the boys, leaving me no choice but to walk with Doreen. I led the way along the narrow sandy path, with Doreen toddler-stepping behind me. I had nothing to say, nor did she.

Duke had selected a table in the back corner of the restaurant by the window. We were the only customers. "Let's have rum and Coke instead of wine," Duke said. I agreed, as the cheapest bottle on the wine list was $50.

"I'll have a glass of red," Mildred said.

"They can't afford wine, so I'll have water," Doreen said.

Our drinks arrived and, just as we took our first sip, the deafening sound of a generator drowned out our voices. "What's that?" I shouted.

"Pooh! What's that smell?" Josh said placing his napkin over his nose and mouth. A cloud of pungent kerosene and insecticide hit us. The waitress approached our table. "That's the fogging machine," she said raising her normally soft voice. I felt a coat of chemical spray lining the inside of my mouth, and as I tasted the bitter poison, I imagined cancer cells multiplying in our throats.

"Duke, go find the owner," I yelled in a panic. All staff members had disappeared except our waitress.

"I think Joyce went home," our waitress said.

"I don't want to eat here," Alec said.

"My throat and mouth are sore," Steve said.

"I bet we get poisoned and die," Josh added, still wearing his napkin as a face mask.

"Let's just leave." I said. We'd ordered our food, but our waitress seemed relieved.

"I understand," she said. "I'm allergic to that spray, too." As we walked downstairs toward the beach, Tania, Joyce's daughter, suddenly reappeared at the bar, as did some of the hotel guests.

"There you are!" Duke said sarcastically to the staff. "You left while they sprayed, and we were stuck with the fumes in the restaurant. Why do you spray during dinner?"

"The mosquitoes out here were so bad, we had no choice." Tania replied.

"I'll talk to Joyce later about our bill." Duke said. He refused to pay a dime.

Doreen and Mildred stumbled along the beach with Duke's flashlight lighting the path ahead. All of us were starving; I opened three cans of spaghetti and toasted some bread. Duke picked a DVD, and we all watched, except Doreen, who picked up her book and sat in the corner.

The following morning at eight, Doreen paced the living room floor. She'd packed her bags, showered and asked Duke where to put her suitcase.

"You still have three hours before you catch your flight," he said. "No need to hurry."

"Would you like a cup of coffee?" I asked Doreen.

"No, that's OK."

Doreen took her departure seat this time, instead of her reading seat. Her back faced me, and she started tapping her foot on the tile.

Both Mildred and Doreen wore the same black suits they'd arrived in. A funeral parlor would have been a more appropriate setting for their drab attire than a Caribbean beach. Duke and I sat at our computers. Both of them were now staring at us. Between the foot tapping and the clock ticking, I was going crazy. There was nothing I wanted more than to yell at the top of my lungs, "Why the hell did you come here? You don't speak to one another, you're not pleasant to be around, you're never funny, you never say 'thank you' and you haven't done or seen anything."

To stop the torturous thoughts chasing around in my head, I decided to clean the shelves in our bedroom. As usual, Duke stayed at his computer, ignoring the sisters. They stared at the kitchen clock. It seemed sad to let precious time simply run by, especially when the rest of your life could be counted in years rather than decades.

Duke decided to take them to the airport earlier than planned. I sat between them. The kids gave Grandma and Mildred a quick peck on the cheek and stayed home.

Duke docked the *Island Rider* at David's pier and found a taxi. Once we reached Tropic Air, Duke ran inside and checked them in. A few minutes later, Doreen stepped inside the building and waited in line. "I've already checked you in." Duke said. "Let's get your bags tagged." Their three suitcases were outside. "Here, Mom, three tags for your bags."

"I don't want my tags stapled to hers," Doreen said.

"Come on, Mom, that's silly," Duke said, separating the tags and throwing Doreen's into her hand.

I wanted to leave, but Duke insisted on making sure they got on the plane. Once the flight was announced, Doreen looked like she was running a senior citizen marathon to board the small Cessna, with poor Mildred hunched over, trying to keep up.

"I hope they're forced to sit next to each other," I said.

The ladder was pulled up and the plane inched forward. The pilot revved the engine for take-off, then pulled off the runway onto some grass.

"Oh, no! Just our luck," I said.

"Another plane's landing," Duke said. "Don't worry. They'll be gone in a second."

CHAPTER THIRTY-FIVE

Work Permit

With Doreen and Mildred finally gone, Duke and I celebrated New Year's Eve with a bottle of French champagne. Duke wiggled the champagne cork between his thumb and index finger, letting the gas hiss out in a slow, controlled manner. He then filled our plastic wine glasses, and I wrapped my lips over the rim to catch the bubbly overflow before it puddled on the kitchen countertop.

"Here's to our six months in Belize and to the start of our successful property management business," I said, clinking Duke's plastic glass. "We need to submit our trade license paperwork to Town Board," I added, handing Duke the paperwork. "I checked, and the next meeting is in two weeks."

"We can't submit anything till we get our residency papers and a work permit," Duke said, leaving the application on top of some old magazines on the coffee table with barely a glance.

Did Duke have amnesia? It couldn't be the champagne. He'd barely touched it.

"What are you talking about?" I shrieked. "The whole reason we paid $5,000 for the QRP was to start our own business. As long as we hire Belizeans, we're fine. Have you forgotten?"

"That's not what I read," Duke said in a tone that signaled the start of an argument.

"What the hell are you talking about?" Now I was worried. *Was Duke turning into my worst nightmare: an expat bum?* He was the one who'd done all the research on the benefits of the QRP program versus the work permit, and we both had reached the conclusion that filing for the QRP was the best way for us to proceed.

"But we still don't have our QRP papers," Duke said.

"So you want us to apply for a work permit?" I said. "That's even worse than waiting for the QRP cards. It could take another two years or more. Remember what we heard from other expats? It's such a pain to get. I'll call Allan right now. He and Patty came in under the QRP."

Allan confirmed I was right. He'd started a tourist shop on the island under the QRP program.

Duke headed over to the refrigerator and took out the bottle of champagne. He topped off our glasses, allowing the fizz to settle before adding more.

Alec and Josh stumbled out of their room with Little Juan chasing them. "Now I hide. You count," Little Juan said. He could play for hours, always hiding in the same spot: behind the rattan couch.

"Let's go outside," Duke said. I swallowed a sip of cold champagne and followed him down the wooden staircase where Steve stood — muscular and tanned — on a tall ladder. He'd borrowed it from Juan and was sanding the exterior wood on our house. Steve volunteered to treat all our wood, both inside and out, with a coat of Cetol — marine varnish — we'd custom-ordered from the U.S. We offered to pay him, but he refused. "I guess he's hoping for that sailboat," Duke muttered. I couldn't believe this was the same Steve who now asked us how he could help.

We sat underneath the palm-fronded umbrella enjoying the late afternoon breezes. "Since you're a lawyer, why don't you fill out our license application?" I suggested. "Once we get our license, we can walk along the beach and introduce ourselves to homeowners. Doesn't that sound like a job in paradise?" I added.

The Christmas holidays were almost over, and the boys were outside fishing from our pier. Steve now begged us to allow him to study from home. He claimed he could work better alone than at Matt's house. He promised to finish all his required units for the entire year in just two months.

"Should we let him?" I asked Duke.

"He's definitely changed, and seems more motivated than Alec," Duke said. "And he's got online teachers for support. We can check his grades along the way."

With Steve seemingly on the right track, my worries had shifted toward Alec. He reminded me of a wilting flower. I worried that his weight loss was due to a growing depression.

After a restless night, my morale received a boost when Duke opened his e-mails the following morning.

"Good thing I left work comp," Duke said.

"Why's that?" I asked.

"Jane e-mailed that the entire California work comp field is being revamped. That's real bad news for attorneys," Duke said, enjoying his morning coffee.

"I'm so glad I quit when I did," he continued. "Where's the application for the Trade License?"

I walked over to the stack of magazines and handed it to him.

"Don't forget we need a cover letter to the mayor with the application," I said.

Duke hadn't lost his attorney skills, and he filled out the paperwork in no time at all. After breakfast I decided to take the *Island Ferry* to town and drop the application off at Town Board in time for the members to make a decision at their mid-January meeting.

Now it was up to the mayor and her staff whether we could get our property management business going.

CHAPTER THIRTY-SIX

The Man with Power

W E'D HEARD SO MUCH ABOUT Mr. Henry from Teresa and Juan, he sounded like a celebrity. Even Little Juan worshipped this elderly gent, who had a reputation as a wealthy and generous man.

"Henry come today," Little Juan said, propelling himself to the top of our stairs like a torpedo, complete with sound effects. In the U.S., Little Juan would probably be diagnosed with ADHD. In Belize, his mom controlled him with spankings, which she called "lashings."

"Mr. Henry always bring me toys and books," Little Juan said.

"Lucky you," I responded.

"He want me go to good school," Little Juan continued.

"What kind of toys? Spiderman?" Josh asked, shoveling frosted flakes into his mouth.

"Yes. He know I like Spiderman and fast cars," he said, making sure we heard tires screeching as he zoomed through our living room.

Henry owned the villa closest to Teresa and Juan's house, and I couldn't wait to hear his reaction to Little Juan's English. Steve had been teaching him the alphabet and sounding out letters at our house almost every morning. I was so proud to see Steve take an interest in helping this little boy learn how to read, something neither one of his parents could do.

"It's not fair," Alec said, carrying his schoolbooks to our boat. "Why can Steve study at home and not me?"

"He studies better alone and wants to focus on his SATs," I said, hoping we weren't making a mistake allowing him to follow his Internet curriculum at home. I had noticed a change in Steve's attitude: He had become self-motivated.

"You do better with a teacher," Duke said, getting the boat engine started.

"Kimberly doesn't teach," Alec said. "She just babysits."

"Well, Matt's following the same grade as you," I said, pushing off from our dock.

"Matt's just like Josh; he doesn't pay attention."

"That's why Kimberly's there, to make sure you get your work done," I said, leaning back in the seat as Duke increased the boat's speed.

"Sharon and I are trying to get more kids to join your Internet school next year," I added.

"I prefer to go back to California."

"That's not an option," Duke said.

"All the kids here are stupid," Alec complained.

I ignored his comment and remained quiet for the rest of the boat ride. I'd run out of things to say to try to make him feel better.

Alec jumped off the boat at Xanadu pier and refused to say "bye." I watched him stride along the beach, his long, ostrich-skinny legs making short work of the walk to Matt's house. I felt guilty forcing him to go to an Internet school he disliked when Steve could study at home.

"He'll be fine," Duke said, turning the boat and heading for home.

"Henry must be here," I said, noticing that his villa had sprung to life, windows wide open and classical music blaring from the stereo in his living room. "I can't wait to meet him."

All morning, I kept peeking out the window hoping to catch a glimpse of Henry. I wanted to find out why Teresa and Juan thought so highly of him. *Perhaps I was jealous that they liked him more than they liked us?* The cynical part of me wondered what he had done or given them to earn their adoration. We certainly didn't get the royal treatment, despite our gifts of food, clothes, paints, canvases and toys for Little Juan. "Perhaps it's because they see us every day, so we're no longer special," I told Duke, trying to justify what felt to me like a slight.

"Why do you care?" Duke said.

"I like people to like me," I said. "Don't you?"

Duke shrugged.

Instead of studying, Steve spent the entire day varnishing the mahogany wooden beams on our living room's vaulted ceilings. The potent smell of varnish permeated every room, making my sinuses feel like they'd been sprayed with a strong chemical. I felt tempted to ask Steve when he was going to do his schoolwork, but decided to let him take charge of it himself. Duke and I wanted to see if, indeed, Steve would take care of his studies on his own. Part of me hoped he had matured and realized this was his future.

When it was time to pick up Josh and Alec, we spotted Henry. From the back, Henry had the physique and posture of a younger man, though his white hair and face showed he was in his seventies. Little Juan jumped into the sea and hoisted himself out onto the dock like a jack-in-the-box under Henry's praiseful watch.

As we strolled down the pier, the weight of our bodies made the wooden planks shake, and Henry turned toward us. He extended his right hand, shook mine firmly and, with a distinguished, Morgan Freeman-like voice said, "You must be Sonia. Such a pleasure to meet you." He did the same formal handshake with Duke and smiled, showing a set of solid, pale, butter-colored teeth.

"Would you like a boat ride? We're heading to town," Duke said.

Henry accepted, saying his fridge was empty and he needed groceries.

"I hear you're from L.A.?" Henry said.

"Orange County, actually, south of L.A." Duke replied.

Henry scooted closer to me on the seat. He had a hearing problem, especially with the engine revving. He asked me about my accent. I told him I was born in Denmark and spent my youth in Nigeria, Paris and England. Apparently I'd forged an immediate connection by acknowledging my Danish background, as Henry had a Swedish heritage. "Did Teresa show you the photos of my house in Michigan?" he asked. "It was in *Architectural Digest*."

"No, I haven't seen it."

"I'll ask her to show it to you. It has beautiful Swedish antique furniture and porcelain."

When Duke docked our boat in town, he said, "We'll meet you here in two hours if you want a ride back."

"I'll be there, thanks."

On the boat ride home, I invited Henry for dinner. He accepted. "I hope you like New York cheesecake," I said. "I have the best recipe."

"I'll let you know if it's the best after I taste it. I'm a cheesecake expert," he said.

I thought it would be nice for the boys to have a "substitute" Grandpa to talk to during dinner, because he reminded me of my dad in many ways.

When my cheesecake was ready to bake, I opened the oven door, lit a match and heard a horrendous bang. The whole family converged on the kitchen. Duke charged outside to close the valve on our missile-shaped gas tank. Steve grabbed one side of the stove, and Duke reached back and slowly edged it away from the wall. The base of the oven screeched as it scraped the coral tile. I pointed a flashlight at the hoses, and Steve and Duke took turns inspecting each one for a leak. "I'm sure it's the valve and not the hose," Duke said. "I'll call Leo and see when he can fix it."

"Why did this have to happen today?" I lamented.

I placed the cheesecake on a cookie sheet and carried it over to Teresa's for help. "Please can I use your stove?"

"Why it explode? It's new, no?" Teresa asked.

"I have no idea. I hope Leo can fix it fast."

"Let me get Miss Maureen's keys," she said. "Miss Maureen no mind if you use her stove." Maureen was the only homeowner we hadn't met, but from what Teresa had told me, they were all friends.

Since gossip spreads faster than a virus, I asked Duke to send Maureen an e-mail informing her I would be using her oven. "If she knows it's for Henry, I'm sure she won't mind," I said.

Henry arrived promptly at 5:30 P.M., dressed in khaki pants, a beige linen shirt and carrying two bottles of chilled white wine, one in each hand.

During dinner, the boys enjoyed Henry's anecdotes, including tales of his former job as a plastic pipes salesman. *How could I have pigeon-holed him as an intellectual snob who'd attended an Ivy League college?*

Henry admitted he hadn't even graduated high school. He claimed he was self-educated and proceeded to explain how his love of books had turned him into a scholar. "I spend my time reading the arts, philosophy and history," he said, taking a bite of cheesecake. My admiration for him grew, based on his honesty and achievements.

"How do you like my cheesecake, Henry?" I asked.

"I'd place it up there among the top New York restaurants," he replied.

Now I liked him even more.

CHAPTER THIRTY-SEVEN

Sailboat

"I HOPE WE'RE NOT MAKING A MISTAKE," I said, twirling my hair, a nervous habit of mine.

"I think the sailboat's a good idea," Duke said. "Besides, he'll want to stay for another year if he's got a boat to fix and sail."

After months of subtle remarks, followed by overt requests, we'd given in to Steve's desire to own a fixer-upper sailboat. "A sailboat's better than a girlfriend," I said, trying to justify the expense.

"Yeah, that should keep him busy," Duke agreed.

The following morning Duke and Steve left together for Belize City. For the first time in years, I watched them walking side-by-side, smiling and chatting while holding onto their lunch packs. This close bond between father and son was what I'd been hoping for; it was a moment to cherish forever.

They sat on the bench at the end of our pier waiting for the early-morning *Island Ferry*. Once in town, they would catch the first *Thunderbolt* to Belize City. Duke planned to register the coordinates on his GPS so he could find his way home with the boat. I tried to stay calm, but worried about two inexperienced sailors crossing the Caribbean on an old, 27-foot Luger. *Was this used sailboat even water safe?* I advised Duke to hire Caesar, an experienced pilot, to deliver it to our boat dock. But he insisted on doing it alone with Steve. Men had to be men. "It's part of our adventure," Duke told me. Later I realized that Duke wanted this father-son bonding experience.

The *Thunderbolt* whizzed to Belize City in 90 minutes, thanks to its two powerful 250-horsepower engines.

With the sailboat's 15-horsepower engine, I had doubts they would make it back the same day. Duke called me on his cell around 3 P.M., his voice drowned by the deafening *putt-putt* of the boat's underpowered motor. I asked Duke to repeat every sentence, and all I could decipher was "home by dusk."

Fortunately, a full moon cast enough light to chaperone them to safety. I could hear the sluggish *putt-putt* as the boat approached our pier; the repetitive hum could put anyone to sleep.

Alec, Josh and Little Juan ran ahead of me to see the sailboat, which Duke and Steve anchored fairly close to shore. As they waded toward the beach, I noticed that Duke's back had the angular look that signaled his back spasms were in full swing. Steve's sunburned face looked painful to the touch, and both claimed they were exhausted and starving. They collapsed on the couch and would probably have enjoyed being spoon-fed, had I offered.

"Hey Steve, like your boat?" Josh asked, filling his water glass.

"It has a small leak, but I can fix that tomorrow," he said.

A symphony of loud snores from Steve and Duke kept me tossing and turning all night.

The following morning I woke up before Duke, a rare occurrence. Alec and Josh's door stood wide open, and I noticed the crumpled sheets on their empty beds. Heading to the balcony, I heard voices echoing from Steve's sailboat. In daylight, I saw the white and navy trim of the boat; it appeared to be in better shape than I'd expected.

Coffee mug in hand, I headed to the beach, Cookie behind me sniffing the sand. Loud hammering noises came from inside the boat, where my boys were working together as a team. A camaraderie had blossomed between the three of them, something I never anticipated prior to our move. I proudly soaked this in as another memory to cherish. This is what I'd secretly been hoping would happen when we left materialism and our family problems behind in Orange County.

"Want to see my boat?" Steve asked, spotting me on the dock.

"Sure," I said. "Let me get my swimsuit on. I'll be right back."

A few minutes later, I swooshed through the shallow water toward his boat. Josh jumped off the bow into the deeper water, where Little Juan was monkeying around, as usual, without supervision. Belizean kids, even four-year-olds, were left unattended for hours. Consequently, they developed a daring streak that would give many mothers in the U.S. a heart attack.

I climbed the narrow steps into the sailboat and landed on a sheet of rotted plywood Steve had removed from the cabin below.

"Come inside," Steve said. I stepped down the wooden ladder backward and landed in the cabin, which boasted a rusty kitchen sink and stained seat cushions. The boat needed work.

Steve pointed toward the leak he was trying to repair.

"Your sailboat's bigger than I thought," I said.

"I can sleep and cook on it," he said, beaming. "Once it's fixed, I'd like to sail across the Caribbean."

"You'll need sailing lessons first, don't you think?"

"I've been reading about it on the Internet," he acknowledged.

Alec spent the entire day with Steve inside the sailboat. I treasured this special moment, watching Alec help his older brother.

This sailboat became Steve's new love, replacing Kari, Mandy and Tina. I was grateful they no longer existed in his life.

Even Alec was coming out of his shell these days. When a San Francisco family with three kids between the ages of ten and fourteen rented

Maureen's villa, Alec approached Brian, the fourteen-year-old. "Want to try my WaveRunner?" he asked.

"Can I?" Brian said, eyes gleaming with excitement.

"Sure. Let me show you how it works."

Alec pushed his WaveRunner and started the engine. The revving sound brought Brian's parents stumbling down Maureen's staircase. Brian's dad asked if the whole family could take Alec's WaveRunner out for a spin, and Alec agreed. I cringed: Belizean gas cost $5 per gallon.

Later that evening, Brian invited Alec to a restaurant with his family, to thank him. Alec accepted, without consulting us first. I was proud of his growing assertiveness.

"Mom, I miss my friends in California. Can I go back for my birthday?" Josh asked when I tucked him into bed. A little disappointed that the issue of returning "home" kept cropping up, I assumed it had to do with Brian and his family reminding Josh of his friends in the U.S.

The following day, when the parents called their kids inside to pack their suitcases, Brian said, "I don't want to go home. Can we stay here?" Brian's dad approached Duke outside.

"I think we're going to buy land here and build a house," he said. Duke handed him our newly printed business card, though we hadn't officially received our license from Town Board to start our property management business.

As I strolled along the beach feeling sad that my kids no longer had playmates, I noticed a new guest by our pool. Henry had so many visitors; as soon as one left, a new one arrived. They varied in age from students to senior citizens, and some traveled from Europe to stay with him. Sue, a friend of Henry's from Michigan, introduced herself. "I met your son, Steve," she said. "What a polite young man."

"Thank you," I said, proud she was meeting him now and not two years ago.

"I asked him how he likes it here," she said, placing her towel on the lounge chair.

"What did he say?"

"I have my boat, my parents take care of me, so why not stay one more year in Belize?"

"He really said that?" I was so happy to hear him say he liked living here. I had been worried that Steve would beg to move back to Orange County so he could finish his senior year at his old school. I had no one except Grandma to send him to, and I preferred that he stay with us. Now I had no regrets about the money we'd spent on his sailboat.

He was on the right path.

CHAPTER THIRTY-EIGHT

In Business

Two weeks had passed since Town Board's most recent meeting, and still no news.

"I can't keep waiting like this," I said to Duke one morning. "Why don't we both go ask the mayor?" Duke nodded and suggested I search for my British passport.

"It might speed things up," he said. Although Belize had gained independence from Britain in 1981, the country maintained a strong respect for Queen Elizabeth II, and my British passport had three weeks left before it expired.

Town Board was a banana-colored, two-story building on the beach. An arrow pointed upstairs to the mayor's office.

"Good morning," I said, exaggerating my British accent for the receptionist. She wore a classic dark blue, knee-length skirt and a creamy silk blouse. Her clothes and high heels looked alien to me after months in Belize. I discreetly pulled my tank top and shorts down as far as they would go, then introduced Duke and myself to Louisa, the receptionist.

"I saw your file," she said. "I'm sorry, but your property management business was not approved by Town Board."

My posture drooped; I felt like she'd announced an "F" on my final exam.

"Please, can we talk to the mayor?" Duke asked.

"Of course," she said, heading down the hallway with our red file in hand. She stopped at the second door on her left, peeked through the glass window and lightly tapped on the door. She whispered to the mayor, then waved us in.

The mayor, a plump, mocha-skinned woman, rose partly out of her executive chair, leaned halfway across her wide mahogany desk and extended her right arm. "Good morning, Mr. and Mrs. Marsh. Please take a seat. How may I help you?"

Duke thanked her profusely for seeing us without an appointment, well aware that old-fashioned British manners carried more weight in Belize than any other approach.

"We'd like to hear the outcome of our business license request," Duke said. The mayor had our file open in front of her. She reached for her glasses and skimmed Duke's letter of request to start a property management business on the north part of the island. We both noticed the red stamp, "Denied," on the bottom right corner.

"I regret to inform you that Town Board denied your request," she said.

"Why?" I asked, a little too abruptly.

"Well, we already have several property management firms on Ambergris Caye," she said.

"I realize that, but ours will be focusing on the north part of the island," I said. "Besides, as you know, contractors are building many new houses up north, and as we already live there, we can specialize in properties up north," I continued.

"Sounds good, but we already have too many property managers on the island," she repeated.

Since we had nothing to lose, I explained that we'd paid $5,000 to enter Belize under the QRP program, which meant that we'd be employing local Belizeans to work for us. I slid my British passport across the table, in front of her eyes, like a bribe. "Does this help?"

The mayor opened my passport and said, "Yes."

I couldn't believe it. She picked up a green stamp marked "Approved" and handed us the file.

I almost kissed her. Before leaving her office, I promised we'd do a professional job.

"Now we can officially hand out our business cards," I said, as Duke and I strolled back to our boat, watching tourists purchase shell necklaces and other souvenirs from vendors scampering to get their attention.

"Let's have lunch before we try to drum up some business," Duke said.

Back home we ate our peanut butter sandwiches, then headed north along the beach holding hands. "Isn't this so much better than working in an office?" I said.

"Yeah. I've always wanted to work in shorts and flip-flops," Duke said with a grin.

Everything was looking up, and things were falling into place.

CHAPTER THIRTY-NINE

Fancy Party

"I'M NOT IN THE MOOD to go to Helen's party tonight," I said. "Jennie told me she's stinking rich, and it's dressy. I don't have any dressy clothes."

"I doubt it's that fancy," Duke said. "Wear your orange dress. It shows off your great figure."

"Duke, it's a Spandex beach dress."

"So? You look great in it."

Most houses on the island had a name. Helen's had a website and a fountain imported from the Palace of Versailles.

"You think this fountain is the real thing or an imitation?" I asked Duke, wondering how one would go about purchasing a fountain from the Palace of Versailles and then importing it to Belize.

"She must have paid a ton at customs," Duke said.

I applied extra eye shadow and eyeliner, and daubed Vaseline on my lips. I'd run out of lipstick, and San Pedro didn't have much to choose from — at least, not any color I'd wear.

When I asked Steve to cook dinner for his brothers, he said, "Why should I? They can get their own food." I stared at him until he said, "OK, I'll cook burgers."

We headed out the door, down the stairs and along the dock. "How do I look?"

"You look great," Duke said.

Helen, a rich divorcee, latched onto Curt, a recently separated man. Men — especially attractive, educated men — were in short supply on the island. After living here for a while, we noticed that only strong marriages survived island life. Too many couples turned to alcohol or drugs as a way to escape island fever or boredom.

"Duke, slow down," I said, as the engine stirred up murky water. "This looks like the house on the website. Look at all the lights on the palm trees."

I asked Duke to carry the wine as we headed toward the mansion. I hid behind some hibiscus bushes to peek at the guests. I noticed some expensive-looking gowns and women sipping champagne from thick crystal flutes.

"Duke, I'm underdressed," I said, refusing to come out from behind the bush.

"Look, there's the Versailles fountain from the website," Duke said, pointing beyond the house. I came out of my hiding spot and noticed that the bartender's counter had more booze than the local wine store. Apart from the ten bottles of red wine already uncorked and waiting to be served, there were champagne, white wine, vodka, gin, Chivas and every liquor you could ask for. The bottles were neatly arranged, along with an array of exquisite Waterford crystal glasses.

"Duke, what should we do with our bottle? Want to hide it in the boat?" I whispered, embarrassed by the cheap Cabernet we'd brought. Duke handed our bottle to the bartender, who thanked us politely and said, "I shall tell Helen that you brought her a bottle."

I was so relieved we didn't bring flowers. I had almost cut a few hibiscuses from the bushes surrounding our house and wrapped the stems in foil. Helen's flower arrangements were like the ones you see in expensive hotel lobbies.

"She must have had those shipped from the U.S.," I said, feeling more out of place by the second.

After the bartender poured us a glass of wine, Curt stepped out of the patio doors. He wore white linen pants with the cuffs rolled up and a dark blue, silk shirt. He also was barefoot. He'd slicked his hair back, which made him look sexier than when I'd met him with his wife a few months before.

Duke wore his old flip-flops, a pair of beige shorts and his sailboat shirt. He'd wanted to wear Top-Siders, but his had rotted since we moved to Belize. Leather didn't last in humidity.

"Take your shoes off," I whispered. "You'll look more hip."

Hors d'oeuvres were visible on every table, and a flurry of waiters catered to everyone's requests. As the evening progressed, the waiters made sure our wine glasses were never empty. Most of the expats living on Ambergris Caye were here, as were the mayor and other important Belizeans. I started mingling and got separated from Duke for a while. Strangely enough, people seemed to know about our new property management business before I even had a chance to bring it up. I started to feel uncomfortable about all their fake-sounding congratulations. *Why were their smiles so plastic?* I didn't understand what was going on.

It was after midnight when Duke drove the *Island Rider* home. I collapsed on our couch after a night of too much wine, feeling dehydrated, ugly and tired; I knew I'd pay for it in the morning.

The aroma of coffee woke me, and I climbed the stairs with three Tylenol in my hand. I couldn't speak until I drank some water. "It seems like we're on people's shit list," I said, throwing my legs over the edge of the armchair. "Everyone knows we're starting a business, and we haven't even told anyone. Are we doing something wrong? We need to make a living, so what's going on?"

"It's probably just island politics," Duke said. "They want to see us fail, and they don't want competition."

"Why? I'm sick and tired of all this pettiness," I said. I placed my mug on my desk and checked e-mails. Jennie had sent me a message: "I have some interesting information regarding your website that you should know about, but it stays between you and me, OK?"

Curious, I called her right away.

"Some restaurant and shop owners aren't too happy with what you wrote about them. This is a small community, Sonia. You can't afford to make enemies." I wasn't sure what she meant. Duke had a web page called *Useful Tips for Tourists*.

"We're only giving information on which stores and restaurants are more expensive and which are cheaper. We're giving the facts. How can that offend people?"

"I know, Sonia, but locals get very upset." After Jennie gave me the name of a storeowner who bitched about our website, I re-read what Duke had written in the *Useful Tips for Tourists* section.

"Get ready to pay more for wine on the island. Everything is imported. If you want to save money, do what the locals do; drink the local beer and rum."

How could that statement cause such uproar in the local community? I'd chatted with the wine store owner the night before at Helen's, and she'd complimented me on my dress and seemed friendlier than usual.

Now I felt betrayed. Negative rumors were spreading about us.

I was no longer sure whom we could trust.

CHAPTER FORTY

What's Going On?

O N OUR WAY OUT THE DOOR, I grabbed two small water bottles from the fridge and slathered on my daily dose of sunblock. Duke dabbed his nose, ears and the back of his neck with a thick coat, leaving blobs of white lotion. I'd grown accustomed to smoothing them out for him.

"Let's head down to the rich doctor's house today," Duke said.

"I'm sure he already has a property manager," I ventured.

"So what? He'd probably prefer us," Duke replied.

I was becoming increasingly aware of the potential dangers of stepping on our competitors' turf. Jennie's comment from the day before, about being careful not to make enemies with the locals, resonated in my head. I was feeling insecure, uncertain whether we were pissing off the locals. This seemed so different from what we were used to in the U.S. There, you were free to start your own business. *Were we making a mistake in Belize?*

After seven months, Duke still had the California entrepreneur mindset. He believed, after listening to complaints from a few disgruntled homeowners, that we could offer them better service.

First, we had to introduce ourselves to as many gringo property owners on the north part of the island as possible. We wanted them to know we could take care of any problem right away, since we lived close by. Word of mouth would help us grow our business.

On our trek, we stopped at Journey's End resort for refreshing lime juice. Listening to tourists, I realized how lucky we were to be living here. They always seemed in a hurry to cram their scuba diving and tours into a few expensive, compressed days before returning to their hectic work lives. Duke and I had all the time in the world to enjoy the moment. It was a concept people try to grasp in the developed world through yoga and meditation, but I realized it could blossom organically from living in a peaceful environment.

I relished the idea that Duke and I could visit homeowners and restaurants along the beach and call it a job. Hopefully, an income would soon follow; then we'd finally be self-sufficient and living our dream.

After I downed my last drop of lime juice, Duke lowered himself off the bar stool and checked his camera. "Let's ask Karen if we can interview her and take some photos. We can add her menu to our website and provide more information to tourists," Duke said.

"Great idea."

Karen, an expat who opened a restaurant for tourists north of town, spotted us as we climbed the rickety wooden steps to her restaurant.

"Careful, that plank's flimsy," Duke warned me.

Karen waited behind the screen door with a broom in her hand. I felt uncomfortable, as though I were intruding, especially when she didn't invite us to come inside. Duke explained the nature of our visit, and I sensed a hesitation on her part. Duke, however, was unaware of her reluctance to accept our free advertising offer.

"I bet Karen heard about our website from Linda. You know they're close friends; plus, she buys booze for her restaurant from her," I said, after we were out of hearing range.

"What's that got to do with anything?"

"Duke, don't you remember what Jennie said? Everyone's pissed off with your website, and they all gossip."

"I think you're exaggerating."

"I trust Jennie. She's been here much longer than we have."

We moved our tired legs along the beach path as fast as we could, arriving home parched and exhausted. Duke grabbed a beer and sank into the couch, yawning. I filled a glass of water, and within seconds Steve and Josh joined us to spill out their ambitious plan.

"Can we build our own boat?" Steve asked.

"You already have a boat," I said.

"I mean a small boat," he said, handing Duke a sheet of paper with a drawing and some measurements.

"What are you going to make it from?" Duke asked.

"The plywood in our laundry room."

"We need that for a hurricane."

"Come on, Dad, we have tons of plywood," Josh said.

"It's not even hurricane season," Steve added. "We'll only need two sheets of plywood."

I was impressed he'd drawn up a detailed plan and recruited his brothers to help. How could we refuse when they wanted to work as a team? The boat looked like a box with a tapered end. Steve had made calculations and scribbled numbers on the paper, and I wanted to encourage him to start. Perhaps Steve would end up an engineer after years spent taking things apart in our garage and designing spud guns from Home Depot plastic pipes back in California.

"You can start it tomorrow, but be careful, as Mom and I will be gone in the morning," Duke finally agreed.

After breakfast, we jumped in the *Island Rider* and headed north to meet more potential clients for our business.

"Think the boys will be OK?" I asked.

"Juan's there to check on them. Besides, you know Steve rarely finishes his projects," Duke temporized. He started the engine, veering left to the northern part of Ambergris Caye. The homes grew larger and sparser, while the beaches resembled perfect postcards of the ideal Caribbean island. Patches of translucent water turned into vivid blues and greens. Bright orange starfish, about one foot in diameter, glowed like scattered markers along the shallow seabed. This was the type of location I'd found irresistible when searching for my paradise on the Internet.

Duke docked at the Portofino Resort. "Let's check it out," he said. "We should take photos and add them to our website." Smiling tourists sunbathed at the end of the resort's pier and swam in a roped-off area.

Duke spotted a "For Sale by Owner" sign on a house just north of Portofino. An arrow pointed upstairs where the owners lived. "Let's ask them how much they want," Duke said. We loved the beautiful location and wanted to own our own property, rather than be tied to a homeowners association as we were in our present circumstances.

We climbed the outdoor wooden staircase, in major need of repair, and stopped on the landing in front of an open screen door. "Anyone home?" Duke shouted through the screen. An older woman with short gray hair and pale skin shuffled to the door.

"Can I help you?" she said in an unfriendly tone, refusing to open the door.

"Yes, are you the owner?"

"Yes."

"We're interested in your house for sale," Duke said. She shrugged, refusing to let us in.

"Which resort are you staying at?" she asked.

"We live here." I quickly replied. Her face lit up, smoothing her wrinkles.

"I'm sorry I wasn't very friendly," she said opening the screen door. "I'm so tired of people from the resorts stopping by with no intention of buying, just being nosy."

Anita invited us in for a Belikin beer and introduced us to Dean, her dark-skinned husband. His large, brown eyes complimented a warm, soothing smile.

We sat on their porch overlooking the Caribbean for two hours, discussing island life. They wanted to sell one-and-a-half acres of land, together with their house and a separate cabana in the back. After a tour of the property, which seemed huge, I was already picturing Steve in the self-contained cabana. It seemed ideal for him to study and finish his senior year of Internet high school in peace, until he left for college. Duke loved the idea of owning 130 feet of oceanfront land. The lot included two storage sheds and access to the golf cart road in the back, where Duke and I were already visualizing construction of several commercial buildings.

Dean and Anita were asking $650,000 US for all this land and the buildings.

Obviously, we couldn't afford it without selling our present villa, but we were running through our savings pretty fast with the extra $600 a month for property maintenance and Juan's little house and salary. Duke wanted the freedom to change things. If we wanted to add a small fence or cut down a bush, we had to ask for approval from all three homeowners. We felt we were back in our strict U.S. homeowners' association, where everything required permission. We'd moved to Belize to be free, not to be subjected to more rules and regulations.

Duke and I grew excited about the possibility of owning our own place and having extra land for other potential businesses. "Perhaps we could start a mini-market for tourists and expats," Duke said. "Or even a DVD rental store, so people don't have to take the boat to town."

We knew we'd be pioneers because very little existed this far north. Both of us felt giddy with new possibilities.

I was so proud of my boys when we returned. They had succeeded in building a small boat in one day. Steve sawed each section of the boat and hammered the pieces together. It looked like a box with a tapered end, and it floated. After attaching Steve's 15-horsepower sailboat engine to it, they took me for a ride on the sea.

It had been an exciting day. At least it was, until the phone rang.

CHAPTER FORTY-ONE

Neighbor Threats

THE PHONE RANG THREE TIMES before Duke hauled himself off the couch to answer it. "Hi, Manuel, what can I do for you?" he said.

Manuel's voice was so loud I could hear every word through the receiver.

"My lawyer's going to be in touch with you," he told Duke.

"Why?" Duke asked in a firm tone.

"Because of what you said about me on your website."

"Fine, let him." Duke responded and hung up.

A tight knot formed inside my stomach. "What's going on?" I asked. "What did you say about him on our website?"

"I just said he charges more than the other boat guys."

Everyone knew Manuel, including Josh, who'd nicknamed him "the hairy gorilla," and that was no exaggeration. His wild caveman look scared me, and I had no trouble visualizing him attacking us in the middle of the night.

"What the hell made him so mad?" I asked. Duke didn't answer.

I pulled up our website on my computer screen and read Duke's segment on *"Beware of being scammed by locals."*

Duke stated that Manuel charged several times the going rate for his boat rides. He also mentioned Manuel's grumpy disposition toward tourists. "How could you say that?" I challenged him. "Now we're in deep shit. You really need to think before you write stuff like that, especially on a small island."

"He shouldn't be getting away with taking advantage of tourists," Duke retorted.

I knew Duke was right, especially as visitors renting our neighbors' villas had asked about Manuel's exorbitant boat fees. Feeling sorry for them, we'd say, "Yes, he does charge more, and we can give you the names of a couple of local guys who are far more reasonable."

Manuel worked for Jessica, a well-established property manager in town. She also happened to manage our neighbors' villas. Whenever I heard a boat racing into our shallow waters, followed by loud screeching and engines yanked into reverse, I knew Manuel had arrived. Like a teenager in a forty-five-year-old body, he enjoyed testing the outer limits of safety.

Now I wondered how we could get out of this mess.

Before bed, I rinsed the last few glasses in the kitchen sink and flicked off the lights in the living room.

"Wait, Sonia," Duke said, staring yet again at his computer screen, "They're trying to kick us out."

"Who's trying to kick us out?"

"Our three neighbors."

"You're kidding. Why?"

"They've listed five new resolutions all geared toward us. They want everyone to vote, and you know they'll win, 'cause they're the majority."

"What do they want?"

"We're not allowed more than one boat," Duke read from the screen. Now I got mad. Steve loved his sailboat and Alec his WaveRunner. Now we were being forced to get rid of them? Duke then read, "We can't have a clothesline on our patio, and we're not allowed another dog after Cookie dies. There's also something about noise. I guess they think Cookie and the kids make too much noise." Now I was fuming.

Duke rubbed his eyes and continued reading. "We can't keep anything outside our house, not even our barbecue. They say it spoils the character and quality of the *resort.*"

"This isn't a *resort,*" I scowled.

"Exactly! But they call it a resort so they can get rental income."

How could all three of them coordinate a detailed list of resolutions so quickly, especially since they all lived in different corners of the U.S.?

Suddenly, we were facing small-town values. We had never expected the American homeowners to turn against us. For the first time in almost a year, Duke was back in his courtroom. His relaxed island attitude had morphed into combative attorney.

I felt sick from betrayal. So many questions spun around my head. This seemed all too abrupt. *How did we become the enemy? What about our dinners and conversations, and the cheesecakes and peanut butter cookies I'd baked for them? How about all the free boat rides we gave them and their guests to town, and the repairs Duke took care of while they were back home in the U.S? Why was this happening? I thought we had become close friends.*

"Sonia, there's one more clause. They say we can't start a home-based business."

"Someone must have told them about our website," I said. "Wow, gossip spreads fast here, doesn't it?"

"I'm sure Manuel bitched about us to Jessica," Duke said. "She must have sent all three of them an e-mail telling them we're trying to take over her job as property manager of Villas Tropicales."

"Jessica must have told them we've pissed off all the locals with our website," I said. Things started to make sense, even the ever-so-slight rift I'd felt growing between Teresa and me, which I had associated with her being more interested in Henry and his *gifts.*

Our neighbors relied on Jessica and Manuel to take care of their rental properties. They probably realized there might be severe consequences, even sabotage, if they didn't stick up for them. We'd lived on the island long enough to learn about sabotage. Even Raul had told me several tales of sabotage between locals, such as neighbors fighting. He told us about one couple who used poisonous meat to kill their neighbors' dogs. This kind of stuff happened quite often, and the longer we lived here, the more gossip we heard.

"You're right. That's probably it," Duke said, finally understanding the consequences of his website.

All three neighbors had signed the long list of resolutions. If we didn't comply, it said, we'd be fined and legal action would be taken against us.

"I think we should sell our house immediately and buy the one up north," Duke said.

"That's exactly what they want us to do. Sell and leave," I said.

Duke turned off the living room lights, and we headed to bed.

When I looked at the clock, it was 2:11 A.M. Duke's breathing was heavy with deep, intermittent sighs. I turned toward him and whispered, "You asleep?"

"No, I can't sleep. I keep thinking of how to fight this."

Had it not been for the humidity, intense heat and a fan blowing gusts of air onto our sweaty bodies, we could have been back in Orange County. I hated nights like this, when Duke stressed over a case. So many nights he'd been sleep-deprived because of his job. Tonight was the first such experience in Belize.

At 5 A.M., I caught Duke looking at Orange County attorney job offers on his computer.

Only a few days ago, things were looking up for us. Now things seemed to be falling apart ever so quickly. I'd never felt more confused in my entire life as to where I wanted to live. A year ago, I knew with all my heart how much Duke and I wanted to get away from Orange County and live in Belize. Now I questioned whether we should return to Orange County and, worse yet, Duke seemed to feel the same.

We were shocked by the turn of events, but I knew Duke was right: We had to defend ourselves. He started typing. When he finished, he handed me a copy of his letter before hitting the "send" button. I liked his approach: gentle first, then the jab.

"I find it quite sad that you target us without any discussion or efforts at resolution," he wrote. Then he continued with the nitty-gritty stuff. "We could pick up after our kids, but what about all your guests? They forget towels, toys, glasses, sunscreen, masks and fins. What are we going to do about them? Isn't that selective enforcement?"

Duke's e-mail then addressed the issue of noise, which was obviously aimed at our children playing outside. "Well, Henry," Duke wrote, "several guests have complained about your loud music. You've also been heard yelling at the kids, including our youngest son for playing with a ball outside. This is a residence, not a *geriatric facility*."

Mentally, we both felt in transition. We were experiencing a different kind of stress than in California, but stress nonetheless. We didn't know what to tell our boys. I tried making a list of the pros and cons of Orange County versus Ambergris Caye, and ended up with the same number for both locations. *Had we traded one set of problems in one location for a different set in another location?* I suppose it didn't matter where you moved; you would always have to deal with a particular community's idiosyncrasies. What upset me was the fact that Duke and I had made all these missteps unintentionally, without any hint of what was to come.

"There is one option," I said.

"What's that?"

"You could delete everything you said on your website."

"Honestly, I don't think that would make a difference. They're out to get us."

Another e-mail arrived later that day, this one from Betty, the neighbor I thought I really got along with. She wrote, "The *Island Ferry* refuses to enter the Villas Tropicales channel because of your son's sailboat; it's blocking access to our dock. You need to move it right away."

I felt their presence around us night and day, yet all three neighbors were back in the U.S. This brought back memories of my visit to East Berlin in the late 1970s, when it was still under communist rule. My parents and I were invited out to dinner by an East German businessman. While we ate our boiled potatoes, another man sat alone at a table next to ours, dressed in a raincoat he never took off — just like in an old spy movie. His job was to watch and listen, and inform the party leaders.

Who were the party leaders here?

CHAPTER FORTY-TWO

Sabotage

"Look at Steve's sailboat," I said, leaning over the patio. "The anchor must have come loose."

Duke hurled himself through the open doors and eyed the boat with laser-like intensity. "That's really weird," he said. "There are two anchors; how could they come loose at the same time?"

There hadn't been a storm or any unusual gusts of wind during the night. Yet Steve's sailboat rested on its side, looking wounded. Duke whizzed through the living room like a firefighter on a mission.

"Steve," he yelled through the open bedroom window. "Your boat's hitting the shallows." Steve flew out of bed in his boxers.

I watched them from the upstairs patio, binoculars ready as they waded into the water to inspect the boat. Duke yanked on the rope closest to shore and almost fell backward as it gave way. He held the rope above his head and pointed to the end, where the anchor should have been attached. Through my binoculars, the rope looked as though it had been cut cleanly; I couldn't see any fraying.

Steve dove and resurfaced with the second anchor in his hand, still attached to its rope. The constant wave motion must have loosened it.

They stood still, studying the ropes and talking. I wished I could hear them. Finally, they headed toward the tipped side of Steve's sailboat, using their lower backs and butts as crowbars to force it upright. With the mast pointing skyward again, Steve climbed inside and bailed. Meanwhile, Duke had donned mask and fins. He floated on the surface with his head underwater. I assumed he was looking for the missing anchor. He found it several feet away. Steve helped Duke secure the boat using the one remaining anchor and a sturdy branch, then continued bailing water.

"What happened?" I asked, rubbing aloe vera cream onto Duke's burned shoulders and back.

"It looks like the anchor was cut off," he said. "I can prove it since the rope isn't frayed."

"Who would do that?"

"Your guess is as good as mine."

Duke joined me on the couch with a glass of cold water. It was clear that some members of the island community reacted on a primitive level when they felt threatened. Rather than talk things over in a civilized manner, someone had chosen sabotage to express his or her displeasure with us. Although we had no proof, something was definitely going on. I couldn't believe it was coincidental.

Alec and Josh helped Steve bail water out of his sailboat. Apart from a minor scrape on the side, his boat seemed unscathed.

Duke decided to check the *Island Rider* next.

After a few minutes, Duke returned, out of breath. "Looks like we have a leak."

"You're kidding," Steve said, finishing his second bowl of cereal.

"What's going on?" I asked. "Did you hit coral?"

Steve took a swig of water and reminded Duke how careful he'd been driving the boat back from Oscar's gym the day before. "Remember, we saw dolphins, and you slowed way down."

Steve was right. And none of us recalled any unusual sounds or scraping noises, so it was unlikely we'd hit any rocks or coral. "I'll have to take the boat in to Tom's place tomorrow morning," Duke said.

The kids were home on Easter break, so we lucked out on the timing of this mishap.

"Can I come?" Josh asked, already bored on his third day of vacation.

"First, help me bail out the water," Duke said, carrying two large plastic Folgers coffee cans to the boat.

"I hope we don't sink," I said throwing my flip-flops onto the front seat of our boat and climbing into a four-inch saltwater bath.

Josh scooped water into the Folgers can and dumped it into the sea as though this were a contest and he hoped to win first place.

"Here, take my container and keep bailing while I start the engine," Duke said, throwing his can to me.

Duke pushed the throttle all the way forward to lift the bow and prevent water from entering.

"Duke, it's filling up," I shouted over the loud engines. "Let's go back. We're sinking." Duke ignored me, and after thirty seconds, water quit seeping in. I slowly leaned back in the seat and reached for my coffee mug, then freaked out when I realized we'd have to slow down at Boca del Rio. "Duke, water's going to gush in again." He didn't comment. He knew we had no choice but to take a risk.

"Look who's coming straight toward us," I said. You couldn't miss the wild caveman. Manuel's boat raced through the *no-wake zone*. I locked eyes with him and flashed him a fake smile, hoping to confuse him. He had threatened us over the phone, and I wanted to show him we had the upper hand. Manuel smiled back.

While Duke dealt with boat issues, Josh and I headed off to the beach. Since this was Easter break, I thought Josh needed some kind of activity to keep him busy. I guess the Orange County mom-manager side of me still existed. "Want to try windsurfing?" I suggested.

Josh picked the surfboard with an orange sail, and we waited for a couple of English tourists to join him for a group lesson. The English father and son looked like they'd been cooped up indoors the entire year. I prayed their milky-white skin was protected with sunblock.

After the free trial, Josh said, "It wasn't fun."

Duke joined us for lunch at Caliente, one of my favorite San Pedro beachfront restaurants. "What did Tom say?" I asked, anxious to find out why the *Island Rider* had a leak.

"The locking plug had been removed from our boat," Duke said. "Apparently, it's impossible for this cap to come out on its own."

"Someone deliberately pulled the plug out?"

"Tom said it was definitely sabotage."

I was in shock. All I could think was: *They're not going to destroy my family.*

On the way home, I tried to fight off my negative feelings. I needed time to digest these recent events, so I took Cookie for a walk on the beach. A golf cart pulled up behind me.

"Hi, Mitch, you're back?"

"I'm here to finish my house," he said. "There's a French guy next door you may want to contact for your property management," Mitch continued. "He's a real ass, so you might not want him as a client."

"We've had a lot of crap going on," I said. "We're thinking of selling our house."

"How come?"

I explained everything, and felt relieved I could trust him.

"Duke should sue the hell out of them. He should subpoena the homeowners and force them to fly to Belize and take depositions. Let them feel like they're in hell, not paradise."

I smiled, then laughed hard for the first time in ages when he added, "Beat the crap out of them."

I cut my walk short and jogged home to tell Duke what Mitch had suggested. As I climbed the stairs, I heard Josh in Steve's room. He was asking Steve to help him design an oarlock for the mini-raft he'd made from a crate.

These were the times when I loved Belize. Strong bonds had developed between my sons. Now they counted on one another more than ever. I kept asking myself the same questions: *Can we hold out? Can we get another business going that doesn't involve the locals? Should we fight our neighbors, move to another part of the island or move back to the U.S.?* Time and money were running out. We had to make a decision soon.

Duke researched houses for sale in our old neighborhood in Orange County. While part of me felt a sense of relief, I dreaded going back.

I knew Duke didn't want to work as an attorney, but how else could we afford to move back? Maybe Duke could teach at a high school and get summers off, and I would work, too. My problem was how to get a decent-paying job after being a stay-at-home mom for so long. I no longer wanted to be a personal trainer, but what else could I do to help pay the bills?

Part of me loved Belize, and I couldn't imagine leaving. Perhaps if we sold our villa we could afford a sliver of beach up north and stick a shack on it. I no longer cared what my house looked like. The serenity of nature — the Caribbean, the sunrises, the birds, the lack of people and noise — had changed me. My boys had learned to entertain themselves without TV, video games and electronic gizmos. They had grown close to one another, played outside, made boats, fished and no longer had to *buy* anything to feel fulfilled. Yes, we did buy a used WaveRunner and a far-from-new sailboat. But the boys didn't plague us with constant requests for useless *stuff.*

The kids overheard many of our conversations and soon began asking, "Are we moving back?" I really didn't know what to tell them. We were in limbo.

After I kissed Alec and Josh good night, I joined Duke on the couch before going to bed.

"Have you noticed how people move to Belize and, as time goes by, they get more and more destitute?" I asked. "Take Rob and Mary; they haven't been able to make a living here, either. Now they're stuck and can't afford to move back to the U.S. I don't want us to make the same mistake."

Duke nodded.

"If only we could have started the transcription business. Things might have worked; what do you think?"

"Come here," Duke said, gesturing for me to sit on his lap. I scooted my legs on top of his and nuzzled my face against his cheek. I realized how much we needed one another. I felt proud of him for standing up for our family. My old Dukie was back, the one who protected his family and took action. *Why was I now longing for all the things I said didn't matter to me? Why did I want my old Duke back when it was the old Duke who was so stressed? Was I a hypocrite?* That night, I fell asleep feeling safe, no matter what we decided to do.

The following morning I found Duke busy typing. "I won't let them destroy us," he said, handing me a mug of coffee. "I had a dream, like the dreams I used to have before a trial, where all the right questions pop up in my head. I wrote them all down. You know I'm good at that," he continued. Duke had prepared for his courtroom battle with our neighbors.

During our boat ride to town, my mind wandered back to Orange County and how Duke used to make enough money to support us, but we never seemed to get ahead. *What about the reasons we left for Belize in the first place?* We'd come hoping to defuse Steve's defiance, gain more family time and bond, become less materialistic, get our kids away from Orange County's entitlement attitude and develop gratitude for what we had.

Belize had helped us accomplish these goals. Yet I felt cheated, as though I hadn't truly found my paradise. *How could I be in the heart of the Caribbean and long to find a new purpose in the heart of Orange*

County? I never expected problems with locals and expats. I felt like we were being forced out against our will. We didn't deserve this. What should we do?

CHAPTER FORTY-THREE

Venting

I DESPERATELY NEEDED TO VENT, but whom could I trust?
On an island where today's friends could easily become tomorrow's enemies, I felt so alone. The urge to spew out my thoughts became unbearable, and I had to find relief. So I called the *Island Ferry* and, without any specific plan in mind, hoped I would bump into somebody I could trust.

Lilly's restaurant was booming with breakfasting tourists and scuba divers grabbing their Styrofoam cups of coffee before their tour with Amigos del Mar, the next pier over.

"Don, why are you eating here?" I asked when I spotted Jennie's husband, a contractor on the island. "I thought this was a tourist hangout."

"I hear you're moving," he said, ignoring my question.

"Yes, and we're looking for a place to rent south of town," I replied, refusing to give Don the pleasure of spreading a rumor that we were selling and leaving Belize. Too many expats moved to Belize and couldn't hack it for one reason or another. Yes, were considering leaving, but I hated the thought of becoming another statistic.

"I don't think you'll find a house to rent for five people," Don said. "Besides, people here only rent to families they know. You and Duke need to learn the way of the Belizeans. It takes time to do things their way. This is not the U.S."

I felt like a first-grader, ordered to stand in the corner for some classroom infraction. I refused to let Don see my tears, so I lied to him. "Have to run. I have an appointment."

Annette spotted me on Front Street and waved from her golf cart. "Need a ride?"

"Have time for coffee?" I asked.

"Sure. Hop in."

Annette zig-zagged her golf cart in between bicycles and pedestrians. Dust blew into our faces, but I was used to it now, as I was used to the familiar smells of chicken stews simmering on stovetops; fry-jacks bubbling in oil; and fresh, Snuggle-scented laundry pinned onto slack clotheslines between buildings.

Annette parked close to Sandbucks. We moseyed into the still non-air-conditioned coffee shop and ordered two coffees. Although Annette seemed more compassionate, she said the same as Don. "Things are done differently in Belize. Why do you think Rick and I stay low key? You can't treat this place like it's the U.S."

"But it's our American neighbors who are causing us grief. All those damn resolutions they've voted on, and we have no say since we're in the minority."

"Sonia, one thing you don't get is what works in the States doesn't necessarily work here. People stab one another in the back and screw with their competitors. Belizeans do that, and I know long-term expats have adopted the eat-or-be-eaten mentality. It's a sad part of island culture."

"But our neighbors live in the U.S."

"I know, but they depend on locals to rent and maintain their houses."

Annette helped me realize Duke and I had been too hasty getting our property management business going. Perhaps Duke had been right to take things slowly. I might have caused this mess by pushing us to start a business and do things the American way.

"Every place has its own pressures," Annette said.

The following morning, a strong, musty smell filled my nostrils. All our ocean-facing windows had a sticky coat of saltwater that smeared when I sprayed Windex on them and wiped it off with old newspapers. For some reason, the ink used to print local papers smudged like mascara. The boys commented on how sand crunched underneath their feet in our living room. It was time to clean the house.

After thirty minutes of mopping floors while Duke lounged a few feet away and read, I snapped, "If you spent as much time working on the house as you do reading, this place would be ready to sell." Duke hurled his book onto the coffee table and stomped toward the front door.

I winced, regretting my words. Obviously I'd pushed him too far, but I hated feeling like the maid, especially when he wasn't working. I guess I had a hard time putting up with the way Duke could escape into his own world and I couldn't. I wanted a solution to our life. Were we going to stay here or move back to California?

Duke stormed out toward his beloved boat, slamming the door behind him.

I continued mopping. "Is the floor dry?" Steve asked. "Can we come in now?"

"Yes. Where's Dad?" I asked.

"He left with his scuba gear."

"What? You're kidding. He went scuba diving alone?"

"Looks like it," Steve said.

If he did, he's more stubborn than I thought. You're never supposed to dive without a buddy. Afraid of what might happen to him, I had to distract myself to avoid an anxiety attack. I packed my gym bag and called the *Island Ferry*. When Marco drove the boat up to our pier, I asked him if he'd seen the *Island Rider*.

"I'm worried," I said. "Duke went diving alone." I immediately regretted saying this in case it started rumors that Duke had left because of a fight. I felt we had no privacy and that everyone knew our business. *Did I have an overactive imagination, or was my paranoia justified?*

"I noticed a lanchon just behind the reef," Marco said. "Don't worry, Miss Sonia, it's calm today."

Sure enough, when I got home from the gym, Duke was standing at the kitchen counter, slathering peanut butter and strawberry jam on white bread. He turned toward me and said, "Hi," as though he'd forgotten our fight.

"You scared me."

"You know I'd never scuba dive alone."

"So why did you leave with the gear?"

"I found a great piece of property for sale up by Mexico Rocks," he said, avoiding my question. "The owners seem like a nice couple from California, and they want us to come up and talk to them about the price. I think they're lonely up there. The bad part is there's no electricity that far north. We'd have to run our own generator."

When Duke had a project or a new goal to work toward, he became the man I loved.

CHAPTER FORTY-FOUR

California Looking Good

DUKE COULDN'T WAIT TO SHOW ME the new property he'd discovered. After lunch, we jumped in the *Island Rider* and continued up the coast. It took forever to reach the spot. My first thought was, *Oh, my gosh, we're even more isolated here than where we live now. How will the kids feel about that?*

The water by Mexico Rocks was like a giant aquarium. You could see coral heads and multicolored fish with your naked eyes. The *Island Ferry* did not go this far north, so we would have to depend on our own boat for all transportation needs. I knew that living here with our boys would be similar to Tom Hanks' life in *Castaway*.

We both agreed it was too far from civilization. Perhaps Duke and I could live here for a few months during the year with no electricity and no phones, but this was not the right place for our family.

Suddenly, I found myself feeling all warm and fuzzy about the idea of moving back to the U.S. I longed for comfort: fresh, scented towels to go along with a nice hot shower lasting more than a few seconds and a glass of chilled Chardonnay.

How could I be dreaming about Target and buying Brie and Boursin cheeses from Trader Joe's when only a year ago I'd fantasized about the Caribbean turquoise waters? What had made me reach the point of wanting to trade the view from my hammock for freeway noise and the fast-paced life of Orange County?

When we moved to Belize, I found everything charming — or perhaps "exciting" is a more appropriate word. The geckos scrambling on the walls; the rain entering the house sideways; the electricity shutting off, forcing us to light a candle and huddle in a circle. It was all so Robinson Crusoe. Now I allowed things to bother me. Perhaps it was a defense mechanism to help me transition back to life in the U.S.

Alec wandered into the living room, and I felt guilty about my son's malnourished, lanky body. He reminded me of the anorexic stray dogs we saw roaming the streets in Corozal. He'd always been a finicky eater. I knew how much he longed for Taco Bell, Crisscut Fries and cheeseburgers at Carl's Jr. Anything to flesh out his gaunt look.

He headed to the corner of our living room, where we kept three fishing rods in a tall, woven basket.

"Why haven't you been fishing with Juan?" I asked. "You used to go all the time."

"Juan can't go," Alec replied, fidgeting with the pole and replacing it in the basket.

Things between Juan's family and ours had deteriorated since the e-mail from our neighbors. Everything changed so abruptly, and I was sure Jessica had convinced Juan and Teresa that Duke and I wanted to take over management of Villas Tropicales. Rumors spread so quickly, and in a way I understood that Teresa and Juan had to show their loyalty to Henry, Betty and Maureen. They had, after all, known them far longer than our family, and their financial stability depended on their relationship with these owners. Although their shift in attitude upset me, their financial security forced them to take sides. I sensed this bothered big Juan and Little Juan, who truly cared about their friendship with my boys, but it was easier for Teresa to pretend we no longer existed. If only we could turn things back to how they were when we first arrived.

Betty and Maureen had each invited us over for cheese and wine, and even Henry had invited us to dinner at his villa. We still liked Betty, Maureen, Henry and, of course, Juan, Teresa and Little Juan. I couldn't understand how we were now perceived as the *bad guys*.

Steve continued to enjoy his sailboat. He had anchored it closer to shore but refused to sell it just because the other homeowners told us we were only allowed one boat. Juan had sold his WaveRunner to conform to the new rules and regulations we'd received, and we knew he'd been forced to do so.

Steve had dreams of sailing from one end of the island to the other, then venturing further on his own. Little Juan's adventurous spirit had rubbed off on Steve, and I relished his new passion for sailing. "I want to sail across the Caribbean to the Leeward Islands, with my pirate flag on top of the mast," Steve had told us. Looking back at his previous girlfriends, Steve's sailboat was also a case of something that needed to be rescued and fixed. This time, however, the romance was healthy, not dysfunctional.

Little Juan meant so much to all of us, and I realized what a positive influence he'd had on teaching my sons gratitude, humility and learning to live with just a few things. Both he and his dad had taught my boys how to build a small shelter using woven palm fronds as the roof, how to find the perfect coconut for milk, how to fish, how to catch an iguana, how to make a fire — and these were just the things I'd witnessed. Little Juan showed us how a kid becomes more creative when he has to entertain himself and the outdoors becomes his giant plasma TV.

Now we realized Henry's money spoke louder than our presence and friendship. Who could blame Teresa, Juan and their son? Henry offered to pay them for Little Juan's private school — the same one Josh attended in San Pedro — and to fly all three of them to the U.S. for their summer vacations. He never stopped showering them with expensive gifts. We couldn't compete, nor did we want to.

Realizing how much Henry wanted us to sell our villa at Villas Tropicales so the "resort" would not be spoiled by a family with kids and a dog, it came as no surprise when Teresa yelled "Ven aqui" every time Little Juan tried to sneak into our house to play.

I was heartbroken, and so were my boys, about not having Little Juan as part of our family anymore.

CHAPTER FORTY-FIVE

Life on Hold

"WHY ARE YOU IGNORING ME, TERESA?" I blurted out one morning. Her new attitude pissed me off, and I could no longer keep my mouth shut, deeply hurt by this shift in our relationship.

"I'm not ignoring you," she said, followed by a snort. "I'm just busy."

Her sister arrived on the *Island Ferry* just as Duke and I were tying up our boat. Teresa, who in the past never shut up, now strutted along the outer edge of the pier to avoid crossing paths with us. She had morphed from Ms. Congeniality to Ms. Standoffish in the blink of an eye.

I no longer knew how to behave in my own house. Crazy thoughts crossed my mind, like what if cameras and tape recorders were hidden inside our home to spy on us? *Why was I feeling so paranoid?*

When the kids left toys or towels outside, I felt like photos were being taken as evidence that we were not conforming to our neighbors' new rules. I rolled our outdoor barbecue to the back of the house and tucked it behind a wooden structure so the homeowners wouldn't say it made our "resort" seem too residential.

For the third night in a row, I woke up in fear, the sheets soggy from my sweaty body. I forced my eyes shut but kept visualizing local thugs breaking in. I opened my eyes to see the curtains fluttering in the breeze, exposing the neck and face of a man. *Was he real?* For a brief second, I thought our eyes connected. But the moon wasn't casting enough light, so perhaps he wasn't there. I rubbed my eyes and felt the salty sting of my own sweat. After my eyes refocused, I expected to see the Creole man, only this time in the flesh. I slid my hand along the moist sheet and Velcroed it to Duke's fingers. As Duke rolled over, I felt the hairs on his chest against my skin. He made me feel safe, like the teddy bear I used to clutch in my arms when I had nightmares as a little girl. I finally fell asleep.

Because our life was on hold, suddenly a busy schedule sounded appealing. I'd never had so much free time in my entire adult life to sit and think. Without television or books to read, I could put together a 3,000-piece jigsaw puzzle in the middle of a school day, something I'd always figured only old people did.

I remembered forcing myself to meditate back in Orange County. The harder I tried, the more frustrated I grew, until the day I said, "Screw meditation." I used to read books and listen to meditation cassettes, but nothing — absolutely nothing — happened. I could never quiet my mind, so I quit.

In Belize, meditation happened when I had nothing to do. I finally understood what "living in the moment" meant. For years, I'd heard Oprah and her guests talk about the importance of living in the "now," but with busy schedules and to-do lists, that was impossible for me. Learning to enjoy the present moment finally happened when I pulled myself away from the rat race. Even then, it took a good six months for me to unwind. Strangely enough, I was able to meditate, despite all the uncertainty going on in our lives. I think it was the only thing I could do to stay calm and in control. I wondered whether I'd be able to maintain this skill if we moved back to Orange County.

In a few days, Duke would be returning to California with Steve so Steve could take the SAT, an exam required for entry to a four-year college. The SAT was offered in Belize City once a year, but applying proved difficult. It was easier for Steve to take the exam in California.

We were proud of Steve. He'd managed to finish his entire junior year of Internet classes by February, which gave him ample time to study for the SAT. He'd done this alone, without any intervention on our part. Alec continued studying in town with Matt.

Duke and I spent hours looking at houses for sale on the Internet in our old neighborhood in Orange County. At the same time, Duke was looking for work as an attorney, and he managed to set up an interview during the eleven days he and Steve would be back in Orange County.

"Maybe we're making a mistake. Perhaps we should look for a house and a job in another state," I suggested, turning to face Duke. Both of us were logged onto real estate websites. "I don't want to go back to the same old," I said.

"I can't practice law outside California," Duke said. "Only a few states offer reciprocity."

"How about a different job? Something less stressful than law?"

"I'd have to start from scratch, and that might make it more stressful," Duke said.

"I could get a job, too," I said. "And if we lived somewhere cheaper than California, we might make enough."

"Maybe, but you know Alec and Josh want to go back to our old neighborhood," Duke said. "We can no longer afford a lakefront house," he added.

"I don't want that kind of house anymore," I said. "Besides, our lake looks shitty next to this," I added, pointing to the Caribbean. "Everyone's too materialistic in that neighborhood, anyway," I concluded.

Belize had forced us to live a simple life, and we wanted to maintain that lifestyle when we moved back. We continued searching the Internet for a small house, even a fixer-upper. I had nothing to prove to anyone.

I had changed, and saving money now felt better than buying stuff. My family and memories meant so much more to me now than a remodeled house with designer furniture.

Receiving e-mails from friends in California helped me realize we were on the right track. Friends complained about their busy schedules, and that they had little time to relax.

Two days before Duke and Steve's departure to California, Teresa knocked on our front door during dinner. She never stopped by anymore, so I was surprised and suspicious.

"When is Duke leaving for America?" Teresa asked.

"This Thursday; why?" I asked, the *why* resonating a tad harsher than I'd planned. Alec gave me a look, which I interpreted as, "That sounded rather bitchy."

"We're also leaving on Thursday," she smirked.

"What?" I almost choked on a piece of chicken.

"Oh, not to Michigan," Teresa said, "but to Progresso to visit my mother," she added, as if location made a difference.

"It's only for five days." She then lifted her right hand and started counting each finger, like a kindergartner practicing her numbers.

"Who's going to be watching the property?" I asked, knowing they usually hired a replacement caretaker when Juan left on vacation.

"Nobody," Teresa giggled. "Jessica tried calling you. Isn't your phone number 2671?" Here you only had to remember the last four digits; the first three were the same for everyone.

"Yes, but we don't answer during dinner."

Teresa stared at me as though I'd committed a sin.

"So it's OK with you?" she asked, all perky.

"No. I'm not happy about it."

In fact, I was fuming. *Had they deliberately planned her family's vacation to coincide with Duke's departure?*

Now Alec, Josh and I would be all alone, five miles from town, without anyone to protect us. At least we had Cookie as our mini-guard dog.

Since the sabotage incident, I was terrified of something happening to the boys and me, especially at night. As usual, I thought of the worst-case scenario: *What if Manuel wanted to take revenge on me?*

Even Teresa had gossiped about Manuel, back in the early days when she still liked me.

"Manuel isn't to be trusted," she had said. Now Manuel knew I'd be alone. News of Duke leaving had probably already circulated through town.

"Goodbye," Teresa said, and pushed the door shut behind her.

CHAPTER FORTY-SIX

Job Hunting

D UKE SEEMED MORE EXCITED TO BE leaving for the U.S. than Steve was. He'd grown tired of the pettiness of the locals and the discomfort of living in a villa where we lacked freedom. *Was he looking forward to working again? Had he realized that too much free time isn't good, either?* "Armin's here," I called from the patio, glancing at my watch. "Something must be wrong; he's early."

Steve and Duke hurried down the stairs with the rest of us, including Cookie, who traipsed behind. By the time we reached the boat, Armin had already loaded all three overstuffed suitcases, which we'd left at the end of the pier. His boat sank a little too low in the water when Duke and Steve wobbled in.

Leaning over, I hugged Steve and wished him all the best on his SAT. When Duke reached for a kiss, the boat teetered sideways. Both Steve and Armin dove to the opposite side to counterbalance the weight. It took five tries before Armin's engine coughed into life. Now I knew why he'd shown up early.

"Why can't I go back with them?" Alec whined, as the boat puttered along.

"Me, too," Josh said. "Steve's so lucky."

"I don't think you'd like to go back to take exams," I said.

All three of us stood like statues watching the boat disappear. Cookie sat between my feet, and I wondered if she understood that they were gone. She hated suitcases; they represented uncertainty in her life.

I had to stay strong, so instead of focusing on my fear of being alone and responsible for Alec and Josh, I visualized this as an opportunity to get things done. The house desperately needed organizing and a major cleanup so we could put it on the market.

"What's for dinner?" Alec asked. He looked pale, almost anemic.

"What do you want to eat?"

"Pizza."

I picked up the phone and called Pauly's pizza, forgetting it was Thursday, the restaurant's day off. Without any other pizza parlors or take-outs, I lifted the lid of our rust-splattered freezer and counted three one-pound packs of ground beef glued together in the bottom right corner. I defrosted one in the microwave and made burritos.

My ears were on high alert for any unusual sounds, so we watched a comedy I knew would make Josh laugh and me forget my fear for a while. "Can I sleep in Steve's bed?" Josh asked, snuggling closer to me than usual on the couch.

"Of course," I replied. At least that way, I wouldn't be all alone downstairs. Alec would sleep upstairs with Cookie.

I hid a solid mahogany rolling pin underneath Duke's pillow and tucked a machete behind some books on the shelf next to my bed. I regretted not following Lucy's advice — she was a 70-year-old woman from Michigan who lived alone in town — "Keep a bullhorn next to your bed. It'll scare the heck out of any thief or rapist."

I managed several hours of sleep that first night. Early mornings were always my favorite time of day. Waiting for my coffee to brew, I savored the morning sunrise with its kaleidoscope of colors. Now, alone, I could finally practice meditating and calming myself down.

When I thought about moving back to our old neighborhood, I longed for a serene space with chirping birds, fruit trees and flowers. The sound of cars, trucks and motorbikes had become so foreign to my ears that I feared moving back to Orange County's noisy freeways and busy streets.

Although we weren't quite sure when we'd be leaving, the pressure of selling our house was getting to me. *Would we find a buyer for our house in Belize? Would Steve and Alec's Internet grades be transferrable to their old high school? Had Alec learned enough through his Internet curriculum to jump into tenth grade? What about Steve and his senior year?*

Duke e-mailed me several times from California. He said his job interview went well and that the company made him an offer. I wasn't sure what to think. Perhaps the fact that he got an offer so quickly meant we were supposed to move back. All he told me was that the position paid less than his previous job and that he wouldn't have to drive as much. The latter point, at least, was good news.

My daily morning meditation on the end of our pier, facing the Caribbean, calmed me during my time without Duke, and I found myself growing even closer to Josh and Alec.

"Want to teach me chess?" I asked Josh.

"You sure, Mom?" he said, bringing out the chessboard in no time at all. "Last time I showed you, you gave up."

"That was in California," I said, pulling the armchair closer to the coffee table. "Now I have time."

We played a "pretend" game, and I saw a skill in Josh I hadn't noticed before. He knew how to explain rules in a concise manner, unlike Duke. Perhaps it had to do with Josh and me thinking alike, and thus understanding one another better.

"Josh, I finally get it."

We played a couple of games, and though Josh won both, I gained a new degree of closeness to my youngest son.

"That was fun," Josh said, lifting the lid of the box and placing all the pieces back inside.

Alec appeared from his room and joined me on the couch. He sat quietly for a change, without fidgeting. I relaxed into my own thoughts, and a great question popped into my head. "Alec, if you could have any job in the world, what would it be?"

"I dunno," he mumbled. I knew he'd respond if I gave him a little time. So I waited and, sure enough, he came up with an answer.

"Perhaps research in genetics or biology." His specific answer surprised me.

"So you want to study genetics?"

"Maybe. I'm not sure yet."

Alec only spoke when the moment was right, and those moments were infrequent. I had to treasure them and be there when they occurred. I was glad to see he still had goals.

I survived eleven days alone with Alec and Josh, free of sabotage, theft or rape. I knew it was all in my head, but now I could return the rolling pin to the shelf above the stove, as Duke's head would rest on his pillow that evening.

"What time are they coming home?" Alec asked, slurping his milk. For almost a year now, my boys had accepted frosted flakes and powdered milk for breakfast without complaining.

"Their plane gets into Belize City from Houston around three," I said. "Let's all go to town. I want to buy steaks for dinner."

"I'll stay home," Alec said.

I no longer argued or forced them to come with me. There wasn't much to do in town for kids, unless they had friends. Josh knew a couple of kids and said, "Mom, can I come?"

"Sure."

"Maybe Pedro can play," Josh said. "Can you call his mom?"

I tried to arrange a play date for Josh. But when Pedro's mom said she wasn't sure where her son had spent the night and would have to track him down, I remembered that pre-arranged play dates were an American concept. Belizean kids had family responsibilities, such as caring for younger siblings, feeding them and generally entertaining themselves. They were shuffled from one relative to another, and parents didn't seem concerned about their whereabouts the way we were in the States.

I brought Josh to town on the 8 A.M. *Island Ferry* and escorted him to Pedro's house.

"Can I knock?" Josh asked.

"Go ahead."

An elderly woman peeked through a small opening. "Can I help you?" she asked in a voice that quavered.

"Josh is here to play with Pedro," I said.

"I'm sorry, Pedro isn't here. I think he's at his uncle's."

"Should we come back later?"

"Josh can play with Pedro's toys in his room," she said pointing to the staircase.

Josh gave me a *should I stay?* look before taking a step inside. I hoped Pedro would return shortly. "I'll be back in an hour," I said.

At Angelo's Meats on Middle Street, I splurged on five small filet mignons, although I knew that Duke and Steve had probably devoured several steak dinners while in California, making up for the lack of good beef on the island. After purchasing the last of the mushrooms and semi-wilted lettuce at the Veggie House, I headed back to Pedro's house. Josh was halfway down the staircase as soon as he heard me knock.

"How was it?"

"Boring," he said, keeping up with my accelerated pace to reach the *Island Ferry.*

"Did you wait long before Pedro showed up?"

"Yeah. His toys suck; they're for little kids."

Belizean kids latched on to one another and made up their own games. They would often play with a small ball, kick a coconut on the beach or fish off a pier. I'd witnessed boys from five to twelve handling sharp pocket knives, fish guts smeared on the wooden docks beneath their naked feet. Their buckets bulging with fresh snapper, they continued to bait their hooks because they were responsible for providing fish for their family's dinner. I worried that Josh might end up with a fishhook in his foot or, worse yet, in his eye if I let him fish with local kids. But perhaps that was my overprotective Orange County mom way of thinking.

As soon as we got home, I unpacked the groceries, changed the sheets on our bed and made a mental list of all the questions I wanted to ask Duke and Steve when they returned. The potatoes were washed and poked, ready to bake; the mushrooms were sautéing on low heat with a lid to keep them from shriveling, and Josh kept an eye on the boat traffic. "Mom, I see the ferry," he said, bouncing up and down as if on a trampoline.

All three of us sprinted to the end of our boat dock. Little Juan no longer ran to greet us. He stayed home, and I wondered how difficult it was for Teresa and Juan to contain his squirmy body. *Surely he missed my boys.* I know they missed their little "brother."

We longed to hear news about our old neighborhood. What had changed? Was the bagel shop still there? Did the local 24-Hour Fitness have new equipment?

Duke wrapped his arms around me, and his familiar masculine smell made me feel safe again.

"I figured you'd enjoy some wine," Duke said unzipping his suitcase and digging his hands into the middle, where he'd wrapped a bottle of Merlot inside a pair of jeans.

Alec, Josh and I hovered over the suitcase like kids waiting for Santa's presents to be distributed. Although the boys didn't really expect anything, they still hoped for something from the U.S.

"Here, Josh," Duke said, handing him a Walmart bag. "This is the game you wanted for your birthday, right?"

"Thanks Dad," he said, glowing with gratitude. This was what I'd been waiting to see in my kids' eyes for years. It reminded me of the look I'd seen in a child's eyes in Kenya when we gave him a stick of gum. Complete gratitude.

"Alec, I got you some new headphones," Duke said, dishing them into Alec's waiting hands.

"Are we going back home?" Alec asked, ripping the plastic off his headphones.

"Yes. I got offered a job, so now we can look for a house."

"Can we move close to Jeff and Jake?" Alec asked, his eyes glistening as he placed the headphones on his lap and waited for Duke's response.

"It depends on what we can afford. We'll see," Duke said.

I smiled at the excitement in Alec's voice, knowing that after all we'd been through, our family had pulled together and was now a unit. It took me a year to realize that paradise is a state of mind, not a place. I never imagined that local threats and other unexpected events in Belize would bring my family to this point. I finally discovered my paradise within my family, and knew it was safe for us to go home.

Duke's enthusiasm was contagious. "I'd forgotten how much stuff supermarkets have in the U.S.," he said, digging into his suitcase. "I really wanted to bring back garlic cheese and crackers, but I got these instead." He threw me a large bag of salted almonds, which I managed to catch in midair. I rummaged in our kitchen drawer for a corkscrew and handed it to Duke while I rinsed out two wine glasses.

"Let's sit down and talk," I said. "I can't wait to hear about Steve's SATs and your job offer." I opened the Merlot and poured us each a glass.

Duke collapsed on the couch, reached for his glass and leaned back into the cushions. "I think you did the right thing not to go back to your old boss," I said, handing him an extra pillow for his back.

"Yeah, that would be my last resort. I won't get paid as well, but I expected that."

"So when do they want you to start?" I asked.

"I told them I could start in a month. That should give me time to find a house when I go back. You know the real estate market is booming. Prices have shot up in one year."

"Think we can sell this one fast?" I asked.

"A couple e-mailed me, and they seem very interested. They're from the U.S. and are looking for a vacation home. They're coming over to see our house in two weeks."

Duke suggested I stay and show them the house while he looked for a house in Orange County. "I can take Steve, Alec and Cookie back first. I'll come back for Josh and more of our stuff while you clean up the house."

I couldn't believe this was the same Duke, the one I thought had become a *lazy bum*.

Steve appeared at the top of the staircase with a towel draped around his waist.

"That felt good," he said. "The pool seems saltier than usual."

As he headed over to the water dispenser, I asked him, "So how was the SAT?"

"I think I did well."

"See any kids you knew?"

"Only Tina. Her parents invited me over for dinner. They wanted to hear about Belize."

I had complete confidence in Steve. He seemed focused on his education and had proved to us that he could complete all his Internet classes alone and in record time. He'd succeeded in pulling his GPA up to a 3.8. We were both so proud of him.

Since returning from California, Steve had lost interest in fixing his sailboat. Every day he had an excuse for not sailing it. His latest was, "I'm waiting for that special worm-resistant wood Dad ordered to replace the rudder." It never arrived, so Duke bought a chunk of hardwood instead, which Steve insisted was inappropriate for a rudder.

"We don't have much time left to fix your boat and sell it. Go help Dad," I ordered.

"Dad isn't doing it right. It'll never work."

He refused to help, and I wondered whether he was sad to be giving up his sailboat without having sailed it on any of his anticipated adventures.

A year and two months after my Orange County garage sale, I was going through the whole process again, only this time on a Caribbean island. The boys helped us load boxes of old clothes, their fishing rods and other items we wanted to sell onto our boat.

From a distance, the *Island Rider* reminded me of an overflowing shopping cart, with the lifetime possessions of a homeless person. With the boat heavily weighed down, Duke drove us to the Palapa Bar boat dock. I grabbed a box filled with old clothes, walked onto the beach at Tres Cocos and scouted around for the perfect spot in the shade. Fresh expats who'd recently arrived on the island from the U.S. asked Duke if the *Island Rider* was for sale.

"Yes," he said. "Want to test-drive it?"

Fifteen minutes later, Duke received a verbal agreement on the purchase of our boat, and later that evening they called us for wiring instructions.

"Aren't you sad to get rid of your boat?" I asked Duke. Things were moving a little too hastily for me.

"I shall miss driving a boat," Duke said, "but I'm glad it sold quickly. Now we only have the house and the sailboat left."

Getting rid of the *Island Rider* felt like losing a family member. We'd had so many adventures on it, and a part of me didn't want to admit we'd failed.

But had we failed? In one way, yes: the way we'd approached starting a business in Belize, with the mentality of American entrepreneurs. But more important, we'd also succeeded. Steve was back on track and focused on his education. We had also instilled a new value system within our kids. All of us had learned to appreciate the simple things in life, something I hoped would remain with us when we returned to Orange County.

"Mom, can you come here?" Alec called from his open bedroom door.

"Why?"

"It hurts so bad," he whimpered.

I jumped off the couch, "I hope it's not appendicitis," I whispered to Duke. This was the third time Alec had pointed to his lower right abdomen, and I had already checked the symptoms online.

"I'm sure it's not. He's had this before," Duke said.

"What could it be?"

"Hurry, Mom." Alec's voice grew anxious.

"I think it's an electrolyte imbalance," said Duke. "We'll buy him Gatorade tomorrow."

"He's way too skinny," I whispered, "I'm scared he's not getting enough nutrients."

"Moooom."

"Coming."

Duke reminded me not to panic. After all, Alec would be back in California in a few days.

I rushed into Alec's room and saw him leaning over with both hands on his stomach.

"Mom, it hurts too much to move."

"Can't you stand?" I asked finding it hard to believe he was in that much pain.

"No. Last time it took me forty minutes to get out of my chair. I really want to get a shower and go to bed now, but I can't."

I bent my knees and asked him to extend both arms to the side. Then, placing my palms under his triceps, I tried hoisting his long torso from the chair. I quit trying when he screamed, "Ooow, oowee, oowee."

"You baby. You're faking it," Josh said from his bed on the other side of the room.

"Stop it, Josh. He's in a lot of pain."

"Let's try again," I said.

This time I mentally blocked my ears to finish the job. Alec shuffled his feet to the bathroom without complaining. For some reason, raising and lowering his body caused him severe pain, but not walking.

While he showered, I rushed to my computer to read the symptoms of appendicitis for the fourth time. Alec kept pointing to the exact spot where I had a scar from my appendectomy thirty-eight years ago.

The website stated, "Severe pain, high temperature and vomiting." Alec had severe pain, but not the other two. He'd had this twice before, and each time he felt better the next morning.

"Duke, I want to take Alec to the doctor," I said. "I just want to make sure."

The following morning, Duke dropped us off in town. Alec seemed relieved that I had decided to get him some medical attention.

A kind female doctor examined him and said he did not have appendicitis. After we described his symptoms, she said that perhaps Alec had been holding in his feelings for a long time and was depressed. She agreed he was extremely thin for his height. I finally realized we might have sacrificed one son's well-being for the sake of another. However, I knew that Alec would soon return to his old friends in California and feel at home again.

CHAPTER FORTY-SEVEN

Special Time

"WHAT HAPPENED, ARMIN? You're late," I said, as he docked his boat, ready to take Steve, Alec, Duke and Cookie to the airport.

"Sorry, guys; my propeller was stolen. I had to locate another."

Duke and I were used to hearing about theft; we now shrugged it off.

This was it. Only Josh and I would remain. I couldn't wait for Alec to get some fat on his bones, and for him to see his friends again. Everyone else, including Cookie, was moving back to Orange County. Duke would be back in a week to pick up Josh. I would stay a few extra days to clean up, sell Steve's sailboat and show the house to the couple who seemed interested.

We each threw a suitcase onboard, as well as the empty dog crate, and Armin took off as fast as his slow engine would allow.

I let Josh sleep through the goodbyes on purpose. No need to hear him complain about staying alone with me.

As I stepped into the living room, I noticed random piles of trash scattered throughout the house. At least this time I'd be able to clean the mess, unlike the previous year, when we'd left our house in Orange County in complete disarray.

I thought Josh and I deserved a mini-vacation first, a little taste of luxury while the guys were settling back into Orange County life. I booked one night in a hotel in San Pedro. We both longed for good food, I craved social interaction, and Josh wanted to watch cartoons on TV.

I was scared to spend nights alone at Villas Tropicales without Cookie to serve as a mini-guard dog. I had no choice, though, as I had to sell our house.

I packed an overnight bag and woke up Josh to catch the *Island Ferry* to town. Josh longed for pancakes at his favorite restaurant, the Blue Water Grill.

Teresa, Juan and Little Juan knew we would never see them again. They were leaving for their first vacation in the U.S., with Henry. I wondered if they would say goodbye or ignore us. I still cared deeply for them, especially Little Juan.

"Come on, Josh, let's go," I said.

"Just a sec, Mom."

I locked the front door and double-checked from the outside that all windows were closed. Little Juan burst into sight with a kite in his right hand. It was one Josh and Alec had given him when his mom allowed him to come over to our house every day.

"You leaving?" he asked.

"Yes," I said.

"You too?" Josh asked.

"Yes. We go to America," he said, beaming with excitement.

Twenty feet behind us, I could hear the wooden planks vibrating from Teresa and Juan's footsteps. They had decided to say "Goodbye." I felt my eyes turning moist. Ten months ago we met them in the exact same spot, when they greeted us getting off the boat. Despite negative feelings over the past couple of months, I wanted to erase the bad and focus on happier times. Based on age, Teresa and Juan could easily have been my own kids and Little Juan my own grandson.

I stepped toward Juan and said, "Thanks, Juan, for everything," then followed up with a warm hug. I noticed a few tears in his eyes just before he turned away. Sadly, Teresa squirmed her way out of my hug. I kissed Little Juan on the cheek and told him what a good boy he was. It suddenly occurred to me that I had never seen his mother kiss or praise him, so I told him how smart he was and to continue practicing his reading and writing.

Josh handed Little Juan the piece of paper he'd clasped in his hand. I watched as Little Juan unfolded the card with Spiderman on the front. I was deeply touched that my son had hand-drawn and written a goodbye note without my knowledge.

As the *Island Ferry* approached, Teresa headed back to her house. Juan held my hand, steadying me as I stepped inside the boat. Little Juan and his dad waved goodbye, and I tried to hide my tears from Josh. I loved this little family and hoped we would stay in contact for years to come.

"Let's get some snacks for our room."

"Even Doritos?" Josh asked.

"Even Doritos."

I booked a room at a small, five-bedroom hotel owned by an American expat. No need to spend extra money at the fancy tourist resort next door when we had the same view. As long as the room offered a TV for Josh and a coffeemaker for me, we were both happy.

"Is this it?" Josh asked as we reached an arched entrance with sea grape growing along the edge. It reminded me of an English country cottage with tropical foliage. The bell jingled as I opened the freshly painted pink gate and followed the meandering gravel path to an "office" sign painted in orange on a lime-colored door. Josh opened the door, and we entered a freezing, closet-size room. Inside, behind a five-foot-tall counter, sat the best-looking expat I had seen during my entire stay in Belize. This guy took good care of himself, unlike so many expats I'd encountered since living here who smoked and drank as though they were getting paid to demonstrate the worst lungs, livers and skin known to a research lab.

He bounced off his stool and welcomed us.

"You'll be staying in room number two, which is downstairs on the beach," he said, leading the way. The room seemed unusually long and narrow, with a queen-size bed, two brand-new futons and a TV. Josh had the TV and remote figured out before the door closed.

"I'm hungry. Can I have pancakes from Blue Water Grill?" Josh asked.

"Let's go."

"OK," he said, already hypnotized by some car commercial on TV.

Josh spent the day flat on the futon, eyes fixed like lasers on the TV screen. I let him watch as much TV as he wanted, and his eyes were red and swollen after five hours.

We had dinner again at the Blue Water Grill. Josh craved a hamburger and fries, and I ordered a Cobb salad with blue cheese dressing. It had been months since I'd tasted blue cheese. After dinner, Josh asked me if he could play some video games.

"Where?" I asked.

"The Chinese take-out has video games."

"How do you know?"

"Pedro told me."

I watched him play and felt sorry for kids living on the island. There were no bowling alleys, laser tag, football fields, ice rinks or golf courses, except for one handkerchief-sized mini-golf course. After a bag of Doritos and 50 cents to play a video game, Josh seemed far more appreciative than when we'd spent $150 or more to invite friends to one of his birthday parties.

On the way back to the hotel, we stopped for an ice cream cone.

"Are you going to miss the island?" I asked, as he kicked sand into mini-dunes with his flip-flops.

"Only Little Juan," he said.

Perhaps I'd been expecting something more profound, but Josh was only eleven. How could I expect him to miss the serenity that I'd only recently learned to appreciate myself?

I woke up early the next morning, started the coffee maker and, with my steaming cup in hand, slid through the patio door. The sun rose just as I settled myself on a green plastic chair, trying to meditate.

I preferred the quiet of living up north. Here, in downtown San Pedro, the buzzing of air-conditioners and the first Cessna flights of the day disturbed my meditation. How would I continue my morning ritual when I returned to Orange County, with its nonstop sounds of traffic, police sirens, helicopters, airplanes and ambulances?

I jumped over the hotel's three-foot wall to get to the beach and strolled toward Ramon's Pier. Tourists waited at the end of the pier to catch their tour boats to the Mayan ruins of Altun-ha and Lamanai, to see the manatees or to try ziplining or visit the zoo. I'd done all of these things and felt more like a local than ever before.

I continued strolling along the beach toward Oscar's gym, a long mile north of our hotel, wishing for access to my computer. *Had Duke found a house for us to buy in our old neighborhood?* I couldn't wait to hear.

When I returned from my walk, Josh had already turned on the cartoons.

"Can we have pancakes again at Blue Water Grill? They were so good yesterday."

"Sure." I was happy to see him appreciate the simple things in life.

After breakfast, it was time for us to head back home on the *Island Ferry.*

Sam, a sixteen-year-old relative of Juan's, greeted us at the pier. He seized the backpack from my hand and schlepped it to the bottom of our staircase. *Was he waiting for a tip?* His teenage energy and looks made me wonder whether I'd acquired another son rather than a man to watch over our safety and protect the property.

"Mom, come see the butterflies," Josh shouted from the pool area. I stopped unpacking and ran outside, where thousands of pale, lemon-colored butterflies flew within a few feet of our balcony, all heading south. The dense cloud of migrating wings took several minutes to pass over us. As I stood in awe of nature's beauty, a single butterfly with saffron-colored wings broke my trance. The butterflies were departing, and so were we.

CHAPTER FORTY-EIGHT

Final Clean-up

I KNEW JOSH WAS BORED when he volunteered to clean my bathroom, then started scrubbing the grout with an old toothbrush. After his tenth row of grout, he still hadn't said, "I'm tired." He was definitely not the same person he had been in Orange County.

By noon, Josh hadn't quit, but I needed a break. "Why don't you pick a game we can play after I check my e-mails?"

"Can we go swimming?"

"Sure."

Duke had sent me some good news. He'd found a four-bedroom house close to our old neighborhood, so the boys could return to the same schools as before. He made an offer without consulting me, as houses were selling like hotcakes. The owner accepted his offer and agreed to rent it to us during escrow. "I think we really lucked out," Duke wrote.

Alec had also e-mailed me and sounded thrilled to see his best friends, Jeff and Jake, again. "I'm very happy with that house, and I already picked my room," he wrote. I hoped Alec's abdominal pains would not reappear and that he would start gaining weight.

"Mommmmm. I'm waiting," Josh hollered from the pool.

"Coming," I shrieked, and hurried downstairs to change into my swimsuit. We had fun throwing a mini-basketball in the pool. Sam showed up and sat on a lounge chair. Most of the time he remained in Juan's house watching TV. As a mother, I felt I should invite Sam over for dinner, but after everything we'd been through, I no longer felt I could trust anyone. The primal instinct of protecting my family surfaced, an impulse I had never experienced in our safe U.S. neighborhood.

Having secured a job and a house, Duke flew back to San Pedro one last time. While Alec stayed at his friend's house, Steve lived with Duke's mom, hoping to cram in a series of driving lessons.

During our final evening together in the villa, we drank a farewell rum and Coke and discussed how the next few days would proceed. Duke would fly back with Josh, and I would remain in Belize alone for a couple more days to sell Steve's sailboat and our house.

I couldn't wait to show our house to Jerry and Lisa, the couple from Washington, D.C., who seemed very keen on purchasing it. "What if they back out?" I said.

"They've seen photos. I'm hopeful," Duke said, massaging the tension out of my neck.

"Please stay. Emily's approaching, and our roof might blow off."

"I can't. I have a meeting for my new job," he said, reaching for my hand. "Don't worry, Snookie. Emily won't hit the island. Besides, Sam's going to put plywood on all the windows."

"I might have to evacuate before I get to show the house."

"You worry too much," Duke said.

CHAPTER FORTY-NINE

All Alone

I WAS ALONE WITH HURRICANE EMILY APPROACHING. Emily whizzed past The Grenadines and Aruba, and was building momentum toward Belize and the Yucatan.

During the night, I tossed in bed as the winds picked up. Struggling to block out memories of our first storm, and how we'd almost capsized on the reef, I tried counting sheep. I repeated silly nursery rhymes from my childhood. Nothing worked. The following morning, I discovered that Emily was heading directly toward Belize, forcing me to change my flight reservation to one day earlier than planned. The hefty airline penalty didn't deter me.

I called the *Island Ferry* and listened to everyone talk on the boat about Emily's approach. This reinforced my fear, and I couldn't wait to get back to Orange County to be with my family.

I'd made an appointment to meet Lucy at Tropic Air before she left the island. She'd expressed an interest in Steve's sailboat, and this was my last chance to sell it before leaving. Inside the small waiting room, every couch and chair was occupied by fleeing locals and tourists.

"Why did you book our vacation during hurricane season?" I heard one wife complain to her husband.

I spotted Lucy on the plaid couch.

"You don't look too good," she said, as I approached.

"I don't feel well," I said, as she scooted over to give me a sliver of couch.

"Are you leaving because of Emily?" I asked.

"Yes. I prefer to be safe, so I'm staying with my daughter in North Carolina."

"Are you still interested in Steve's sailboat?"

"Depends on the price."

"Well, it's got a brand-new engine, so how about $2,000?"

"You sure?"

I should have asked for more, but Duke wanted to get rid of the boat so we wouldn't have to pay storage fees at the boat yard. With Emily on her way, I thought $2,000 in my pocket was a better deal than a smashed sailboat.

Lucy rummaged through her purse.

"Will you take a U.S. check?"

"Sure," I said.

As she wrote the amount on the check, I tiptoed to the water dispenser. I couldn't help but think: *What if her check bounces?* Such was my growing mistrust of people on the island. Lucy handed me the check, and then her flight to Belize City was called.

"The sailboat's in front of our house," I said.

"I'll get it when I return." We waved goodbye. In less time than it took me to buy a swimsuit, I'd sold a sailboat.

With only two hours left before the arrival of Lisa and Jerry, I rushed home on the *Island Ferry*. If I could sell the house as fast as I had sold the boat, I could leave San Pedro with the feeling of mission accomplished.

I planned to give Lisa and Jerry a quick tour of the house. Then Armin would pick me up in his water taxi while Sam boarded up all our windows. In case the American couple wasn't interested in purchasing our villa, I had a backup plan. Debbie and Rick, expats in desperate need of cash, agreed, for a fee, to show our house to other potential buyers. Somehow I felt confident we wouldn't need their help.

Lisa and Jerry, a pleasant couple in their early sixties, arrived precisely on time. I gave them a five-minute tour of our house, and I could tell they were ready to buy it.

"Sonia, we'll be in La Jolla next week. We could meet you and Duke for brunch and discuss the purchase then."

Everything had fallen into place as though choreographed to perfection. Sam waited next to our storage shed, plywood sheets, hammer and nails in hand, ready to board up all our windows the minute Lisa and Jerry left our property. In the distance, I heard the familiar *putt-putt* sound of Armin's boat approaching our dock. Before I knew it, I was out of Belize and heading for Orange County.

When I realized I'd never wake up to the Caribbean outside my window again, my eyes filled with tears.

CHAPTER FIFTY

Back in Orange County

After one week in Orange County, the kids fit right in, but not me. Part of me worried that if we grew comfortable, we might become materialistic again. Of course, we'd changed — how could we not, after living in a third-world country? However, we were back in the same place, and I didn't want to revert to our old ways.

I no longer worried about Steve; I was confident he would remain on the right track. I knew with all my heart that Duke and I did the right thing in moving to Belize. Our desire to solve our family problems and reconnect with Steve by moving *our family* away, instead of sending *him* away to a behavior-modification school, showed our commitment to him. I know he now realizes this and is aware of the sacrifices we made, which contributed to his willingness to work as a team member in Belize.

During his senior year of high school, Steve focused all his attention on researching and applying for engineering colleges. This was his goal, and we did not interfere with his choices or help him with the application process. He only asked Duke for guidance with the Free Application for Federal Student Aid (FAFSA), which required parental tax information.

We were grateful his grades from Keystone National High School were transferrable to his Orange County high school transcript. Furthermore, his success in raising his GPA to a 3.8 enabled him to apply to some top-notch engineering schools. Steve believed it was the essay he wrote about his experience in Belize, and mentoring Little Juan, that helped him get accepted at the University of Michigan and Georgia Tech.

Now that we'd returned to Orange County, I tried to maintain the new values we had learned in Belize. We had become a close family unit; the boys continued to help with chores and to have conversations during mealtime. I often found all three of them huddled together in the living room talking like close friends. In Belize, that happened when the electricity shut off. In Orange County, it wasn't due to lack of power. We also managed to keep our house free of TV and video games, which made us unpopular with other kids. They thought we were strange, but our boys didn't seem to mind.

Our new house remained empty for several months — except for four mattresses and an outdoor patio set that stood in as dining/living room furniture. Duke and I felt like we were reliving our post-honeymoon days, when we took great pride and joy in decorating our house. This time around, though, we were older, more practical and a lot more frugal.

The new me was thrifty. Belize had taught me not to try so hard to conform. I no longer cared if my furniture was a mishmash from Craigslist or if I didn't own a set of matching dinner plates. I *wanted* to be different. I was proud of driving a used Saturn, although I knew we were ruining the upscale look of the neighborhood with our three old and unattractive cars — all used Saturns.

Shopping for food made me feel like a small kid again: There were too many choices. As I stared at the fully stocked shelves, assistants invariably came up and asked me, "Is there something I can help you find?"

I wanted to say, "Yes, help me decide."

Our experiences in Belize made me aware that each one of my boys is different, and that I had made a mistake assuming Alec and Josh would respond to Belize the same way Steve did. However, we each learned something unique from the experience. Despite Alec's hardships in adapting, he benefited by learning to be more independent, assertive and helpful toward others. Yes, Alec had complained the most, but I realized that his health is more fragile than his brothers', and I remembered how traumatic his birth had been. Born a month early, he needed a blood transfusion to keep him alive. Now the tallest of my sons, he was still more prone to allergies and sickness. I accepted that Alec does not like change, and I felt enormous guilt about uprooting him from Orange County. Still, I was pleased when I discovered a copy of his college application essay, which stated: "I truly believe that all my experiences abroad made me the person I am today."

I took Alec to an Orange County orthodontist, who said Dr. Afonso did an excellent job on Alec's teeth. "We couldn't have done it better ourselves," he concluded. I almost wrote a letter to Dr. Afonso complimenting him on his work, but decided it might come across as condescending: "American orthodontists think that your standards are as good as theirs."

Alec was right when he said Duke and I had been selfish in uprooting our family. I did have my own selfish reasons for moving to Belize. Not only did I want to escape our problems in Orange County, but I was also looking for my own *paradise:* a place that could fulfill me. Ironically, Belize taught me that paradise is a place in your mind and your heart, not a physical location.

Duke also had his own selfish reasons to move. He was fed up with his job and traffic, and he wanted some adventure in his life. When I asked him how he would sum up Belize, he said, "An idyllic landscape isn't idyllic when you have to fight for basics like water, food and jobs." I believe Duke thought he was escaping the pressures of Orange County, only to realize that no matter where you go, you still have to face the burden of work, especially when you have a family to support. Neither one of us expected the struggles we encountered. However, we both agreed we would not trade what Belize had given us in return.

I noticed changes in Josh, too. He'd become more aware of nature and his surroundings. When his friend Ryan, also eleven, spent the day with us, Josh asked me to take them to the beach. Driving on Laguna Canyon Highway, we stopped at a red light. Josh looked outside while Ryan played with his Game Boy. "Mom, look at those beautiful flowers; what are they?" Josh asked. While strolling around downtown Laguna Beach, Josh pointed to a huge poster of an angel with a beautiful blue sky behind her. "Look, Mom. That's the kind of picture you like." He was thinking of my inspiration cards, the ones with pictures of angels, which he'd seen me reading while I meditated on our boat dock in Belize.

Ryan didn't appear to "see" anything unless it was pointed out to him.

I took Steve to visit the two colleges that accepted him, Georgia Tech and University of Michigan. We rented a car at the airport and stayed in a hotel room in Atlanta. That evening, we enjoyed a nice dinner together. What a change from two years ago, when his fist came so close to hitting my face and he punched a hole in the wall. During orientation at the University of Michigan, I knew Steve belonged there. Everyone in California warned him about the terrible weather in Michigan, but that did not deter him. Not once did he complain about anything, not even the freezing winters in Ann Arbor, Michigan. He enjoyed studying mechanical engineering, and I realized that he needed — and wanted — to grow up.

When he returned for his first Christmas back in California, we had downsized to an even smaller house and no longer had a bedroom for him. A week before his arrival, we installed a primitive shed. It was just big enough for an extra-long twin bed and a dresser. Without a bathroom, heating or air-conditioning, it brought back memories of the simple life we'd lived in Belize. Steve appreciated everything, including the shed. I continued to see gratitude as he matured.

A year and a half later, we still hadn't caved in to television, and we were never too proud to pick up what others had sitting on their lawns, marked "free." That was how we got our dining room chandelier. We continued to turn off faucets while brushing our teeth or doing dishes, remembering how precious water can be.

Realizing that paradise is a state of mind rather than a place, I was able to find my passion through writing. Duke's creative outlet is making movies, which allows him to escape the mental stresses of being an attorney.

CHAPTER FIFTY-ONE

Changes

Aꜰᴛᴇʀ ꜰɪᴠᴇ ʏᴇᴀʀꜱ ʙᴀᴄᴋ ɪɴ Oʀᴀɴɢᴇ Coᴜɴᴛʏ, Josh decided he wanted to go to New Mexico Military Institute to finish his last two years of high school. Belize opened Josh's eyes to the world beyond Orange County. His sense of independence and his compassion grew in Belize, and he told us, "I don't think like the kids in my school. They all want to show off what they have. I want to be different." He begged us to allow him to attend military high school.

I remembered when Duke and I had threatened Steve with military school; now our youngest son chose that option. When I asked him why, Josh said, "Mom, you have no idea how many kids do drugs at my school. They judge other kids by what they have. I need a change." This came as a huge surprise to me. During our tough years with Steve, I feared Josh would follow the same path, and perhaps be even worse. With his growing entitlement attitude, his obsession with video games and his lack of interest in school, I had believed he would turn into a problem teenager.

Duke and I have decided to move to Naples, Florida, when we no longer have kids in college. We both miss the warm waters of the Caribbean, and we discovered Naples while on vacation in 2009. We know we made a huge mistake thinking we could run a business in Belize according to the American paradigm. The Gulf Coast of Florida offers us a Caribbean *feel,* without the threat of job loss or sabotage. We long to further simplify our life and experience our next adventure.

When our family is together during the holidays, we often discuss our time in Belize, especially Little Juan. My heart has pulled me back there three times in the past five years. I feel a love for Belize and for how, despite all the trials and tribulations we faced, it brought my family back together. I shall always have a soft spot for Ambergris Caye.

I paid a return visit to Belize in 2008 and stayed with my friend Jennie. Not much had changed except for the new bridge joining both sides of Boca del Rio, where the hand-drawn ferry once plied the waters. As I pedaled to town on Jennie's bike, I heard, "Miss Sonia?" Turning, I saw Teresa and Juan on a shiny red motorcycle. "You visiting?" Teresa asked, sounding like the friendly Teresa from earlier days.

"Yes," I said, happy to see them. "Where's Little Juan?"

"He go to Island Academy. Mr. Henry pay for it. He know how to read and write now," Teresa told me proudly.

"Can I see him after school today?"

"Yes, he's back at four."

"I'll take the *Island Ferry* up to visit."

My heart beat so fast; I couldn't wait to see him. All my life I had said I could never adopt a child, but my feelings toward Little Juan had changed me.

I was disappointed when the *Island Ferry* dropped me off at Villas Tropicales and he did not show up. But as I headed for the pool, I saw

Little Juan rolling Alec's old skateboard on the coral tile. He looked almost the same, perhaps a couple of inches taller.

"Hi Juan. Remember me?"

"Yes," he said, giving me a quick glance with those chestnut Bambi eyes and long lashes.

"Is that Alec's skateboard?"

"Yes, he left it."

"Do you know how to ride it?"

He got up and demonstrated his skills.

"Wow. Good job."

"Want to see the toys I play with?" His English had improved tremendously since he'd started attending the Island Academy.

I followed him. "Can we go inside?" I asked, as Little Juan led me up the stairs of our old villa and into Alec and Josh's bedroom.

"Yes, come in," he said, bouncing around like he used to. He opened the closet, and I found all my boys' toys still on the bottom shelf. "I come here every day. Miss Lisa said I can." He sat cross-legged on the cool tile and gazed at the toys, not yet bored with them.

I watched as he opened Josh's old box of magnetic blocks. It's what he used to do every morning before my boys went to school. Tears rolled down my cheeks as I remembered the good times and the life lessons this little boy had taught my family: humility, gratitude and *joie de vivre*.

"Would you like to see Steve, Alec and Josh again?

"Yes, when?" he asked, raising his head and giving me a huge smile.

"One day, we'll all come visit."

"You can stay here," he said. "We still have toys."

I followed him back home to say goodbye to his parents. Juan wanted to know if Steve was in college. I told him Steve was studying engineering and that Alec planned to study biology.

"They miss you," I said. "A pity we're not here; they would have enjoyed helping Little Juan with his homework."

"Juan know more reading and math than us," he said. "We cannot help with homework."

I remembered when Juan told my boys he had to quit school at twelve and how lucky they were to get an education. That had been a defining moment in my boys' lives.

Little Juan stayed with me as I waited for the *Island Ferry*. He could not sit still and had to climb on things.

"Monkey boy," I said.

He giggled.

Epilogue

HAD IT NOT BEEN FOR A LEAKING TOILET, we might never have healed our family.

That is the thought going through my mind as Duke and I get soaked through our flimsy ponchos outside the University of Michigan football stadium.

I'm wearing high-heeled leather sandals, and a new cream and taupe sleeveless dress purchased for this special occasion. Duke is in his business suit. It's barely six in the morning and pitch dark.

Together with hundreds of other parents, we're waiting for the lightning to stop. Security is tight, and no one is allowed inside the stadium until the airport-style body scanners start working again. Secret Service officers are standing on the stadium rooftop, binoculars glued to their eyes, scanning the crowd. We're waiting for President Obama to arrive to give the commencement address at Steve's graduation.

It seems ironic that Steve's graduation — a moment of immense pride for Duke and me — should fall on a day when weather conditions are similar to those of our year in Belize. A thunderstorm is causing havoc, and the electricity is out. Inside our ponchos, the humidity matches the microclimate of Belizean jungles.

When a wedge of sunlight appears, we hear the drone of a helicopter circling the stadium. President Obama is here, and all eyes look toward the sky.

It's hard to believe that Steve is graduating with a degree in mechanical engineering, and that the president of the United States will be congratulating him and 40,000 other students for their success.

I wish Alec and Josh could attend, but they are in college and high school, and it's too expensive to fly all of us from California to Michigan.

After the president's commencement address, we found ourselves among thousands of parents and graduates heading to Union Hall, where a hostess directed us to our table. We had brunch reservations, and I waited impatiently for Steve to join us in his black cap and gown with the orange tassel.

He arrived, his gown still damp from the early-morning showers.

"I've been offered a paid position over the summer to do research with a professor," he said.

Duke and I reveled in Steve's enthusiasm, playing the role of proud parents to the hilt.

"I'd like to get a paper published and go to grad school," he told us.

Steve, my defiant teenager, not only graduated with a bachelor's degree and congratulations from President Obama, but also plans to continue working toward his doctorate.

Alec is now in his third year at the University of California, Santa Barbara. He was offered a summer internship in cancer research at Stanford University. I had worried that following the Internet high school program in Belize might hinder his chances of doing well, but my fears proved unfounded. His aim is to become a doctor of medicine, and we are so proud of his hard work and ongoing dedication to doing well.

Josh is in his senior year at a military academy in New Mexico. He enlisted in the National Guard at seventeen. Josh is passionate about his career in the Army, something I had never expected from any of my sons. He has turned into a compassionate young man who is intent on "one day giving back to my country." How can I not be proud of my boys?

All of us, my sons included, have learned to take risks in life, to embrace adventure and to accept different ways of thinking about life's challenges. And though Belize failed to live up to my clichéd vision of paradise, it taught me that paradise is not a place but a state of being. I discovered my Caribbean paradise within my family, a gift far richer than I could have imagined possible. And for that, I shall remain eternally grateful to Belize.

Acknowledgments

MANY GREAT PEOPLE HELPED ME create this book.

I am grateful to my very first editor, Debra Ginsberg, who started me on this journey of transforming my Belizean journal into a final story.

Editor Dale Griffiths Stamos guided me through the process of developing a structure for my story. I am grateful for her expertise and help in focusing on the "heart" of my memoir.

I'd like to thank my outstanding copy editor, Eve Gumpel, and my talented proofreader, Tracy Gantz, who edited and polished the book for the discerning eyes of my readers.

I have gained tremendous appreciation for the blood and sweat authors put into completing a manuscript from start to finish, and I thank all my writer friends for their amazing support. My close friend Kimberly Brower deserves a medal of kindness and patience for her hours of coaching and encouraging me to "finish the book."

I am grateful to Shirin Taber, my first writing instructor, and I apologize for the regrettable remark I made at the time: "How can it take someone six years to write a book?" (I can now be counted among those who take years to complete a manuscript.)

I wish to thank my close friend Sylvia McDonald: She came up with the title *Freeways to Flip-Flops* when she first heard about my book.

I still have the flip-flop gift bag she offered me with her note, "Keep this for your future fan mail."

My cousin, Pia Nielsen-Wagner, has been a fan from the beginning, and deserves credit for listening to me complain and cry while I struggled. I am grateful for her continual cheer-leading from start to finish.

My wonderful husband, Duke, has been my pillar of support throughout my entire literary journey. I thank him for staying married to me during the gestation and birth of my book. I don't think I could have put up with as much whining from him as he did from me, had the situation been reversed.

I am grateful to my three sons for allowing me to share both the good and the less favorable events on our family's journey. They know how proud I am of their individual accomplishments, and the fact that they have turned into fine young men with a global outlook on life.

Finally, I wish to thank my father, who still lives in Paris, for instilling his love of travel and his "gutsy" tendencies in my veins. I wish my mother had been alive to know Duke and my three sons. I always admired my mother's energy, compassion and ability to care for others. She would have been proud of me. Thank you, Mum.

And to Belize, I shall remain eternally grateful for our year of adventure, friendships and personal growth.

About the Author

HAVING LIVED IN MANY COUNTRIES — Denmark, Nigeria, France, England, the U.S. and Belize — Sonia Marsh considers herself a citizen of the world. She holds a degree in environmental science from the University of East Anglia, U.K., and now lives in Southern California with her husband, Duke.

Sonia prides herself on being a "Gutsy" woman who can pack her carry-on and move to another continent in one day. As a motivational speaker, she inspires audiences to get out of their comfort zone, take a risk and pursue their dreams. Sonia welcomes new friends, bloggers, writers and readers at Soniamarsh.com (http://soniamarsh.com) Contact her at: sonia@soniamarsh.com, www.facebook.com/GutsyLiving or Twitter.com @GutsyLiving.